VOICES ON THE EDGE

PLAYS &
SCREENPLAYS
1980-2018
RON IANNONE

Destination Press
Morgantown, West Virginia

© 2019 Ron Iannone

ISBN: 978-0-9982020-5-1

DEDICATION

To my good friend
Ralph Brem.

CONTENTS

PREFACE — VII

VINNIE SERRANO — 1

RECOVERY — 89

THE GENE NETTIE SHOW — 173

THE BOILER ROOM SCHOOL — 229

THE COMEBACK — 317

PREFACE

In this work are plays and screenplays I have written, dating back to the early eighties. My greatest influence in writing these pieces was from my participation in a workshop entitled "A Map of New World Players," taught by West Virginia University theatre professors Frank Gagliano and Patrick Murphy. The driving idea for this workshop was to have playwrights, directors, and actors work together on developing plays. From that time on, I have been writing plays and screenplays. Included are five of these works, presented as the original manuscripts, in chronological order of their composition: *Vinnie Serrano, Recovery, The Gene Netti Show, The Boiler Room School,* and *The Comeback*. Each piece is preceded by a brief synopsis of the plot, and a note about its production.

My stories frequently come from either fascinating characters I dream up, or from observing people, places, and events in my life; from there, I'll imagine histories, futures, and worlds where these elements can grow and blossom into their own true selves.

I've been thinking about my fictional character Vinnie Serrano for nearly forty years now, and he shows up here in the first play, as well as in *Recovery* and *The Boiler Room School*. In each story, he is presented differently, and the course of his life is explored independent of the other stories, chronicling just a few of the possible lives this central character could have lived. In *The Boiler Room School*, I placed Vinnie in a setting I knew from personal experience, teaching and developing a curriculum for Appalachian school children, which I wrote about in my 1972 book, *"School Ain't No Way . . ." / Appalachian Consciousness*. Later, I would revisit the play *Vinnie Serrano* and adapt the story for my first novel, *A Boston Homecoming*, published in 2017.

The Gene Netti Show was inspired by a brief visit to a small radio station in Myrtle Beach, South Carolina. I combined my observations with my imagination and ended up with a hostage situation. Finally, the screenplay *The Comeback* is the story of a young person overcoming physical and social obstacles as he struggles to regain his place on the football field. This story was inspired by the moving strength and determination of someone very dear to me, who has dealt with more than their fair share of struggles.

At this point, I would like to thank and dedicate this compilation to my friend Ralph Brem. When I was writing the earlier of these plays, he was the editor of the *Dominion Post* in Morgantown, West Virginia. His editorials read like beautiful poetry. We would spend several early morning hours at Shoney's restaurant on Monongahela Boulevard talking about the art of writing. He also helped me develop a screenplay, but because of personal reasons I had to let it go. Ralph was kind and gentle with me when I was writing weak characters and scenes, and he taught me how to bring depth to my writing. Sadly, my friend Ralph has Alzheimer's now and his memory is vanishing quickly. But Ralph, we will be together again where everything will be the same as it was at Shoney's.

I also would like to say here, thank you to those who helped with *The Comeback*: Bret Martin, who took my story and turned it into the screenplay presented here, and Mark Castaldo from Destiny Pictures who, as a consultant, gave us many excellent ideas. Finally, another thanks goes out to Populore Publishing, for their multi-talented assistance in bringing my various writing projects to fruition.

VINNIE SERRANO
A PLAY

This play tells the story of Vinnie, a confused college professor and writer who suffers a nervous breakdown and returns to his Italian American family in Boston to attend his uncle's funeral—and in hope of a little support and comfort. However, he finds that he hardly knows his family anymore. Confrontations ensue among Vinnie, his mother, and his overbearing father, who refuses to accept that his son has reached his psychological limits.

Throughout, Vinnie's alter ego voices his profound self-loathing and anger—anger at university bureaucracy, anger at himself for not pursuing his desires, anger at his inability to deal with a failing marriage, and anger at Catholicism. As tension mounts, the Serrano family learns painful truths, and each person has to come to their own decision about how to respond.

Vinnie Serrano was presented as a staged reading on Saturday, November 1, 1980, at Fairmont University and on Saturday, November 8, 1980, at Parkersburg Community College, and was partially funded by the Humanities Foundation of West Virginia.

Scenes

Act I   Scene 1 - Jimmy Serrano's Hotel Room
             Scene 2 - Angie Castro's Apartment
             Scene 3 - Longo's Funeral Home

Act II   Scene 1 - Mario and Theresa Serrano's Apartment
             Scene 2 - Concetta Serrano's Apartment
             Scene 3 - Angie Castro's Apartment
             Scene 4 - Mario and Theresa Serrano's Apartment

Cast of Characters

<u>Vinnie Serrano</u> is in his early thirties. He is short and thin. He has a pointed face with long black hair parted in the middle. Dark, tunnel-like eyes give him a sad and tragic look. He has been teaching English at Wheeling University in West Virginia when he decides to return home to Boston to attend his Uncle Louie's funeral.

<u>Theresa Serrano</u> is his mother. She is in her early fifties. She is a tiny, pretty, bleached-blonde woman.

<u>Mario Serrano</u> is his father. He is in his late fifties. He is broad-shouldered and large-chested. There is a soldierly quality about him. He has thick, graying hair with very few wrinkles on his face.

<u>Alter Ego</u> looks a lot like Vinnie, except for having light blonde hair and a rounder face. He moves about the stage as if he owns it. That is, he speaks to Vinnie and the audience from wherever he's sitting, lying, relaxing, etc., on the stage.

<u>Jimmy Serrano</u> is in his late thirties and is the son of Concetta Serrano. He's a part-time actor and sometime dilettante. His age is showing; his face looks gaunt and hair seems to be thinning on the top. However, he still has a fairly good build.

<u>Patsy Serrano</u> is the oldest son of Concetta Serrano. He is older than Jimmy and Vinnie. He has the same kind of squinting face as the TV detective Columbo. His hair is frizzed and curled like an afro. He talks and gestures in an effeminate way.

<u>Concetta Serrano</u> is in her late forties. She is a very successful business lady, and is presently an editor for a publishing house in Boston. She has very few wrinkles on her face and has a fine stately figure that would still tempt many men. She's the type of woman that needs to dominate whatever situation she's in.

<u>Angie Castro Rogers</u> is in her early forties. She looks like Jacqueline Kennedy. She is tall and has lion's mane-like black hair falling over her square shoulders. Everything about her is elegant.

<u>Phil Cassallaro</u> is a brother of Concetta and Theresa Serrano. He is all Italian. Black hair streaked with gray, and dark brown eyes. He also looks like a fat slob as fat and hair squeeze out over his belt.

<u>Rose Serrano</u> is the only daughter of Concetta Serrano. She at one time was very beautiful but now looks like she doesn't care about her appearance. Everything about her looks worn out. Specifically, she has too many crow's feet around her eyes and mouth, her hair is unkempt and she has a body too big for her clothes.

Louie Serrano looks like his brother, Mario, except he has more of a gentleman quality about him. His features are more finely shaped than his brother's.

Mike Conklin is a friend of Jimmy's. He has an ape-like face and is built like a hulky guard on some professional football team.

Sharon Kelly is a friend of Jimmy's. A very thin girl with long silky blonde hair. Her features are very plain-looking.

ACT I - SCENE I

[*A hotel room in Boston. At the center of the stage is a bed, the size of a sleeping cot. There is a white bed spread on it and a pillow facing back stage. On the left of the bed is a night stand with a small lamp and phone on it. There are two chairs located at the foot of the bed. There are also two door frames located stage left and stage right. Behind the stage left door frame, there are two women and a man sitting on a bench with glasses in their hands.*

As the curtain rises, the light comes up on Vinnie and his Alter Ego entering the stage right doorframe.]

    Jimmy
    Come on, sit down and relax, Vin. I'll get you a drink. I'm just having a small get-together celebrating his death.

[*Alter Ego goes over and sits on the bed in a cross-legged position.*]

    Vinnie
    You're really unbelieveable, did you really hate him that much?

    Jimmy
    Yeah, and more. But, shit, Vin, let's forget that crap. Tell me, my boy, what's been happening with you. Eight years is a hell of a long time, man. That asshole taxi cab driver wouldn't let me get in a word. I could give shit about how expensive it is to own a cab. The world sucks. So what? Anyway, my mother is really grateful that you came, she tells me you're a big shot writer and a professor in West Virginia. Jesus, how the fuck did you end up in that place?

    Vinnie
[*Goes over and sits down in a chair.*]
    I don't know. I just did. A great place to raise kids and to be bored. I love its second-class reputation, I guess.

    Jimmy
[*Goes over to nightstand.*]
    A scotch, okay?

    Vinnie
    Yeah, fine

    Jimmy
[*Takes out a bottle and two glasses from underneath the nightstand and pours the drinks.*]
    Jesus, I still can't believe it. I still remember the little pisspot of a kid who was scared of his own shadow. And now look at you. A famous writer and getting all the cunt you want, I bet. No wonder you stay in by-gosh-West Virginia, you don't have any competition. [*He hands Vinnie a drink and sits down.*]

Vinnie
[*Shakes his head.*]
 Still as gross as ever, huh, Jimmy? Time wears well with you.

Jimmy
[*Gulps a large portion of his drink.*]
 Oh, come on, Vinnie, tell me is it true what they say about those southern girls? You know...

Vinnie
 I don't know, I'm really quite straight.

Jimmy
 Sure, I bet you are.

Vinnie
[*Sips his drink.*]
 What if I told you I was celibate. And I have been for years.

Alter Ego
[*Yells out to the audience.*]
 Little does shithead's cousin know how true that statement is. You see, shithead has been competing for years with the biggest stud of all, the one and only, the best, the cleanest nobody could do it like he could, not even MacDonald's, he has quality, taste, and tradition, the Grand Dad of them all... Jesus Christ!

Jimmy
[*Laughs.*]
 Sure you are, you're probably King Dick among the Hicks.
[*He laughs again.*]

Vinnie
[*Pleading.*]
 Please, Jimmy, let's change the subject, enough dumping on Vinnie for a while. Okay? I am out of practice.

Jimmy
[*Takes another gulp of his drink.*]
 Okay, champ, I always loved to watch how you would cringe at good basic filthy street talk. And so, my boy, we both haven't changed that much. Have we?

Vinnie
[*Coldly.*]
 I guess not.

Jimmy
[*Gets up, pours himself another drink and sits down again.*]
 My mother gave me some of your books to read. Not bad. A bit too preaching, maybe, but not bad. I just wish you would let the animal in you come out a little. That's all.

Vinnie
Look, I'm tired and don't feel like getting into anything too heavy. But I will tell you this, that art should lead. It should give people something to believe in. And it should not offer people how many times a day a person's glands are working. That stinks. Now let's forget the academics and tell me when is the funeral?

Jimmy
Okay, no arguing, I promise. Monday morning is the funeral. But, Jesus, Vinnie, I must tell you this, you sound like a right-wing politician. I mean it.

Vinnie
[Laughs.]
Perhaps, now enough. Tell me where's the wake being held, your mother's place or at a funeral home?

Jimmy
At Longo's. Nobody in the North End has it in their houses anymore. So Longo has become richer than hell over the last few years. You know old Man Longo died last year and now his crazy son, Butch, has taken over. Jesus, what an asshole he is! Remember him, Vin?

Vinnie
I think so.

Jimmy
[Gets up and goes over to the nightstand and pours himself another drink.]
So more scotch, Vinnie?

Vinnie
No, I'm still working on my first one.

Jimmy
[Sits back down.]
Shit, I drink too much. I can't stay away from it. Women and drinks are killing me, Vin. [He laughs.] Well, anyway, that asshole Longo last year got divorced on one day and on the very next day he married some blonde broad who weighs about two hundred pounds and has tits the size of watermelons.

Vinnie
[Forces a laugh.]

Jimmy
The cocksucker wears green, pink, rose, yellow, white, all kinds of loud-colored shitty suits at the wakes. He's a fraud like all of them. Shaking hands, hugging and kissing my mother. All of them pretending that they loved him. Christ, they hated him as much as I did...

Vinnie
That's really sad. I always felt your father was a good and decent man. How couldyou have so much hatred for him?

Jimmy
Oh, my poor, poor Vinnie, still as fucking naive as ever. Jesus. [*He shakes his head.*] Look, I wish I'd never come back. The only reason I'm here is because of money. I'm doing some work for my mother. One of my kids in Georgia is going to a psychiatrist. Nine years old. If you believe that. Nine years old. I feel terribly guilty about that. His bitchy mother won't even let me talk to him on the phone. Divorces, Jesus, two of them in five years almost killed me. Then on top of all this crap, that son of a bitch had to die. Never will I go to his wake, never, man. Not after all the shit he laid on me. My mother says it doesn't look right, I give a shit. My fucking sometimes doesn't look right either. So what. But I think she understands and that's why I promised her I would stay in Boston until after the funeral. My brother and sister are useless to her and she might need some support. Hey, Vin, ready for another drink yet?

Vinnie
No, I'm still doing fine.

Jimmy
[*Finishes his drink and gets up and pours himself another one.*]

Alter ego
Watch your dear old cousin now get loaded, shithead. That's what the glamorous hollywood life does for you. Ask him why he doesn't get any big parts on TV and in the movies. Ask him. Ask him why if he's supposed to be friends with big movie stars like Frank Sinatra, Clint Eastwood, and Burt Reynolds, why he doesn't get bigger parts. You know why. He's a fake...

Jimmy
[*Sits back down and now speaks sluggishly.*]
Vinnie, I bet you didn't know that I also had a ten-year-old boy who is the captain of his little league team. That helps to soften all the fucking alimony I have to pay out for two wives and four kids. Of course, Vinnie, my children have to have everything, private schools, expensive clothes, large suburban houses, good teeth, guitars, mini bikes... you name it, they got it. Thank God for my mother and the extra money I get from her. That son of a bitch wouldn't give me anything, he loved to see me suffer...

Vinnie
Are you getting yourself together now?

Alter Ego

[*Talking to the audience.*]
There he goes, people, playing the priest again. He loves to do that. It's so safe. Now watch him get his asshole cousin to spill his guts in the next five minutes. Watch, now.

Jimmy
You know, Vin, all my mother talked about when I was growing up was you. [*His voice is not as sluggish as before.*] She would always talk about how smart you were and how every time she saw you you had a book in your hand. Boy, was I jealous of you. I just wish I was able to discipline myself like you did. Females were my problem. I had to fuck and fuck every minute of the day. That's what ruined my marriages. I got tired of fucking the same cunt time after time. I needed fresh ones. I paid out a thousand bills to a shrink to find that out.

Vinnie
You were disappointed in yourself, huh?

Alter Ego
Listen to that, people, didn't I tell you, he would start playing Sigmund Freud... [*He turns to Vinnie and cups his hands around his mouth.*] Hey, shithead, how about you, who's helping you with those thoughts about that night with him, huh, shithead, who...

Jimmy
A little bit. But what hurts me is the people I work with. Vin, film people are the dumbest people in the world. All they want to talk about is who's fucking who, the new mercedes they bought, their guilt-ridden liberal causes... I just don't have anyone to discuss with me the important questions of life. So lately I've buried myself into books on all sorts of subjects. My mother has helped here. I really love to read weird macbre things. I don't know why. It may be because I keep thinking there might be a candle hidden in one of those weird stories which might light the world... Oh, that's bad, that sounds as bad as some of the shit I have to read in scripts.

Vinnie
That's okay. There's some deep truth behind all corny lines.

Jimmy
Yeah, I think you're right. Anyway, you know what I'm really into now?

Vinnie
No.

Jimmy
Noses.

Vinnie
[*Laughs.*]
Noses!

Alter Ego
Oh, great, fucking great!

Jimmy
Yes, my dear cousin, noses. I know, I know you think I'm crazy. But wait until I tell you what I'm into.

Vinnie
Okay.

Jimmy
I know it sounds stupid. But listen, I was reading an unpublished manuscript that my mother gave me and it said that the nose was one of the most important organs man has. It does more than smell. This Matt Ziegler who wrote the manuscript says it has the ability to taste and even see in certain cases. And listen to this, if stroked properly it gets sexually aroused just like a fucking prick.

Vinnie
You can't be serious?

Jimmy
[*Excitedly.*]
I am, I am, man. Listen, this Ziegler says if pinched just right it could knock a person unconscious. It's all very simple really, with a quick but strong twist like this. [*He twists his thumb and forefinger together as if he was winding a clock.*] The person is shocked into unconsciousness. [*He taps the end of his nose with his forefinger.*] This area is called the Kissebock Triangle.

Vinnie
[*Sarcastically.*]
Really interesting.

Jimmy
Okay, don't believe me, but I'll tell you Ziegler thinks the nose may be related to the missing link in the theory of evolution. A perfect murder can be accomplished by knowing about noses this Ziegler says. He says all you need is a glass tube curved at one end and a couple of tiny pieces of chewed meat.

Vinnie
What?

Jimmy
Chewed meat, I said. You know why chewed meat, don't you?

Vinnie
No, please tell me... Jesus, this is unreal.

Jimmy
I would think my smart-ass couson who graduated from Harvard would've already guessed. Well, stupid, you use the chewed meat to blow it through the glass tube and up someone's fucking nostril. [*He clenches his fist and blows hard into it.*] Something like that. You see, my dear bright cousin, the chewed meat travels up the nose cavity like a pinball rebounding off the sides of a machine and then wham it lodges itself in the windpipe. The person then chokes to death, Ziegler says, in about sixty or ninety seconds. Something, huh?

Vinnie
Yeah, really something.

Jimmy
Hey, Vinnie, no shit, think of the lives that could be saved if armies fought battles with their noses. And then just think what would happen if we could find a way to have sexual intercourse with our noses. I'm serious. I doubt we would have to worry about the population explosion, right? [*He laughs cocky-like.*]

Vinnie
I think you have been hanging around with too many pin-up and porno freaks.

Jimmy
[*Laughs.*]
Okay, okay, don't believe me, man! But you wait and see, in a couple of years everybody will be into noses. The nose knows more than you think. Well, I've said enough now, let's see how the party is coming along.

[*The three people sitting on the bench behind the doorframe get up and enter. They form a circle near the bed and act as if they're having a conversation with each other.*
Jimmy and Vinnie get up and go over to them.]

Jimmy
Hey, guys, I want you tp meet my cousin, Vinnie, he's a smart-ass professor and writer from take-me-home West Virginia.

[*The three people all nod in Vinnie's direction.*]

Jimmy
Vin, this is Sharon Kelly, a friend. [*He winks.*] And this is Angie Castro, a friend of Shar's. [*He winks again.*] And this monster, is big Mike. [*He laughs.*]

Alter Ego
[*Gets off the bed and stands behind Vinnie.*]
Wow, shithead, look at that Angie. She looks just like Jacqueline Kennedy. I wonder what she would look like without clothes on. Now, don't screw up. You've always wanted to screw a beautiful older women who looked like Jacqueline Kennedy, right? Well, here's your chance, kiddo!... Look, shithead, she's looking at you... [*He goes stage left and sits down on the floor.*]

Jimmy
You know, guys, if Vinnie's students only knew how naive he was when he was growing up, I think they would be quite surprised. Hell, remember old Vinnie how you would have to go to bed at seven each night while the rest of us guys fooled around. His mother was always scared poor Vinnie was going to get hurt. She was kinda nervous, right, Vinnie?

Vinnie
I guess.

Alter Ego
[*Faces the audience.*]
Nervous is right, in fact they say Vinnie was an accident. Hey, people, something else I better get straight with you, especially now because I am going to be quiet for a while. And what I want to get straight with you is that even though I call him shithead all the time, that doesn't mean I don't care for the shithead. I really do... Now he is a bit of a dummie when it comes to dealing with life and that's because I think all the junk he's carrying around with him, but otherwise the kid has got a lot going for him. Okay, now, I'll keep my mouth shut for a while and see how old shithead makes out with that good-looking head.

Jimmy
Well, guys, you should've seen Vinnie this one night, hell, it was as if he had seen the devil himself. Too much. [*He laughs.*]

Vinnie
Hey, come on now, please, Jimmy, don'g get into that.

Jimmy
Oh, don't worry, Vinnie, these guys know life quite well. Right, guys?

Mike
Sure, sure.

Sharon
[*Nods her head shyly.*]

Angie
I don't know, Jimmy, if you should. He seems a bit embarrassed. Leave him alone. And please cut out that guys crap. Do I look like a guy?

Jimmy
Oh, Vinnie, I forgot to tell you we have a feminist in our midst. Sorry, my dear.

Angie
[*Shakes her head in disgust.*]
I give up, Sharon, where did you meet this asshole?

Sharon
He's just teasing you, Ang, don't pay any attention to him. He does that to me all the time. He's really for all the things women are striving for.

Angie
[*Sarcastically.*]
I bet he is.

Jimmy
Well, look, my dear Angie, if you don't want to hear a funny story, shut the fuck up. Okay. But I know Sharon and Mike will get a bang out of it. And don't worry about poor Vinnie, he isn't embarrassed. He loves the attention. Hell, that's why he writes. Right, Vin?

Vinnie
[*Coldly.*]
No, and I don't appreciate...

Jimmy
Oh, be quiet, Vinnie, and let me go on.

Vinnie
I really don't think...

Jimmy
[*Suddenly puts his hand over Vinnie's mouth.*]
Oh, professor, be quiet. Here's what happened, guys. [*He takes his hand away from Jimmy's mouth.*] This one time Vinnie wanted to know where some of us guys were getting this extra money we had to spend. Well, we told him he could make some too if he would join us this one night. Now us guys realized that Vinnie being so goody-goody wouldn't go along if he thought we were doing something bad. So we assured him that it wasn't stealing or anything like that. Anyway, this one night Vinnie, Tony Rossetti, and myself met in the front of Don's grocery store on Salem Street. Well, old man Dipietro who owned it lived over the store with his son Peter, who was a bit slow in the head. God, did Peter stutter. Okay, so this one night

we all met in front of Don's. Then we go in and tell old man Dipietro we're going up to see Peter and play cards. Now when we got up to Peter's room, Tony and me started to talk to Peter about money. Well, while we're negotiating for something like two dollars apiece, Vinnie is standing in the background wondering what the fuck is going on. Finally, after about a half hour we convinced Peter to pay us something like two and a half apiece. Then, right afterwards, Peter, who had hot pants, turned the lights off! Then he started fucking stuttering, you... you... wan... wanna do it now? And as we started laughing at Peter's stuttering, I turned and saw Vince running out the door screaming, Oh, Jesus, no, oh, Jesus!

Angie
Thanks for sharing with us a sick adolescent peek-a-boo story, now what? [*Turning to Vinnie.*] And you call this jerk your cousin?

Vinnie
[*Visibly shaken, he mumbles something to himself over and over.*]
Beneath the subtle murmurs of the sea, I hear someone playing a song for me, playing a song for me, playing a song for me...

Angie
I'm sorry, I didn't hear you. What did you say?

Vinnie
[*Shaking his head as being awakened in the middle of a troubled dream.*]
Huh, oh, nothing, really nothing.

Jimmy
[*Angrily.*]
Will you guys let me finish, the real funny part is what has happened to Peter. Okay, first of all he's serving a six-month term in Walpole for being a peeping Tom. They tell me over the last ten or fifteen years he has become quite skillful in peeping. Now listen to this, guys, after they arrested fucking Pete, they found a book of peeping Rom routes he was using and also selling to other peeping Toms. Do you believe that? I heard also they found all sorts of peeping Tom equipment in his room; ladders of all sizes, rope, binoculars, bricks, cement blocks, cardboard periscopes, sketches of window shapes, planks of wood, all the tools of his trade were there! But this is the beauty of this whole fucking story. The night the cops caught him he was standing on a homemade scaffold, looking in on a young couple's room in a motel outside of Newton. Somehow the fucking scaffold got loose and he fell. Later he told the cops that he was too involved and excited to stop his fall. That's what I call dedication and commitment to one's job. Do you believe that shit?

Mike
[*Laughing.*]
Too much.

Sharon
[*Laughing weakly.*]
   Well, at least he was interested in improving his craft. Good for Peter. I wish we had more people like him.

Angie
   I think you're all a bunch of sickos.

Vinnie
[*Numbly.*]
   Hey, Jimmy, I think I'd better go.

Jimmy
   You're not mad are you?

Vinnie
   Oh, no, it's just that I'm beat from the flight and I would like to get to the wake before I see my parents.

Jimmy
   Why bother, Vinnie, I told you they're just a bunch of phonies. Forget it, man, stay here and party with us. Mike got hold of some great grass from Mexico. Man, I tell you after puffing on a joint of that stuff, oh, wow, everything becomes fantasy world. Join us, Vin.

Mike
   Hey, man, it's a great turn-on. It's so, so relaxing.

Vinnie
   I'll see, maybe later.

Jimmy
   Look, cous, just come into the other part of the suite and see for yourself. They're some great looking broads. Yeah, tell him, Angie, about all the good-looking broads with big tits and small asses. [*He laughs.*]

Angie
   You're such an idiot, Jimmy.

Jimmy
[*He leans over and whispers in Vinnie's ear.*]
   A fine cunt if you could put up with her mouth.

Angie
   Christ, Shar, where did you find this punk?

Sharon
[*Laughs.*]
   Oh, Ang, he's just showing off because he knows it's bothering you.

Jimmy
Hey, really I'm not a bad guy. Just ask my ex-wives. [*He laughs.*] Come on, both of you, join us. Later tonight I'm having some great Italian food catered in from a friend's restaurant. Come on, guys.

Angie
Sorry, not this girl. I just don't think I could listen to any more of your stupid adolescent stories. [*Turning to Sharon.*] Sorry, Shar, I just can't relate to the people and what's happening in the other room. I don't know why I came.

Sharon
Okay, hon.

Jimmy
Oh, shit, guys, come on. She's one of those broads who's a relater and probably can't relate to her ass. I hate those kind... Come on. [*He speaks over his shoulder as he heads toward the stage left doorframe.*] See you later, Vinnie.

Vinnie
Perhaps.

[*The three sit down on the bench and stare out at Angie and Vinnie standing now in the center of the stage.*]

Angie
[*Shaking her head.*]
Wow, he's something else.

Vinnie
Yeah, I guess so.

Angie
Sharon told me his father just died and he's celebrating it. That's hard to believe. Were you close to his father?

Vinnie
Not really.

Angie
How come you came back to Boston?

Vinnie
I really don't know... Perhaps, hope... I don't know.

Angie
I don't understand.

Vinnie
I don't either.

Angie
Okay, I won't pursue it. How about having a drink with me before you leave. I know we won't have to worry about them coming back in here for a long time. [Nods her head in the direction of the stage left doorframe.] In there, macho man will have an audience that will massage his ego for hours.

Vinnie
A drink sounds okay.

[She takes his glass from his hand and goes to the nightstand and fills up his glass and hers. She then comes back, hands him his glass, sits down in a chair, and he does likewise.]

Vinnie
What do you do?

Angie
Teach high school art.

Vinnie
Do you like teaching?

Angie
Some days are better than others.

Vinnie
That's my problem of late, I have very few days that are better than others. I've come to feel in the last few years that I really can't influence anyone. Sometimes I feel that my students could learn more in their bathroom talking to themselves. I don't know. I lecture, they nod, smile and take notes like good students. Then they show me on tests how much of my ideas they know. How do you stop doing this? While my individuality is being taken away by the silly games the university plays, so are my students.

Angie
Yeah, I know.

Vinnie
I see myself doing this all the time in a composition class I teach to seniors. What I do is to force them to learn how great writers wrote and then I ask them to write like these great writers. And all I get back are papers with some style but with very little substance. I'm forcing them to use ideas, their own ideas in forms that are not theirs. You see, I feel why I'm so unfair is that not only does each person generate his own ideas but each person's ideas have their own form inherent in them. So what kind of sense does it make when I write comments on students papers such as lack of coherence, lack of unity. Hell, what I'm really doing is destroying whatever unique way students have of putting their ideas

together. All great writers like Shakespeare, Dante, all of them
invented their own form to go along with their own ideas. What right
do I have to impose my logic, society's logic, my form, society's
form on the inner logic and form of students? What right do I have?
[*He shakes his head.*]

Angie
I agree in a way but we all need the tools, the grammar, the
techniques of a specific art. And I see no problem in giving students
just that, but when you have to evaluate, then the real problem occurs.
In fact, that's why I only teach technique courses in art. I could
judge techniques, but I feel very uncomfortable judging the painting
itself. There's too much of the student's soul in a painting to say I
like it or I don't like it.

Vinnie
Yeah, I feel the same way. I'm so glad I stayed. Then you could
see that the world works the other way. The world loves to judge the
results, the painting, the essay, the novel, the finished product.
Very, very seldom do we applaud the doing of the activity. Teachers
are the worst sinners in doing this. We force our external judgments
on students without giving them a chance to discover their own inner
way of looking at the world. I don't believe it's the students who
are stupid, it's the teachers and it's the system that are stupid.
We are the uneducated.

Angie
Well, I haven't thought about teaching that much. I know what
you're saying and I agree with you. But I still feel we need teachers.
I just started teaching again after eighteen years and I feel so lucky
that I have an eighteen-year-old daughter who has helped me understand
today's students. I think students today want the rules, the techniques, but I don't think they want anything else from the teacher.
You know, they want the product but not the salesperson. And how many
times have teachers asked them to accept them as God and as absolute.

Vinnie
But, you see, I think the real Gods want us to help students
discover truths. Not external truths but inner truths that can hold
humanity together

Angie
God, I haven't had a discussion like this for years. Gee, it
feels great.

Vinnie
I've been thinking the same thing.

Angie
Good.

Vinnie
You don't really have an eighteen-year-old daughter, do you?

Angie
Yep, and thanks for the compliment. I was married for twenty years until last year when I got divorced. In fact, that's why I'm here at your crazy cousin's party, Sharon teaches with me and she's been trying to get me out for months. And now I never realized how much I hated these parties. Everyone is always hiding behind some shield.

Vinnie
I think so, but tell me, was it hard going through a divorce after twenty years? Maybe I'm getting too personal now.

Angie
[*Reaches over and gently touches Vinnie's hand.*]
Don't worry about being personal. I'm enjoying your company. It means you're recognizing me as a human being and I like that. I hate talking about why the mayor didn't get the snowplows out or why the Bruins are doing so terribly. All so trite. Anyway, at first the divorce did hit me hard. But I'll tell you the freedom and happiness I experienced afterwards made it all worthwhile. You know the biggest decision I had to make before the divorce dealt with what country club to have lunch at, what to wear to play tennis in, what to serve for a party, where we should go for our vacation, France, Italy or Switzerland. Then just one day I saw that all of that was attached to my husband's life, the hundred thousand dollar house, country clubs and all. I had no life except what belonged to him.

Vinnie
What did your daughter think about the divorce?

Angie
I think she thought it was best for both of us, but hell, it was my family that gave me all kinds of shit. An Italian just doesn't get divorced. You know what I mean.

Vinnie
I thought you looked Italian or Spanish. I wasn't sure because of your last name being Castro.

Angie
My married name was Rogers. Angie Rogers. How's that for a good melting-pot name?

Vinnie
[*Laughs.*]
Pretty good. I wonder how many people have told you that you look like Jacqueline Kennedy.

Angie
[*Embarrassed.*]
A few.

Vinnie
Another drink?

Angie
Okay.

[*Vinnie gets up and fills their drinks.*] Well, tell me about your good Italian family and their reactions to the divorce. I'm really curious. [*He comes back, hands her her drink and sits back down again.*]

Angie
Well, first of all, let me tell you that my mother always treated everything in an antiseptic way, especially sex. Everything about it, for her, was dirty. To this day I haven't lost all the shame and guilt she taught me. Pleasure was always bad. Once when I was sixteen I told her about a dream I had about a boy in my class. Before I knew what was happening, she had me kneeling next to her on the floor saying the rosary and praying for forgiveness to the Virgin Mary. Heck, when I was in college I was always running to a priest after a boy tried to kiss or feel me. That was until a young priest tried to lay me in the confessional. Still, when I first got married I used to shake if I had to talk to men other than my husband. And if I found myself in such a situation at a party, shivers used to run down my body and eventually I would get sick to my stomach. I'm still at times terribly frightened of men. I must say that Ed, my former husband, did help me in this area of my life. Well, anyway, with that kind of background you can imagine my family's reaction when I told them I was getting a divorce.

Vinnie
Yeah, I could.

Angie
Well, my mother thought I was going directly to Satan. Both my mother and father said that I would suffer the rest of my life and my daughter would grow up to be a whore because of not having a father. That was a laugh. Living the way we were, it was the only choice for her... I guess you got the picture. It took a year before my parents started to talk to me again. It was hard for a while dealing with that. Then I figured I didn't care, I was in charge of my own life now. But it was the loneliness that was really hard to deal with. No one understands loneliness until you have to experience it. I'm sort of used to it now but at times it's still hard to accept.

[*Vinnie reaches over and lightly strokes her arm.*]

Alter Ego
[*Gets up and moves toward Vinnie.*]
I'm sorry, shithead, but I have to interrupt. Look, you'll never get a chance like this again. She's really beautiful and very vulnerable. And she likes you. God, she just told you her whole life story in five minutes. I know, I know what's going on in that pea brain of yours, well forget it. Saintly Chris won't give a shit, she's too busy rolling on the floor with those other religious nuts. For Christ's sake, shithead, can you see that fucking once or twice a year is unhealthy. Come on, kiddo, turn the old charm on...

[*After placing his glass on the floor, Vinnie gets up and then she does the same.*]

Vinnie
Angie, I... [*He pulls her close to him and then tenderly kisses her.*]

Angie
Let's get out of here, okay? My place is nearby.

Vinnie
Okay.

[*As they turn and walk toward the stage right doorframe, Alter Ego moves to center stage.*]

Alter Ego
Hey, shithead is doing okay. Jesus, most of the time he's out in left field. Yeah, he's pretty good at discussing Plato, Hegel, Dante, but when it comes to love and sex, he's an idiot. You see, he's got to dig deeper into himself without fighting it. Somehow I must get him to trust his emotions without thinking about it. Always fucking analyzing, analyzing. He wants everything to be rational and logical. That's why his novels are so dull and boring. They're too analytical and too philosophical. Why can't he see that? All that shit about truth and goodness. He's too much of an impersonator. God, if he would only trust his own sense of being. Damn it, he knows that one night nothing was rational, it was all emotion. Pure emotion. Jesus, why does he always have to hide behind those characters of his that are always so intellectual. Everyone could see that the flesh and blood of his characters are missing. But not him, no sir, not him. Hell, I was feeling good when I started talking but now I'm getting depressed. Shithead will do it to me every time. I bet you wouldn't believe me if I told you that the son of a bitch writes some great poetry. He does. But do you know what he does with the it? The fucker hides it in the back of his file cabinet... in the back of his file cabinet.

[*He shakes his head, turns and walks toward the stage right doorframe.*]
[*The curtain and the lights come down.*]

ACT I - SCENE II

[*Angie Castro's apartment. As the curtain and lights come up, there is at center stage a large bed with Vinnie lying on top of Angie and kissing her passionately. A white sheet covers their bodies. Next to the bed is a night stand with a Tiffany lamp on it. There is only one doorframe which is located stage right. At stage left, there hangs as suspended in mid-air three paintings of old ships lying on shore. They are all in a different phase of decay.*]

[*The Alter Ego is sitting cross-legged, almost off stage at stage left.*]

Vinnie
[*He stiffens, rolls off Angie and quickly sits up. He's bare-chested.*]
 Damn! I just can't, I just can't. I'm sorry, Angie, I'm so sorry.

Angie
[*She slowly sits up and puts her arms around him. She is wearing a white bra.*]
 It's okay. Don't worry, my dear, I don't like instant sex either. [*She strokes his hair.*] A good warm-up always makes it a lot better.

Vinnie
[*Shakes his head.*]
 Yeah, but it's not fair to you. I acted like an insecure teenager making out for the first time. Damn sex!

Angie
[*She kisses him lightly on the cheek.*]
 Please, don't worry about it, you know sex is never perfect. Love, it was still very beautiful.

Vinnie
 Heck, I just don't know... Maybe it's the violence in sex I don't like, then maybe... I just don't know. It scares me sometimes.

Angie
 It scares me, too, love.

Vinnie
 I didn't hurt you in my bumbling attempts, did I?

Angie
 Oh, no, dear, it was really lovely. Please believe me. Vinnie, just accept that this is where our relationship is. You know, dear, I really love beginnings, especially in relationships, the new feelings, the new sensations, I love it all. God, do I hate it when

relationships become old and stale. So let's enjoy our beginnings. Okay? [*She reaches up and pulls him toward her. They kiss*]

Vinnie
God, Angie, you're so understanding and so, so beautiful. I can't believe it. Every time I touch you, my body trembles with excitement. How could I have blown it with you? [*He shakes his head, feeling sorry for himself.*]

Angie
You didn't, my love, you didn't. Please don't say that.

Vinnie
Okay. I guess when you don't do it anymore than once every six months that also doesn't help.

Angie
You practice rhythm with your wife?

Vinnie
Yes, and it's a bitch.

Angie
I can't see how people can keep their sanity doing it that way.

Vinnie
I can't either. And listen to this, on top of that, I was also a virgin when I got married at twenty-four. You're probably talking to the only guy who grew up in the North End of Boston and got married as a virgin. Do you believe that? I still carry a lot of those insecure feelings of a virgin. Even with you, tonight, I was worried I would end up with some disease or that I would get you pregnant. You see what I mean?

Angie
Yes, but don't worry, dear, I'm safe on both accounts.

Vinnie
It's so crazy.

Angie
Yeah, but it's okay. We'll grow together, love. I got a lot of hang-ups, too.

Vinnie
But Angie, you don't know what you're getting yourself into with me. I got some dark monsters hanging around in my head.

Angie
I don't care. I just know I'm feeling real good about you.

Vinnie
[*Feeling sorry for himself again.*]
God, how I wish I could be like a normal guy. How many guys my age are scared to buy condoms. A teenager, yes, but a guy in his thirties, no! You know about two years ago I decided I was going to buy them. So here I am walking into a drugstore, sweating and shaking like hell, you thought I was going to rob it. Well, anyway, I first bought toothpaste, then deodorant, then mouthwash, then shaving cream, everything but the condoms. I kept looking for them but I couldn't find them. Finally, I got up enough courage to ask this pimpled-faced clerk where is the medicine for venereal diseases, figuring they had to be in the same area. Well, this clerk looked at me as if I was some kind of weirdo and then afterwards he said something like Aisle B. Quickly I rushed over and thank God they were there. Sweat was really pouring off me by now. At first I didn't know what brand to get but then I thought about the brand Trojans because that's the brand the guys in North End used to talk about. So I picked up a pack and then slid it underneath the pile of other stuff when I came to the check-out counter. Well, when I got out of the drugstore, you should've seen me. Hell, you thought I just won the Irish sweepstakes. I was so happy. I wanted to scream to the world, see Vinnie Serrano can buy rubbers, see...

Angie
[*Laughing hard.*]

Vinnie
Of course, my wife wouldn't have anything to do with them because she said they were filthy and unnatural. Well, one night I tried using them anyway, but after taking one from the package, I threw it away. I couldn't stand to touch that slimy thing. Ugh! I don't know how people use them.

Angie
[*Laughing not as hard.*]
Oh, God, Vinnie, you're too much. There's a gentleness and innocence that you have that men I know just don't have. You know I don't fear you like I fear other men. I feel so safe with you.
[*She reaches up and kisses him hard and long.*]

Vinnie
Then you won't ask me to buy condoms? [*He laughs.*]

Angie
No, darling, I won't ask you to buy condoms. Now tell me more about yourself. Are you really that against teaching?

Vinnie
I don't know. I don't think I'm really against teaching because I love working with students. I think I'm really against the university and what it forces me to do to students. Universities really

don't understand what it means to pursue truth and goodness, even though they may have those words in their mottos. They ask you to be nice to students and also to teach students to be nice to each other and then the very next minute, the administrators tell you to give exams so that students will learn how to beat the hell out of their neighbors. God, Angie, you should see the guy I work for. What an ass. He's my chairman. He has a mouth that twists to one side when he talks. And he hates any conflict situation where we question his policies. He also thinks discussions about such questions as what is truth, what is goodness, or why we're doing what we're doing, he thinks all these questions are useless. All he wants to talk about are promotion policies, leave policies, how many hours you should teach, and how other departments are beating us out in designing new courses. How the hell can you design new courses if you don't first state what you believe about man and his world, about his ideals, his myths? How can you design new English courses if you don't do this? I'm so happy he graduated from Yale because his memos about making sure we throw our soda cans in the trash cans are really beautiful. I remember him saying something to the effect if ecologically there are problems, then cups will be my only choice. Or another time when he wrote a memo explaining how faculty members should review each other. Something like each department faculty member shall be randomly assigned by the chairman to a three-member, anonymous peer review committee... On and on his bullshit goes.

Angie
It's the same shit that goes on in the high school I teach in. Perhaps it's not as sophisticated.

Vinnie
What a stupid system, what does all that have to do with students finding out about themselves and how they can gain control of themselves? What? I really think universities should've never left the medieval period. Then they understood their roles, they understood about beauty and truth then.

Angie
Do you talk to your wife about these things?

Vinnie
No, not any more, all she would say when I did was you're making things too complicated. We all have to suffer, she would say. Sometimes when I would show her what I was writing, she would say it's too abstract. She doesn't understand that I want to show the world what abstract really is. She just can't understand why I won't give myself over to Jesus as she does in her charismatic group. She can't see that Jesus Christ was a great prophet, giving us myths and stories so that we can get to a higher level of knowledge. Her emotionalism will never get her to that level, but she doesn't care, she's got the Lord. Anyway, that's what she keeps telling me...

Angie
So, she's one of them.

Vinnie
Sure is. Almost every night, she invites one of her holy-roller friends over. God, I can't stand their piety! I lost her and my children to Jesus a long time ago. And so it goes, my dear. She hides herself away in prayer and perhaps I do the same in trying to write novels that give people insights into their lives. I don't know. I failed miserably doing this with my other novels, but I hope I'm on the right track now...

Angie
Is it another novel?

Vinnie
Yes, and I hope my characters and dialogues will help people see that they are living in a pseudo-material world. I want it to show the world that their culture, their art, their religion, their education, their relationships are all pseudo. I know I could do this if my characters do a good job in explaining the major esoteric principles underlying mathematics, philosophy, science, religion and art. I hope people will see that there's a chance for their souls to be in flight toward truth and goodness while their bodies live on in this greedy world.

Angie
Those are very noble ideas, Vinnie, very noble.

Vinnie
Oh, I don't know about that. I just feel a book like this must be written if the inner life of man is to survive.

Angie
I agree, Vinnie, I just hope you never leave teaching because students need to hear your talk about these thoughts. And with your compassion for them, it's a must.

Vinnie
Well, we'll see once the book gets finished. Hey, dear, I must go. I really want to get to the wake before I see my parents. Boy, that's a whole scene I wish I could avoid.

Alter Ego
Would you listen to him? [*He gets up and goes over to Angie's side of the bed.*]

Angie
Do you have to go?

Vinnie
[*He gets out of bed and picks up his pants from the floor.*]
Yes, I don't want to, but I must. [*After he slides his pants on, he sits on the edge of the bed and gives Angie a short but loving kiss.*]

Angie
Vinnie, will I see you again, this is not a good-bye, is it?

Vinnie
Oh, no, Angie, I'm looking forward to getting back to your warm soft skin. I think I want you more than ever, but there's too many blocks right now.

Angie
[*She hugs him tightly.*]
I really like what I'm feeling for you.

Vinnie
Good, I liked everything that happened here tonight, even my fumblings.

Alter Ego
You notice, shithead, I didn't say anything during this whole scene. I thought you would be able to handle it. But, no, you blew it, of course. Look at her, look, how beautiful she is, look at those eyes, those eyes that want you, look, shithead...

Vinnie
God, I wish I could stay but I've got to go. [*He gets up and finishes dressing.*]

Angie
[*She gets out of bed and walks over to Vinnie with only her bra and panties on.*]
I'll miss you.

Vinnie
So will I.

Angie
[*She hugs Vinnie.*]
I don't want to lose you, Vinnie. I don't want this to end up as a one-night affair.

Vinnie
It won't, I promise you that. It just won't. [*He kisses her and keeps kissing her while Alter Ego speaks.*]

Alter Ego
He sits on the edge of the bed and faces the audience.
I give up, shithead, how did I ever get mixed up with such a screwball. Can't you see, idiot, she's real, real flesh and blood? She's not a character in one of your inane novels. She's a real person with real needs and her major need right now is to be fucked by you. Stay, shithead, and fuck her, please... People, he thinks those tablets-in-the-sky thoughts of his are more important than making it with her. For Christ's sake, when will he accept that those goddamn thoughts of his and his prick are all part of him... he must accept them, both parts, if he's going to feel whole again.

[The lights and curtain come down.]

ACT I - SCENE III

[*Longo's Funeral Home in the North End section of Boston. The North End is the Italian-American section of Boston. There is a stage right doorframe and a stage left doorframe with a bench behind it. Next to the stage right doorframe is a stand-up writing desk with a tiny lamp clamped on at the top. A large ledger-type book lies on the desk where visitors sign in.*

At center stage there is an open coffin with Louie Serrano lying inside. In front of the coffin, there is a red-cusioned kneeler. A reddish glowing light seems to envelop the coffin. In the background a girl's high pitched voice is loudly singing a rock song with the following lyrics.

I talk, babe, you listen,
You talk, babe, I listen,
Hoping each time
It will glisten,
But like the unending
Circle of time,
It goes on and on
And it's not
Worth a time.
I talk, babe,...

As the curtain riases, the light comes up on Vinnie, his Alter Ego and Longo standing in front of the stage right doorframe.]

Longo
[*Shouting in the direction of the stage left doorframe.*]
Alice, turn that damn thing down.   *He turns to Vinnie.*   Sorry, man, we're closed. The family left about three hours ago. [*The rock song has been lowered.*] Do you realize, man, it's close to two in the morning? Who the hell are you? Are you a member of the family?

Vinnie
Yes.

Alter Ego
[*He walks over and sits on the red-cushioned kneeler.*]
Well, fucking Lou, I brought over your asshole nephew to say hello. Yeah, I know, I bet you really care. You and I both know what he's avoiding. He'd do anything to avoid facing those memories, anything... But look, Lou, the fucker really has problems. Analysts would come down on him like vultures if they knew about him. He's an intellectual, a fairly good-looking guy, broads like him. But still he fucks up. You know I think Groucho Marx was thinking of people like Vinnie when he said about himself that he would never join a club if it had him as a member. A pure black and white figure, Lou, that's what he is. No color at all in his life. Everything he touches turns into shit. Pure black and white shit. A neurotic fly

paper. Yeah, that's another way of thinking of him, Lou. He attracts shit and it never leaves him, sticking to him for life... Oh, God, I get so depressed when I think about him and his fucked-up life... See what you can do for me, Lou. Right now, I'm going to sit here and think about a beautiful broad he just blew it with... Oh, Angie, come to me, I'll make you happy like no one else will... Your skin, oh, your beautiful warm and soft skin wrapped around me. Please, Angie... [*He stares off into space.*]

Longo
Hey, who are you?

Vinnie
I'm Vinnie Serr...

Longo
[*He quickly grabs his arm and pulls him over to the lamp on the stand-up writing desk.*]
Holy shit, Vinnie, I didn't recognize you. God, the last time I saw you you were wearing short pants. Jesus, I can't believe it. Vinnie Serrano. Mario and Theresa's son. Jesus.

Vinnie
Do you mind if I visit for a few minutes?

Longo
Hell, no. I heard you were coming, but I thought someone said you would be here earlier.

Vinnie
I thought I would be, too, but I had some problems.

Longo
Could I get you something, Vinnie, wine, food, what, anything?

Vinnie
No, thanks.

Longo
[*Shaking his head.*]
Vinnie, Vinnie, where does the time go?

Vinnie
It goes.

Longo
You sure you don't want anything.

Vinnie
No, really, all I want is to sneak in and see my uncle for a minute or so. Okay?

Longo
   Sure, man, you got the whole place to yourself. *[Jokingly.]* The show must go on, you know.

Vinnie
[Laughs forcefully.]

[Longo and Vinnie move toward center stage.]

Longo
   Look, make yourself comfortable and please stay as long as you want. I got to go and get some sleep, man, got another body to pick up in about couple hours. Like God, my work is never done. *[He laughs.]* Hey, just one thing, Vinnie, I haven't fixed your uncle up for tomorrow. You know he was really a mess when I picked him up from the hospital, especially his nose. The doctors tell me that they think he got that way because of the way he fell when he had his heart attack. I don't know. I just know I'm having a hell of a problem trying to make his nose look normal. Hell, man, every night it discolors on me because all the insides were screwed up. All the blood vessels and mucus membranes were twisted and mashed. Jesus, you should've seen it. The right nostril was twice as big as the other. I don't care what kind of undertaker you are, it's hard to patch something up that is that bad. So I hope you don't mind. It's not very nice to look at. *[Alter Ego gets up, turns around and stares down into the coffin.]* I wish to hell I could've used an artificial one. They're tremendous. But Concetta wouldn't hear of it. Well, anyway, Vinnie, take your time. I must go now and get some sack.

Vinnie
   Well, thanks, I appreciate your letting me in.

Longo
   That's okay. Old Longo believes in serving the public.
[Laughs and pats Vinnie on the back and hurries toward the stage left doorframe. Once there, he sits on a bench and stares out.

Alter Ego moves to the stage left side of the coffin while Vinnie walks toward the red-cushioned kneeler The rock singer starts singing again but the sound is quieter like background music one hears in an elevator.

> *I search in vain*
> *Among my friends*
> *Lovers and Strangers too,*
> *They talk, babe, I listen*
> *I talk, babe, they listen*
> *So like me and you.*
> *. . . . . . .*

All the lights are low except for the reddish glowing light which now envelops Vinnie and his Alter Ego. Vinnie stares down at his uncle.]

       Alter Ego
    Yeah, look closely, shithead. I know you can't believe it. But it's true. Your fucking crazy cousin killed his father. For Christ's sake, how many people have to deal with nose murders in their families? Sure, just tell me how many people in this country have asshole cousins who twist noses, stick pea shooters up them and then blow chewed meat through. Jesus, I just don't know, shithead, how much more you can take... I should have seen it coming. Do you have the courage to turn that fucking Jimmy in? No, of course not. Shit, why is it in this country everyone is so fucking scared. The Shhhh generation! That's it. *[He puts his forefinger in front of pursed lips.]* Yes, power and violence always win out in this country. Shove a fist or a huge cock in someone's face and you could do whatever you want to them. God! How much easier my life would've been if I attached myself to a sharp mugger or raper. But, no, I have to get mixed up with shithead, whose life dwells in confusion and in fear. Beautiful targets for the Jimmy's of the world. Well, I'll tell you this, shithead, I don't think I could take much more. *[He fades into the blackness behind the coffin.]*
       Vinnie
    God, Uncle Louie, I feel so sorry for you... That nose, it's so terrible looking. I just can't believe Jimmy would do that. My God, it's so purple and coal black. *[He shakes his head and cringes in disgust.]* Oh, Uncle Louie, how I wish I'd talked to you more... but you only said hello and good-bye to me when you visited him.... why didn't we say more... there's too much lipstick on your lips... Hey, Uncle Louie, that pin stripe suit with wide lapels and that new white shirt you're wearing are too big for you... and those unseamed cordovan shoes... Uncle Louie, you just don't look right in those things... you always wore an old tweed suit coat and underneath you usually wore one of your soiled green polo shirts... yes, and always that thick rope belt that held up your dark gray working pants... that rope belt... I always wanted to ask you about that... God, Uncle Louie, I hardly knew you!
    I want to laugh, Uncle Louie, come on, Vinnie, why do you always have to at times like this... stop it... please, God, help me... Uncle Louie, are you looking down at me... I know, I know, you're probably saying we're all fucking nuts... Gee, that's the first time I've used that word in a long time... Oh, never mind, tell me, Uncle Louie, what's it like where you are... God, I wish I could talk to you about that... You know, I'm sort of writing a book about heaven, my heaven is getting people on the path to truth... Is there a hell, Uncle Louie? I still can't figure out how I'm going to deal with that... maybe you're better off... the world screwed you enough like it has done to millions of others, but some are able to break through to that esoteric world where the hidden meanings of myths lie... You know, Uncle Lou, I think I envy you. This phony world can no longer

distract you... Hail Mary full of grace, the Lord is with thee... [*He mumbles the rest of the prayer under his breath, and then he turns and slowly sits down on the kneeler. He rubs his eyes with the tips of his fingers.*] You know, Uncle Louie, I still remember those late night talks you would have with him in the kitchen. I always felt secure when you two were talking. The world seemed right. Perfect. I was also glad Grandmother Serrano had taught me Italian because I loved to listen to the words as they flowed from your mouth. It was nothing like the stop and jerky sounds of the English language where too many words need some kind of tongue action... I also remember how when you and him drank too much, your voices would increase in volume and intensity. I love it... I think, Uncle Louie, I did understand something about you which very few around understood... I always felt a very real part of you, Uncle Louie, was your strong belief in the Italian code of ethics, especially those things dealing with man's honor and respect. But you were never able to get it. No, never. I remember how you couldn't get a permanent job because of your refusal to learn the English language. As a result the jobs that were available were very menial... Sometimes I remember you working at the statehouse as a part-time doorman, other times I remember grocery store owners in the North End having you sweep out their stores in the early morning hours...

I often wondered why most of the time you seemed depressed. I think I know why now. You were carrying shame and guilt because you were not able to support your family like other men in the North End... I also remember how you became a servant in your own household. Night after night you used to bitch to him about having to clean Aunt Concetta's house, having to shop for her, having to wash for her, even her underwear, having to fix meals for her... God, Uncle Louie, I'm so sorry I never said anything, nothing. I remember you were an Italian father without any authority and power, you were you said just a slave to a woman and her family. That you said was the most severe suffering God could give you. Nothing in hell could be as bad you said.

Those Cassallanos were at fault you always said to him. That was the cross you said to him that you had to bear... I think, Uncle Louie, you were right. They never give you any peace. The apartment you lived in was owned by the Cassallanos, they were always around making fun of you and giving gifts to your kids. I remember you telling him once that the only place you could find some peace was when you were taking a shit. And that you said sometimes was taken away when the Cassallanos consumed too much food and drink...

Hell, my dear Uncle, your burden was the Italian-American world you lived in... To outsiders, this world supposedly offered affection, emotion and communal sharing. To you it was all a lie... [*He stands up, looks at his uncle, and then faces the audience.*]

Remember, Uncle, the story you told us about Italians in America always wanting to be shining red apples instead of beautiful strong olives. I think it was one Christmas Eve. They laughed and called you stupid. I didn't. Those assholes.

    I listened to every word you said as you went on to tell us that when shining red apples get ripe, they get soft and rot, but not so with olives, you said, they become firmer and more beautiful. They still laughed, especially when you said that ripened olives give off a glow that warms like the sun... Oh, yes... beautiful... I thought for the first time in my life I was hearing real poetry. And they kept laughing... I'm so, so sorry I never said anything to them. [*He starts to sob a bit and slowly sits back down on the kneeler again.*] Jesus, Uncle Louie, how I wish I'd talked to you more, you were probably the only one that would understand. A cross, yes, Uncle Louie, I have one, too. I've been carrying it for years.. Oh, Uncle Louie, help me... [*He sobs louder as he covers his face with his hands.*]

    [*The curtain and lights come down.*]

ACT II - SCENE I

[*Mario and Theresa Serrano's apartment in the North End. At the center of the stage is a large round table with three wooden chairs placed around it. One chair faces the audience, one faces stage right and the other faces stage left. To one side of the table and to the rear is a sink and stove unit. There is a glassless window frame suspended over the sink and stove unit. Blackness is behind the window frame. There are also four door frames located around the stage. One is stage right, two are stage left with small beds behind, and another is near the sink and stove unit. There is also a small table with a phone on it near the stage left doorframe nearest the audience.*

As the curtain rises, the light comes up on Vinnie and his Alter Ego entering the stage right doorframe. His mother is standing on the other side of this doorframe. Behind the doorframe near the sink and stove unit sits Mario Serrano, his father.

Vinnie kisses his mother on the cheek. His Alter Ego goes over and sits in a cross-legged position on top of the sink and stove unit.]

Mother
I was so worried, what happened?

Vinnie
Nothing, I'm sorry. Avoidance behavior, I guess.

Mother
What, I don't understand.

Vinnie
Oh, nothing, nothing.

Mother
You should've called.

Vinnie
I know, but I just couldn't because of the circumstances.
[*He sits down in the chair facing the audience.*] God, I'm tired.

Mother
[*She moves over toward the sink and stove unit.*] Have some coffee?

Alter Ego
[*He jumps down from the sink and stove unit.*] Have some coffee, is that it, bitch? After eight years, Jesus. Yeah, I almost forgot how much practice you've had in keeping your feelings locked deep inside of you. My God, woman, why are you so scared of him? Why?
[*He goes over and lies down on the table.*]

Vinnie
Okay, I'll have some.

Mother
[*She comes over and places a cup of coffee in front of him.*] How about some nice homemade cookies? [*She goes back to the sink again and bends over to get something out of the cupboard underneath.*]

Alter Ego
Jesus, shithead, remember how fucking happy she would be when she was helping Aunt Concetta prepare a large feast for the Cassallanos. Hell, shithead, you and I know that fucking serving is really what the Italian woman is all about. And, of course, cleaning, remember fucking cleaning. Now you remember, Vinnie, how many times a week she would scrub the kitchen floor, vacuum the furniture and rugs, and wash the fucking outside steps to the apartment... Jesus!

Vinnie
Please sit, mom, you look tired. Never mind the damn cookies. The coffee is good enough.

Alter Ego
[*He now gets into a cross-legged position.*] Woman, oh woman, can't you see how difficult it is for you to speak to each other. Never mind the fucking cookies, he's right. Tell him what you're really thinking. Up-tight bitch, come on. Pretending is an art that you both have developed over the years. But no one is fooled. Come on, will you both stop playing this fucking game.

[*She's holding a cup of coffee as she comes over and sits down.*]

Vinnie
How's Aunt Concetta doing?

Mother
I'm worried about her. I just hope everything will go all right with the funeral and all.

Vinnie
[*Sarcastically.*]
It will, don't worry, mom, she's been planning it for years.

Mother
Vinnie, please don't you start, one's enough. [*She nods in the direction of the doorframe where his father is sitting.*] I'm so happy I have the brothers I have. They've been a Godsend for Aunt Concetta during this sad time. You know they made all the arrangements for Uncle Louie's funeral without anyone ever asking them. They've been wonderful.

Vinnie
I wonder what they are expecting in return?

Mother
Come on, Vinnie, be nice. They're my brothers.

Vinnie
[*He reaches over and gently strokes her hand.*] I'm sorry, mom.

Alter Ego
[*He jumps off the table and goes to the doorframe where they entered. He leans against it.*] Great, shithead, now tell her what's been crying inside of you for all these years. Please. Don't be afraid. She'll understand...

[*Both Vinnie and his mother seem embarrassed as their hands quickly slide apart.*]

Alter Ego
Oh, God, no!

Mother
Vinnie, I've been worried. I don't want you to start with him. I don't care what he says. Right now he's in the bathroom and he's as mad as anything because he figures a son who comes home to make up should at least be here on time. So let him be. Please... for me, Vinnie.

Vinnie
Make up, don't tell me he's starting on that shit again.

Mother
Ssshh, he might hear you. Whisper. [*She leans over the table, stretching her head closer to his.*] And, please, Vinnie, don't use that language. I can't believe my boy who at one time was going to become a priest swears now. My God, Vinnie, a professor is not supposed to swear. Wonder why today's kids don't have any respect for anything. Their professors and teachers teach it to them. I hear them talk on the street corners. It's terrible the way they talk so filthy. They're bums, today's kids. You've changed, Vinnie, I just knew you would.

Vinnie
Not exactly, mom, I'm just starting to enjoy sinning more. The other way is so boring.

Mother
Don't say that. You know I was always so proud of you when you used to serve mass for Father Charles. You looked so holy. Everyone thought you would make a fine priest. Father Charles told me that time after time. He always said you had the brains to be one.

Vinnie
Come on, mom, how did he know, he was drunk half the time I served mass for him. But I believe he, too, understood that sinning gave a chance to a person to enrich and deepen his life. The good and decent people are bores. They know nothing of life. The sinner is the only one who understands passion and the mysteries of life. Poor suffering catholics have been fooled because they rarely understand this. Father Charles understood, he sinned and he did it joyfully.

Mother
Vinnie! Stop saying that about Father Charles, he was a good priest. I don't understand what you're saying. He helped me through a lot of bad times with your father. I mean it, he was good to me. And I don't think it's right of you to make fun of him.

Vinnie
I'm not making fun of him. What I'm trying to say is that most of the priests don't understand the hidden meanings behind their saying mass externals. But Father Charles I believe understood that there was something more. That there were internals behind what he did. He understood that there were inner truths behind the stories and myths Jesus Christ used in his teachings. You see the only real sin we can commit is when we move away from searching for truth. It's not the same kind of sin that the majority of priests and nuns invented about missing mass on Sunday and eating meat on Friday. Sober or drunk Father Charles was always trying to get this message across. But very few understood. And it was only in the last few years that I have come to realize what he meant when he used to say to me over and over again. Vinnie, you must use your intellect and your passion to strip away the veils of life. You could never pay too high a price for this. I wish he hadn't died because I would say to him now I understand and in time I will be shouting it to the world.

Mother
I'm confused. Your thoughts confused me, Vinnie, you didn't talk like that when we would kneel down each night and say the rosary. Do you remember, Vinnie, how before you went to sleep you used to love to hear me read something from the Bible? You said it always made you feel dozy inside.

Vinnie
You're right. It did make me feel cozy inside. It made me feel like I did when I went to communion. Holy and clean. But the feeling was all emotion and you can't get close to truth by just feeling emotion. Your mind must also understand what's happening to you. All parts of you must understand the hidden truths behind experiences. And no way, my dear mother, are you going to get on this path to truth by attending some superficial mass for one hour a week. The catholic church today is too much of this world to ever see this.

It's soulless like so many other things in this world today. It's fine to have a bureaucratic structure in a city's clerk office where marriage licenses are given out. It doesn't need a soul, it only needs to be efficient, but to run a church the same way is pure nonsense.

Mother
I still don't understand everything you're saying, Vinnie. I feel bad that you don't care about the church anymore, especially when I think about all those five-thirty masses you served for Father Charles. [*She shakes her head.*]

Vinnie
But I do care about the church. In fact, I hope to show the world how much I care in the book I'm now working on. You see I still love to go into churches because of the beauty that exists there. The quiet, the semi-darkness, the feeling you get that someone is bouncing your thoughts back to you, mom, I love all of that. That's why I used to love to serve mass. I just loved the color and beauty of the whole affair. There were the candles inside the vigil lights which became dancing shadows on the walls. Are the walls at Sacred Heart still banked with vigil lights?

Mother
Yes.

Vinnie
Good, I must go over and make a visit before I leave. Oh, yes, the statues, I was fascinated by the early morning light and how it would play with the statues. It would make them move, so eerie but so lovely. Sometimes I even imagined that they were talking to me. See the beauty was in all of this. It was also in the smells of Sacred Heart at that time in the morning. The candles burning, the leftover incense from novenas held the night before, the fresh wine, even Father Charles' alcoholic breath... all of it touched my senses. Of course, Sacred Heart was my sanctuary. A relief from his bitching and yelling.

Mother
Vinnie, please, he might hear. Now, whatever he says, just listen. I don't want this to be another day to remember like that time. I still feel bad that your wife had to see it all.

Alter Ego
[*He goes over and leans against the doorframe where the father is sitting.*] Don't worry, woman, his wife is a saint. That's what everyone says. Always taking care of others and their pain. Feeling so sorry for them, but, of course, never seeing shithead's pain. Right, shithead? Saints breed on troubles and sufferings. So, woman, the day shithead brought her home to meet him and he called a whore. That was nothing. She loved it. She was able to show shithead how

strong she was. Remember, shithead, what she said? Pray for him, remember she said, he is too ignorant to appreciate love. Oh, God, how wrong she was.

  Vinnie
I won't start. I promise.

  Mother
[*Her eyes filling with tears.*]
  Thank you. If you only knew, Vinnie, what it's like living with him now. I have kept so many things inside of me for too many years. No one knows except for my sister, Concetta, what it's like living with a man who hates the world. He's just like his brother Louie. Full of misery. I just don't understand what happened to him. He treated me so wonderful for so many years, and then as you got older something just seemed to snap. I can't tell you, Vinnie, how many times I wanted to write and tell you how bad it is. I tried to tell you when we talked over the phone on holidays. But I couldn't. I figured you were free of him and why should I burden you with my problems. Concetta wanted me to fly down and talk to you. When I asked him, he said if I went he would leave me. Maybe I should've gone, huh? I don't know. It's not right that I shouldn't be allowed to see my son and my grandchildren. And you know what the worst thing is? Having him hate my family. He says he would rather burn in hell than be nice to my family. Now he's saying that my family killed his brother. He talks so stupid sometimes. I don't understand how he could say that after Concetta and my brothers have supported his brother all these years. His brother and his pride. And always talking about the old country. They were still in another century. Thank God your father learned English because of his business. That's one good thing.

  Vinnie
That's enough, mom, please. I feel so bad that you had to put up with all of this by yourself.

  Mother
Don't feel bad, Vinnie, I've just been wanting to tell you these things for so long. I'm doing fine, really. Aunt Concetta has given me a great deal of support over the years. And, Vinnie, she thinks so much of you. She's been telling everyone how wonderful you are to come all the way from West Virginia for Uncle Louie's funeral. She wants you to come over tonight and have something to eat. Okay?

  Vinnie
I'll see, mom. I don't know if I could put up with all of them... At least not now.

  Mother
Please, Vinnie, you've got to go! She's been so good to you and to me over the years.

Alter Ego
[*He is now standing directly in back of Vinnie.*]
   Hell, woman, he never wanted any of those gifts. She just sent them hoping it would relieve the guilt she had for shitting on you. I told shithead to send them all back. The silverware for his wedding, the clothes for the kids, the fifty dollar bills on their birthdays, the electric ovens... But no, shithead was too scared it would hurt you. Asshole. [*He goes over and sits in front of the stage right doorframe.*]

Vinnie
   Hell, mom, I just don't know if I could put up with all those loud-mouth brothers of yours and then watch you wait on her like she was some kind of royalty.

Mother
   Vinnie, please. Only my brother Phil will be there. The others will be at the wake.

Vinnie
   Okay, but sometimes, mom, you must admit that your brothers, especially Uncle Phil, are too much to take.

Mother
[*Apologetically.*]
   I know, I know. But they have changed since you last saw them. They really have.

Vinnie
   Well, I just can't believe Uncle Phil has changed. Always trying to prove the Cassallanos are smarter than the Serrannos... Mom, I'm above all of that now. Understand?

Mother
   Yes, I know you are. But believe me he's changed. He teaches in Braintree and loves it. You'll see.

Vinnie
   I hope so.

Mother
   Listen, Vinnie, if Phil starts anything, do what I said to do with your father, just listen, keep your mouth shut and pretend whatever he's saying that he's right.

Alter Ego
   Sure, shithead, just like all good Italian boys do. Can't you see what she's doing to you? Please, shithead, stop playing these fucking games with her, please...

Vinnie
Let me see how I'm feeling after I get a couple of hours rest. Okay? I'll probably be there, so don't worry.

Mother
Good.

[*His father now stands up and begins to gargle loudly.*]

Mother
[*She brings her forefinger to her pursed lips.*] Ssshh.

Vinnie
[*Shaking his head.*]
I just can't believe that he's still mad. You would've thought after eight years he would've mellowed a bit.

Mother
Please, Vinnie, he might hear you.

Vinnie
Okay.

Mother
Since his brother's death, he's been drinking worse than ever. You'd never have expected it - a man who was so good at one time. Where would you be if it wasn't for that money he saved for your education?

Vinnie
I don't like talking about that, it hurts too much.

Mother
I'm sorry, Vinnie, but it's true. You know it. He could be so good. Sometimes I think it's because his business in the last few years has not been very good. The one piece rubber sole has hurt him. People instead of getting old shoes fixed, buy new ones and throw the old ones out. So now because he doesn't have too many customers, he has all of this free time during the day to think about himself and whatever he does on those nights he disappears.

Vinnie
I didn't realize he was still doing that. I still remember how mad you used to get when he didn't get home until the next day. I wonder what he does on those nights. I have...

Mother
Bitterly.
I don't know what he does on those nights and I don't care anymore. He goes his way and I go mine. I'm not going to spend the rest of my life worrying where he goes at night. No more... I'm finished with that business... [*She pushes her chair back, stands up and goes*

over to the stove and pours herself some more coffee. Tears come to her eyes again. Vinnie gets up and goes over to her. She waves him away. Setting the coffee cups on the stove, she rushes by him into the stage left doorframe.

The light comes up on her lying on a small bed on the other side of the doorframe. Vinnie enters.]

Vinnie
You okay?

Mother
[Weakly.]
Yes, I'll be fine in a few minutes. I'm just tired.

Vinnie
You sure?

Mother
Yes, I'll be okay. Please don't make a fuss and let me be for a few minutes. Please, Vinnie, he might hear and that's all I need.

Vinnie
Okay. [He leaves, and after a long minute she gets up and follows.]

Mother
I'm okay now, I'm not going to lay there and mull over things. I'm finished with that too. Just promise me, Vinnie, you won't start with your father, please.

Vinnie
I won't.

Alter Ego
[He gets up, goes over to the stage left doorframe which she just went out of and leans against it. Now the father walks out. Quickly the mother sits down in the chair that is facing stage right. Vinnie stands in back of her.]

Vinnie
[Trying hard to sound friendly.]
Hi, dad.

Father
[He nods sadly as he goes to the sink while coming his hair with his hand. He stands there for a long moment, his back facing Vinnie and his mother.]

Vinnie
It's been a long time.

Alter Ego
Oh, what a wonderful line, shithead, it sounds like something from a soap opera. And you're the one they look to for the most eloquent comments at staff meetings. That's a laugh, look at you now, Mister Helen Keller.

Father
[*He drinks a glass of water, makes some funny sounds in his throat and continues to stare out the window frame.*]

Mother
[*She gets up.*]
I'm late for mass, I'd better go. I just put some clean sheets on your bed, Vinnie, so you go in and have a nice rest and I'll see you later at Aunt Concetta's, okay?

Vinnie
Fine.

Father
[*He shouts angrily without turning around.*]
Go, go help the big shot.

Mother
[*Smiling.*]
You two have a nice long visit. And welcome to happiness valley, Vinnie. [*She hurries out of the stage right doorframe.*]

A long pause.]

Vinnie
How have you been feeling, dad?

Alter Ego
[*He goes to the table and sits on its edge facing Vinnie and his father.*] Please, fucker, speak to your son before he goes bullshit. I can't stand the tension...

Father
[*Stiffly.*]
Not good, all this funeral business for my brother has taken a lot out of me. They pretend they love him now when everyone of those sons of bitches have put more than one nail in his coffin. I wanted to tell them all of last night, but I had too much respect for my brother's sake.

Vinnie
[*Sympathetically.*]
Well, all of this wake stuff will be over pretty soon. Then you won't have to deal with them any more.

Father
It won't, it won't be over. My brother only wanted to have a place of his own where he could raise his family without the bloodsucker Cassallanos around. But Miss Big Shot didn't want to because she wanted to be around people who would kiss her ass.

Vinnie
Perhaps he's better off dead.

Father
Maybe... But I just wish I had told those assholes off a long time ago.

Vinnie
Why didn't you?

Father
[*Shouts loudly.*]
You know.

Vinnie
You're not going to start with that stuff again... Jesus, I'll leave. Remember we've gone through this before.

Father
[*Shouting again.*]
Look at your own family, Miss Big Shot would say. A lazy bum who treated you like shit. He takes all your money for schooling and then he lies to you...

Vinnie
Please, dad.

Father
[*Sarcastically.*]
Mister Hot Pants couldn't wait. Sure, sure, those goddamn Irish didn't want to lose a good catch. Any mother or father would want the same thing for their daughter. They're smart. Hell, they figured with you they could be set for life.

Vinnie
That's not true. They could care less. My God! The father makes at least two hundred thousand a year. How ridiculous can you be? I don't believe this. I don't believe I'm arguing with you about this same old shit again.

Father
You always have an answer. A good education means your son becomes a good bullshitter. You think your father knows nothing except shining and cutting leather. Well, I'll tell you this, buddie, I know a lot more than you think. I was already ready to screw the

other guy before he screwed me. Like it or not, fellow, it's a
dog-eat-dog world. I know with all your education you still don't
understand that. That's America and that's why you'll never have
anything. Learning fancy words and ideas doesn't put food on the
table. I was lucky I worked for myself, no one ever knew how much I
really made. Where would you have gotten the money for all those good
schools I sent you to, huh?

    Vinnie
Come, on dad, I've heard all of this before. I don't want to
argue with you, please.

    Father
No, you couldn't listen to me eight years ago. Without a family
you would've been able to save and invest your money. A doctor. A
lawyer. That's what you should've become, not a school teacher.
There are millions of them.

    Vinnie
I'm a professor, not a school teacher.

    Father
No difference, you still have to work for someone.

    Vinnie
Please, dad, I told you I don't want to argue and I really
don't care. Money is not that important to me. Period. There's so
much more I want to talk to you about. Eight years, my God!

    Father
[*He starts to pace, firing up his anger with each step.*]
You're crazy. Look at Carilucci's son, he's a doctor now.
[*Vinnie shakes his head as if to say I give up.*] He makes a hundred
and fifty thousand dollars a year. Last year, he built a new home for
himself and his father in Newton. But no, right after you got your
degree from Harvard, you had to get married. My priestly son couldn't
contain his sexual juices, right? A whore comes to his doorstep and
he follows her like a male dog smelling a female in heat. Watch
out for the quiet ones, they say, they're the worst ones...

    Vinnie
[*Putting his hands to his ears.*]
Stop it, I won't listen any more.

    Father
Oh, yes, you will. I won't ever forget the day you said don't
worry, dad, once I've finished at Harvard, I'll still live with you
and mom for at least three years. I need to get myself established,
you said, yes that's what you said, that you needed to get yourself
established before you moved on. And so what does my lying son
do, he brings home a fresh whore and then tells me he's getting married

and taking a job in West Virginia. I'll never forget that, never.

Vinnie
[*Takes his hands away from his ears.*]
You don't understand, dad, I needed some order for my writing. I really didn't want to leave, but I just couldn't take any more of your bitching and yelling. Day in and day out.

Father
Listen to him, I needed some order for my writing. Bullshit. You don't know what you put me through. You don't know.

Vinnie
Hell! What do you want from me? I never gave you any trouble. I never stole anything. I didn't murder anyone. I never did anything that would embarrass you. Jesus, I went on to tough schools, worked hard, got my Ph.D. from Harvard. What else? God, what the hell else do you want from me? What...

Father
[*He moves toward Vinnie as if he were going to hit him.*]
You didn't do all those things for me, you selfish son of a bitch.

Vinnie
[*Helplessly.*]
You're just like Uncle Louie.

Father
So what? I'm proud to be compared to my brother. He was not a liar like my son.

Vinnie
Hell, I never asked to be born to you.

Father
[*Backs off.*]
That's right, mister sensitive, get mad now. I didn't mean that. I was just talking.

Vinnie
[*Tears in his eyes.*]
Talking, my ass.

Father
You're like your mother, you take everything so personal... I can't talk to you. Eight years makes no difference. Go, go where you have to go. I don't care. [*He goes over to the sink and takes out a bottle of red wine from underneath.*]

Vinnie
You bastard! Why do you do this to me? Oh, God, I hate you.

[*He runs and throws himself on the small bed which is behind the stage left doorframe nearest the audience.*]

   Alter Ego
[*Moves toward the audience.*]
  Destroy someone and then afterwards pretend it's the other person's fault. A great Italian trick. You've had a lot of practice, haven't you old Mario? I'll say this for you, you still know how to rattle him. How many more times will you turn his love into hate, huh, old man? So your wife has her Concetta. And now you have your bottle. But what does your poor shithead of a son have, huh?... Do you remember how he loves you. Do you? That's what I want to know. Did you ever really talk to him afterwards? No, of course not, you just became mean and belligerent. Not helping his mother, forgetting to flush the toilet, spending too much time reading; these, old Mario, became great excuses for you to unleash your anger on him. Why, old man, why do you hate so much? [*In the background, the father is gulping the wine down from the bottle.*]

  [*The light comes down on the father and the Alter Ego. A single spotlight now shines on Vinnie twisting and turning in bed.*

  Finally, after a long pause, the spotlight goes out and the curtain comes down.]

ACT II - SCENE II

[*Concetta Cassallano's apartment. There are two doorframes, one is stage right and the other is center stage and is located directly behind a large oval-shaped table which has a white tablecloth covering it. A large bowl of fruit and three bottles of red wine are on the table. There are also glasses half-filled with wine in front of everyone.*

Concetta Serrano is sitting at the head of the table facing the audience. Sitting on her left are Theresa, Patsy, and Rose. Sitting on her right are Jimmy, Phil, and Mario whose head is on the table, asleep.

The light and curtain comes up on Vinnie and his Alter Ego entering from the stage right doorframe. The Alter Ego goes over and sits in one of two empty chairs which are located to the stage right side of the oval-shaped table. Vinnie goes over and kisses Concetta on the cheek.]

Vinnie
I'm sorry.

Concetta
Thank you, dear, I'm so happy you came. We just finished eating. We'll fix something for you. Patsy, please get Vinnie a chair and put it next to me. I want to talk to him. It's been too long since we've talked.

[*As Patsy goes over and gets him an empty chair, Vinnie goes over to Rose and kisses her on the cheek.*]

Vinnie
I'm sorry, Rose, is everything okay?

Rose
Yes, thanks for coming, Vinnie. Isn't it sad that the only time Italians get together is at funerals and weddings?

Vinnie
Yes, I agree.

Concetta
[*She is waving to him.*]
Come here, Vinnie, let's hear about you and we'll get you something to eat.

[*As he goes back to her, Patsy is placing the empty chair next to her. He shakes Patsy's hand.*]

Vinnie
I'm sorry, Patsy.

Patsy
Nice seeing you, Vin. What will it be, a dish of homemade spaghetti with some spareribs and sausage?

Vinnie
No, nothing, thank you.

Patsy
Oh, come on, you've been living with those poor people in West Virginia for too long. Eat something.

Vinnie
No, thank you, I'm really not hungry.

Patsy
Well, then, how about something to drink? Wine, scotch, bourbon, anisette. Anything. We got it.

Vinnie
A scotch and water will be fine.

Patsy
Good. [*He goes out the doorframe behind the oval-shaped table.*

Vinnie nods in the direction of Phil as he sits down.]

Phil
So the Prodigal Son returns.

Vinnie
Not exactly, but close.

Rose
Vinnie, you sure you won't have anything to eat? Your mother and I cooked most of it.

Vinnie
No, really. A drink is all I need.

Concetta
You sure, we have so much. The others that have already left for Longo's. They hardly ate anything. My dear brothers, I don't think they have slept at all since it happened. I know Joe, Cosmo, and Nick will be glad to see you. But now tell me, how's your wife and kids?

[*Patsy places a drink in front of him and then goes back to his place at the table.*]

Vinnie
Fine, they're doing really fine. [*He takes a sip of his drink.*] Thanks, Pat.

Patsy
That's okay.

Concetta
I told your mother the other day you were lucky to find such a nice Irish girl like Chris. We would like to get to know her. How long has it been since your wedding?

Vinnie
Eight years.

Concetta
No!

Vinnie
Yes.

Concetta
Maybe I'll come to visit you with your mother some day.

Vinnie
Good.

Concetta
I travel a lot on business now and I've always wanted to go to West Virginia. I could use the excuse that I'm making contact with a famous writer who might publish with us. Right?

Vinnie
Right.

Concetta
I also have more time now because Rose is running the antique shop for me. I just wish she would get married. Look at her, she's getting fat. Do you remember, Vinnie, that summer when you worked for me cleaning up some old brass bedposts. The sweat poured off you as you worked hard getting the black-greenish tarnish off. I remember asking you, Vinnie, is that the kind of work you would like to do for the rest of your life? You said, trying to be nice because you're the type that wouldn't hurt anyone's feelings, you said you didn't mind as long as it helped me but I knew in my heart you were too good for that kind of nigger work. That's why I never asked you to help in the store again. I told your mother I wanted you to get working on becoming a genius.

Vinnie
I'm grateful for the compliment, Aunt Concetta, but a genius I'm not. I just have a little talent for being very, very tolerant of boring hard work. But, enough of me, Rose, mom wrote and told me about you running the antique store. Good for you.

Rose
Well, I'm enjoying it but sometimes it gets tiring. The help you get today is terrible.

Concetta
If she would stop playing around with those young immigrants she always hires, she might get something done.

Rose
That's not true.

Concetta
Well, that's not what I hear...

Patsy
Please, mom, she's not feeling good.

Concetta
Okay, should I tell Vinnie about my dear son who has had a degree for six years but the only job he was able to get was counting basketballs. And should I tell him that the only reason he got the job was because his mother knew the guy who was running the community center. Should I go on?

Patsy
Come on, mom, I do a lot of other things, too.

Concetta
Like what? Tell us, please.

Patsy
A lot of things, I said. I make up schedules for senior citizens. I help to write proposals for grants. I counsel people, and so on.

Concetta
Big deal! Vinnie, only you have done well in this family. You were the smartest. I'm proud of you.

Vinnie
Well, I don't know about that. Jimmy seems to be doing well. I talked to him last night. [*He looks over to Jimmy who flashes a smile at him.*]

Concetta

Oh, sure, the biggest part he's had in a movie was for three minutes. And in those three minutes, all he was was Robert Redford's punching bag. He said ouch and ouch and ouch. And that's it. I remember this one time when he called and he told me he was in a movie with Clint Eastwood. So I waited until the movie came to Boston and when it did I went to see it with some of my friends. You know what he was, he was a nude statue who I guess all these people wanted to capture. I told him a long time ago I would give him the money to go and study at a good acting school. A friend of mine in the film business told me Jimmy will never make it big in the movies because he still speaks like he's from the North End of Boston.

Jimmy

Mom, don't you think you're exaggerating a bit? Are you forgetting that last year I played Richard the Third here in Boston.

Concetta

Oh, I almost forgot. You did. But the critics tore you apart because of your accent.

Jimmy

I don't care what the hell the critics said. I felt good about my performance. And that's what counts. My own sense of worth.

Concetta

Vinnie, Jimmy could've been like you, he had the brains. He has a great analytical mind. I see it all the time when I ask him to read some manuscripts for me. I also wanted him to go to night school like I did and get a degree. I wouldn't be where I am today if it wasn't for that damn piece of paper. I remember my mother and father thinking I was wasting my time. Everyone thought I was crazy, working all day in the store and then at night working on a business degree. I'll tell you, I was years ahead of the so-called feminist movement. Well, it payed off. I could get Jimmy a job just like that if he would start working on a degree. I've worked myself up from sales to executive editor in just a few years. Maybe you can talk to him, Vinnie, he won't listen to me.

Jimmy

You can't tell, mom, I still might take your advice. I'm just coming alive. I've always wanted to be an archaeologist. I love discovering what we're connected to. Digging and finding something centuries old, I think, would give me a feeling of continuity. I need that, especially now. Maybe, mom, I'll just do that. We'll see.

Concetta

Well, I hope you do something with your life, son, instead of playing around with those phonies in Hollywood. Vinnie, how many mothers do you know that are still supporting their children who are all nearing the age of forty. Still, I love my kids and one thing I must say about them, they've always been good to me. Considering what they had to live through, I think, they've also done pretty good with their lives. Sure, I guess I've spoiled them, too, but I couldn't help it. [*She sniffles, but then quickly gains control of herself.*] You have to do the best you can when you're raising your kids almost all by yourself.

Jimmy
Hell, mom, we've done more than pretty good. Look at how much more interesting we are because of our experiences with him.

Concetta
Stop it, Jimmy, you're being disrespectful.

Vinnie
I just wonder if experiences ever have to be judged.

Jimmy
I don't understand.

Vinnie
Well, I guess what I'm wondering about is how we decide what a good experience is and what a bad experience is. I mean, is there a universal criterion or conscience we could use. Now I don't mean God, here. I just wonder if there is a great experimenter somewhere who's evaluating our experiences or our actions. Are we his laboratory and I wonder who of us are doing well in this experiment? You see what I mean?

Jimmy
Are you talking about morality?

Vinnie
Not exactly, but it's related to morality. The morality we now know is constantly controlled by those who are in the majority. And I believe this majority are the ones who lead us into wars, who teach us how to murder, to rape, to steal, to destroy our environment, and so forth. You see this morality is part of our civilization, which never learns from history. It keeps having wars, murders, destruction, and so on. But I believe there is another civilization, a civilization that separates itself from the civilization we are now living in. And I think you reach this civilization when you start getting closer to the hidden and esoteric knowledge of humanity. Let me be more specific. I believe this esoteric knowledge is like the knowledge one gains after reading a poem. A worthwhile poem, of course. What happens after you read this poem, you get an implicit understanding of life. And sometimes this type of understanding is very hard to put into words. You see, this type of knowledge is different from the explicit knowledge one gets from science. And so, I guess, what I'm searching for are ways of getting us closer to the esoteric world.

Jimmy
Whoa, boy, you've lost me. It's a funny thing how you're more talkative than last night. It must be the audience.

Concetta
Theresa, would you listen to your son. Wow! I don't understand very much of what he's saying, but I'll tell you, it really sounds impressive. I always said, Vinnie, that you had a way with words.

Theresa
Now you see, Concetta, what I meant earlier when I told you he has changed. He thinks too much now. Why does he have to make everything so deep? The next thing you know, he'll be throwing himself off a bridge. I worry about him.

Vinnie
Look, mom, if I find this esoteric world, it doesn't matter what I do to my life in this civilization... Well, not really...

Concetta
Oh, Three, stop worrying. He's exaggerating just like my Jimmy does. All writers are great liars. Right, Vinnie?

Vinnie
That's right. You have to twist the facts of this world to get closer to the real truths.

Theresa
I'm so confused.

Concetta
Don't be, Three, look at Einstein, very few understood him at first...

Vinnie
God, don't compare me to him, you're doing him an injustice. Please.

Concetta
You're too modest, Vinnie. You know, I've read some of your books, Vinnie, and I must admit that I couldn't follow very much of what you said. I guess that's why I only work with trade books. Your books are a bit too philosophical for me.

Vinnie
I agree. They were. However, I think with my next book, it will be different. Everyone will understand what I'm saying if they work hard at it. Truth is the language of all men. And that's what I hope my novel will deal with.

Concetta
You know, Vinnie, since I've been in this business of publishing, I've come to understand a few things. Nothing will sell unless you really simplify it for the public.

Vinnie
But I think that's the whole problem. In the process of making it simple, we lose the difficult truths. You see I don't plan to entertain people with my words like a writer of a best seller. Great books were never made simple to read, if they were, we would have nothing now. Do you see what I mean?

Concetta
Yes, I do, but I know a lot of publishers would argue that readers don't want to think about what you call difficult truths because it makes them too depressed.

Vinnie
I don't care. What these publishers usually give the public are lies and more lies.

Concetta
Didn't Smith and Brothers publish your books?

Vinnie
Yes.

Concetta
A fine company. Are you also thinking of publishing your next book with them?

Jimmy
Yes.

Concetta
Well, look, why don't you share it with us? Maybe we could work out a better deal.

Vinnie
I'll see, maybe I will. If you can give me wider distribution, I might go with your company.

Concetta
Good. I just hope it's not as weird as some of the stuff Jimmy loves to read. I don't know how he could stand to read all that crazy stuff.

Vinnie
Last night he told me about one manuscript he was reading. I found it interesting. In fact, after going to Longo's, I thought a great deal about it.

Jimmy
[*Laughs nervously.*]
　　I can't remember too much of what I said. I was really out of it. You know, mom, how I get when I have a bit too many.

　　Concetta
　　Yes, I do, my poor Jimmy sometimes doesn't know when to be quiet. He's so impressionable. Every week he's into something different. One week it's hypnosis, another week it's sufi, another week it's macrobiotics. In fact, a lot of kooky actors go to him to get advice on their bodies, diets, and skin. I'll tell you that whole Hollywood bunch is crazy. You know our worse writers come from there. Well, I guess Jimmy could be doing a lot of other things a lot worse. So I'm really grateful he knows how to keep busy.

　　Alter Ego
[*He stands up, facing the audience and walks stage left.*]
　　Oh, yes, good old Concetta, killing is a wonderful way of keeping busy. Wonderful. I'm so disgusted with the whole fucking bunch of you. Do you believe, people, not one asshole here has shown any sympathy for Louie. Selfish bastards. I can't believe shithead, he usually has too much sympathy for people, but not today. Him and his fucking medieval ideas about truth and esoteric civilizations... Well, good for you, Mario, sleep your ass off. The rest are a bunch of unfeeling bastards. I'll tell you, Mario, if you wake up, tell the son of a bitches that. Will you? [*He fades into the darkness.*]

　　Jimmy
　　You know, mom, I'm just working at being a good dilettante.

　　Concetta
　　Well, I just wish you would center on one thing. I don't care what it is, even basket weaving. But take one thing and do it well.

　　Jimmy
　　Maybe, Vinnie, with all his great thoughts, could help me with this. [*Bitterly.*] Or maybe he's just too smart to bother with peons like us.

　　Concetta
　　Oh, stop, Jimmy, you're just jealous.

　　Jimmy
　　Yeah, you're probably right. I got to talk to you more, Vinnie, okay?

　　Vinnie
　　Okay, I just hope I have time before I leave to go back.

　　Jimmy
[*Authoritatively.*]
　　We will.

Mario
[*Slowly raises his head from the table, shakes the sleep from his head, and then looks around.*]
Talk! Talk! Talk! Nobody ever says anything. What do you people remember about my brother? That's what I want to talk about. He was nothing to you people. He was must somebody who came in for meals and when he talked you told him to shut up. Let's talk about that. Yeah, let's talk about how when he was around you pretended he didn't exist. [*He fills up with emotion and now the words come out sluggishly.*] Day in and day out he was burning in hell. Oh, God, I'll never forget what you people did to him, never. You damn murderers...

Theresa
Oh, Mario, go back to sleep. You had too much to drink.

Mario
Yes, woman, I did have too much to drink just so I could forget you bastards. Do you know he wanted to love his family, that was his dream. But no one would let him. His thoughts were always of his family, but his family only laughed at his ways. My poor brother, I loved you so. You were just a good man. Yes, Louie, these bastards wanted you to feel ashamed because you loved your far-off country from which you came. Couldn't they see that's the only place where you had your dignity, couldn't these bastards see that? It held your immorality also...

Theresa
[*Gets up.*]
Come on, Mario, let's go home. I will not sit here and listen to you hurt my family, especially at a time like this. Come on...

Mario
[*Slowly gets up.*]
Yeah, bitch, I'm going, but I'm not going with you. I can't stand to sit here and watch you people celebrate and mock my brother's death. I want to get away from here before I throw up on all of you. And you don't deserve that. None of you do. I just hope before my brother died that he cursed you all with the worst sicknesses and sufferings that exist on this earth. A cancer sickness would be too good for you animals. He deserved so much better... [*He staggers toward the stage right doorframe.*] Oh; my dear brother, I'll miss you, I have no one now, no one...

Theresa
Mario!

Concetta
[*Gets up.*]
Three, let him be, he doesn't bother me, they all say stupid

things when they drink. He did the same thing. He... [*She suddenly gets sad and begins to sob a bit.*] If he only knew how hard I tried, how much I loved him... I can't talk about it. [*Jimmy comes over and comforts her by putting his arms around her waist.*] Come on, we've got to get over to Longo's, the others will probably be wondering what happened to us. Theresa, you stay here and feed yourson. He looks terrible. And Phil, you take Three and Vinnie over to Longo's when they're finished.

Vinnie
Really, Aunt Concetta, I don't...

Concetta
You eat something, Vinnie, or I'll get mad. And you know how I can get when I get mad.

Vinnie
Okay.

[*Concetta goes out the stage right doorframe and Jimmy, Rose, and Patsy follow. Theresa then goes out the doorframe which is directly behind the oval-shaped table.*]

Theresa
[*She sits on the bench behind the doorframe and picks up a plate which has a sandwich on it.*] Want a meatball sandwich?

Vinnie
Yea, that'll be fine.

Theresa
Concetta is right. You don't look good. You need some color in your face. [*She gets up and comes back in and places the plate in front of Vinnie. Phil now gets up and starts moving toward Vinnie.*] Eat now. I just wish your stupid father didn't say those things. He's stupid, Vinnie. He never saw how terrible Louie treated my sister. He never saw how moody Louie was and how no one would dare say anything to him for fear he might explode and be violent. Yes, Vinnie, your stubborn father never saw the big bruises on Concetta's body because of his beating her. No, Vinnie, he wouldn't believe me when I told him these things. He just would say I was on her side. I feel so embarrassed now.

Vinnie
Don't be. His heart is carrying a huge amount of anger. He has to strike out, I guess. He started with the same old crap with me, too.

Theresa
No.

Phil
[*Standing now next to where Vinnie is sitting.*]
Forget it, Theresa. Forget it. He's crazy like his brother. Plain and simple. Now I want to talk to the big university professor. Maybe I could learn some things. [*He sits down next to Vinnie.*]

Theresa
Phil, please don't start with him now. I don't want another eight years to go by before I see my son.

Phil
Oh, stop worrying about your son, Three. University professors need to be strong if they are going to save the world. [*He sits down next to Vinnie.*]

Vinnie
It's okay, mom.

Phil
[*Taunting.*]
It's okay, mom, listen to that.

Theresa
Listen, Phil, you be nice to him. I got to go in and get supper ready before I leave for Longo's. I want Concetta to find everything done. That poor woman, all she's been through. But, Vinnie, don't pay any attention to him. His bark is bigger than his bite.

Vinnie
[*Biting into the sandwich and staring down at the table.*]
Okay.

[*Theresa goes into the doorframe behind the oval-shaped. She sits and stares out.*]

Phil
[*Backing off in his attack.*]
Hey, I heard what you were saying to my sister. It looks like you're into some deep stuff with that book you're planning to write.

Vinnie
[*Icy voice.*]
Yeah, it looks that way, doesn't it?

Phil
You know, Vinnie, someday I hope to go on and finish my Ph.D. degree in education.

Vinnie
[*Without any enthusiasm.*]
Good. They need all the help they can get.

Phil
Well, I could've been working on it now if I didn't spend so much time commuting to Braintree. I wish I could've gotten a job teaching here in the North End. But the Catholic schools didn't have any openings. And there's a good possibility that all the Catholic schools in the North End will go public in a year or two. And if that happens, that means niggers.

Vinnie
So?

Phil
[Angrily.]
Well, I'll tell you, Mister Professor, if people thought it was bad in South Boston, wait and see what happens here. You know, just two months ago some nigger tried to move in with a white girl and in one night they were burned out. I'll tell you the Italians here won't stand for any niggers taking over their neighborhood. There'll be more killing here than they ever thought of having in South Boston.

Vinnie
It's a reality, Phil, you have to face. Like it or not.

Phil
Not me, buddie, not this guy anyway. I won't be forced to live with them and I'll be damn if I'll teach them. It's liberal professors like you who have given the niggers the feeling that they're better than everyone else.

Vinnie
So what, after three hundred years they deserve the right to feel better than everyone else. It's about time.

Phil
That three-hundred-year stuff is pure bullshot. We've given them more time than anyone else to make it. Sure, I know they were slaves and all that shit, but still they had a good head start on Italian immigrants like my parents who worked their asses off for their children. You know what the niggers problem is, it's that they are too damn lazy to make it on their own.

Vinnie
[Shaking his head in disbelief.]
I don't believe you said that. You sound like a bigoted southerner that was around in the fifties and sixties.

Phil
I don't care who I sound like. I won't give them any respect until they work for things just as I had to. Believe it or not, I don't really hate them. Look, I teach with one in Braintree, and we get along fine. Even he agrees with me. I'm just saying, I'm being

discriminated against when a nigger gets ahead of me because of his color.

Vinnie
I think you're scared, Phil, scared to accept the fact that the scales have to be balanced in their favor until they have the same equal opportunities as we do.

Phil
That's bullshit, too. Hell, they're taking over in politics, in businesses, in education, in everything, even in the rackets. What else do they want, my home, my children, my religion? Tell me, Mister Professor, what else do they expect to be handed to them?

Vinnie
You're being melodramatic.

Phil
No, I'm not. I'm just asking for my rights as a citizen of this country. This country is founded on the right of Americans choosing the right to send their kids to a school in their own neighborhood where they will be with their own kind. And that's really the issue.

Vinnie
No, the real issue is that you can't accept blacks. Period.

Phil
Would you have your daughter marry one?

Vinnie
That's not the point.

Phil
Oh, come on, Vinnie...

[*Theresa gets up and comes in.*]

My God, Phil, I could hear your yelling all the way in there. Leave him alone, please. Can't you see he looks tired?

Phil
Oh, Theresa, stop babying him, we're just talking. One educator to another. Right, Vinnie?

Vinnie
[*Dully.*]
Yeah, I guess so.

Theresa
Well, let's go. I'm ready. Vinnie, you're coming, aren't you?

Vinnie
Yeah, but you go ahead. I want to call home and see how everything is in West Virginia.

Theresa
That's nice, you miss your family, huh?

Vinnie
Yeah, so go ahead. [*He stands up.*] I'll be there in a little while.

Phil
Some day, Vinnie, I would like to have about four hours with you, then I think I could straighten you out about higgers.

Theresa
Come on, Phil, let him call his family in peace.

Phil
[*Gets up.*]
Of course, if we do get together, you must tell me what professors think about while they sit on their asses all day.
[*He laughs as Theresa angrily shoves him into the direction of the stage right doorframe. He turns just as he's going out the doorframe and winks.*]

Vinnie
[*Gets up.*]
Asshole. [*He goes over to the small table, picks up the phone and dials.*] Operator, could you give me the number of Angie Castro or Angie Peters? Thank you.

Alter Ego
[*He comes out of the darkness and stands center stage, facing the audience.*]
I'm scared, people. I just don't know why. I got this uneasy feeling that something is happening inside of shithead and it's something that I have no control over. You know, people, for some many years I've felt that I was his wings. At times I even felt like an attendant in an insane asylum, he was do damn dependent on me for support. But now, I don't know. I don't like it. I'm feeling like an empty boat in a stewing sea. Hell, a few days ago shithead would've never stood up to Phil and his fucking arguments about niggers. Shithead just doesn't like to argue or hurt people. I mean, really, he's pure chickenshit. But today, this was a Vinnie I've never seen before. You know, I really didn't feel needed in this whole scene. And that's not good. I think, people, I'm starting to need him more than he needs him. And that, people, is a no-no in my job. You see,

my role is defined by his soul, but in this scene, I felt his soul slipping away from me. And, God, what if that should ever happen? What the hell would I do? Who would I be then? What neurotic would have me after being with shithead for so long. Jesus, I just don't know how this could've happened, I mean his type never sheds me until death. His type has just got too many things screaming in his mind in anything he does. I like to tell him he's got it all under control, but I know it's not true. Hell, psychiatrists love using that bullshit about control all the time. Shit, if we didn't have psychiatrists, schools, nut houses, people like me would be out of work. All these institutions are obsessed with developing a normal personality. Guilt and shame are their greatest weapons and, of course, it keeps guys like me working. And so you see my role has been clearly defined for centuries.

Hell, wait a minute, I might be getting hyper about nothing. We all have our downs, even people like me. I guess with shithead I'm not used to it because it seems he always needs me. I've been spoiled... Hey, what the hell am I worrying about, huh? Isn't he talking to lovely Angie [*Cocky-like.*] Wonderful, he'll never in a million years make it with her. I know, believe me. He's got too much loyalty for the saint. Oh, saints are also good for our business. You know, loving pain, suffering, hating sin and all that shit. Yeah, why should I sweat it, the thoughts about the saint, his kids, and I almost forgot Father Charles screaming in his mind that it's a terrible sin to selfishly desire another person only for sex. Hey, I got it made. Did I mention that priests and nuns are also great in drumming up people for my business? Oh, I feel better already. I'm ready to work again... Come on, shithead, let's get going. You got a date with a beautiful broad... [*He turns and goes over to Vinnie who is still talking on the phone.*

The curtain and lights come down.]

ACT II - SCENE III

[*Angie Castro's apartment - Everything is the same except this time there are three rolled-up cigarettes, a pack of matches, and an ashtray on the nightstand.*

When the lights and curtain come up, Angie and Vinnie are embracing and kissing. They stay like this for a long moment. A sheet half covers their bodies. Like before, Vinnie is bare-chested and Angie has a bra on.

Also, the Alter Ego is lying beneath the bed.]

Angie
I told you it would help, love.

Vinnie
Yes, it sure did.

Angie
[*She leans over and picks up a rolled-up cigarette from the nightstand. She lights up and lets Vinnie take a puff as she holds it. Then she takes a puff.*]
How do you feel?

Vinnie
I feel fine, just finne.   [*She laughs.*]

Angie
[*Laughs, too.*]
You look wonderful. I love your body. [*She lays the rolled-up cigarette on the ashtray and gives him short, quick kisses on his chest.*]

Vinnie
God, I never thought it could be so great.

Angie
[*She strokes his hair.*]
I told you, dear, you didn't have to worry about performing with me. If you let nature take its course, eventually everything will work out.

Vinnie
[*He lightly kisses her forehead.*]
You're wonderful.

Angie
So are you. You know, darling, I think I could easily say I love you. And mean it.

Vinnie
[*Sits up and leans against the headboard. She does the same, staying wrapped in his arms all the while.*]
Don't, it may spoil everything. I don't know exactly what love is. I do know, however, caring is involved. And, God, I do care for you.

Angie
So do I. Then let's just feel and be.

Vinnie
Good.

Angie
Vinnie, please tell me something more about your wife. I know I should say it doesn't matter, but it does.

Vinnie
That's okay. I don't mind talking about her. I think I already told you that she's really into the charismatic movement.

Angie
Yes.

Vinnie
Well, to be perfectly honest, she does try hard to be a good wife and mother. It seems all she lives for is her Jesus and her family. She's almost too good. A saint, really. Her model is the Virgin Mary. So, you know what I mean. Sometimes I've thought of leaving her. But I worried about the kids. I still believe a child needs a strong anchor to get through this fucked-up world. And I don't care what psychiatrists say, divorces do fuck up kids.

Angie
Love, you know I used to feel the same way about leaving my husband. But I think I was kidding myself. Kids had a wonderful way of coping. I believe they're better at it than adults. It's really too bad my daughter is away. I would love to have you meet her. You could see how together she is, probably more than I ever could be.

Vinnie
You know, maybe you're right. I just don't know. I would do anything to say fuck it, pick up and fly off to a small island in the Caribbean. You can't believe how many brochures I've collected on the different islands in the Caribbean. Late at night when I'm alone, I'll pull them out and dream about escaping to one of these islands. It's the kind of thing that helps me get through all the shit that goes on at the university. Oh, God, I hate the games we play. Everyone uses a little of this idea and that idea so that they'll be noticed and then eventually promoted. You know about the whole

tenure game. And if you're real good and use such words as humanistic, feedback loop, ad hoc, interfaces, and so on, you might even get a raise. I also hate it how everyone learns to say yes and yes and yes because you see it's really difficult for the university to say no to someone who is constantly reaffirming its existence. It shits. If you don't learn what the safe and unsafe areas are in the university, you're either forgotten or dismissed. I'll tell you, Ang, to be free of that shit would be so great. I think then I could really concentrate on my writing. [*He laughs.*] How about it, would you like to run away with me?

Angie
I would love to. I could maybe help you get closer to your ideas by having you answer some of my stupid questions.

Vinnie
Ang, you could never ask me a stupid question. Could a beautiful figure sculptured by Michelangelo ever ask a stupid question? Nothing that is beautiful could be stupid. I know anything you ask me will have to be answered if the world is going to understand me... And, God, Angie, do I need someone like you. Up to now, I've had no one to share my ideas with. Damn it, we just might leave for that island. The more I think about it, the more I like the idea. I'm serious.

Angie
So am I serious about joining you. I would do anything to get away from people like Jimmy, his phony friends and their disgusting materialism. My daughter already has her own life. She doesn't need me anymore. I could paint. We could get just a small place with very little furniture. Maybe a desk so that you can write and a bed, of course. [*She moves in closer to him.*]

Vinnie
[*Laughs.*]
A lot of books, also, especially dealing with eastern religions. I just haven't had the time to concentrate in this area. And I know some answers for my novel are in those books.

Angie
What do you mean, dear?

Vinnie
Well, we know that there existed similar teachings of Christ and Christ-like figures in eastern religions centuries before Christ was born.

Angie
I guess I have read where archaeologists have found tablets and writings to support that claim.

Vinnie
Right. You see, Ang, I believe Jesus Christ was only a prophet like so many prophets in other religions who wanted to help people to understand that they were self-evolving beings, and that their salvation was not to be found in worshipping them as Gods, but to find their salvation in themselves, in their inner circle which would connect them to higher forms of consciousness. You see, I think this inner circle of man is the link. And I also think the Bible, Koran and other major works of religions use myths and allegories to help us get closer to this truth.

Angie
Love, I don't know if I quite follow you.

Vinnie
Okay, let me use Noah's Ark as an example. You know it's an allegory. Right?

Angie
Right.

Vinnie
Well, in this allegory the flood is usually considered the most important symbol.

Angie
Why?

Vinnie
Because the flood usually symbolizes death and destruction which we know is unavoidable. But what is important in this allegory is not the flood, but the building of the ark...

Angie
Go on.

Vinnie
Okay. Well, I believe man can build within himself an ark and assemble in it parts of everything that is valuable in him. In this case, these parts will not be destroyed but will survive and be born again. I feel other myths and allegories in the Bible also reach the same conclusions about man's salvation. Now, let me get back to the inner circle of man idea. I think when all the inner circles of men can connect up to higher forms of consciousness, then we'll have something called God, love, Heaven, or whatever name people would like to attach to it. Some philosophies call this ideal state a cosmic force that moves the world. I really don't care what people call it, I just know that people like my wife who are into that praise the Lord shit are missing the boat. I believe no one can be saved by pure emotionalism because it goes against the real thoughts expressed by Jesus Christ in the Bible.

Angie
That makes a lot of sense, Vinnie.

Vinnie
I'm glad it does. I feel so good talking to you about these things. Like I said, I have no one in West Virginia to talk to. They're all fucking bores. My wife has these get-togethers and they're terrible. I usually end up getting drunk so I could get through them. The conversations are always the same. Football, zoning laws, blacks, more football, crab grass, dogs shitting on beautiful manicured lawns, then more football... and on and on the shit goes.

[*Angie laughs and then passionately kisses him. As they are moving down into the bed, Jimmy and Mike walk in through the stage right doorframe. Now the Alter Ego sticks his head out from underneath the front of the bed.*]

Alter Ego
I've been screwed, people! This is not supposed to happen. How am I going to explain this to the others? Please, Jimmy, do something, do anything! I'm losing him! Jesus, I just can't believe this is happening to me... [*He slides back under the bed.*]

[*Jimmy goes over to Vinnie's side of the bed, raises his right hand in the air, and with an exaggerated gesture of putting his thumb and forefinger together, he jumps on Vinnie and twists his nose. On the other side of the bed, Mike forces Angie out. He then hands her her bathrobe and begins to push her toward the stage right doorframe.*]

Angie
What the hell! Vinnie, help...

[*Angie and Mike are now gone and Jimmy begins to slap Vinnie's face. The blows are hard and violent.*]

Jimmy
Wake up, asshole! Wake up! Come on, I only tapped you. You should see what I really could do with my Kissebock triangle twist. Come on.

Vinnie
[*Moans as he tries to shake the dizziness out of his head. He looks over to where Angie was lying.*] Where's Angie? What did you do with her, you crazy son of a bitch?

Jimmy
Don't worry about your precious whore, she's down in the car with Mike. He'll take good care of her. I wanted to be with you alone. I just knew you wanted in her pants as soon as I saw the look in your eyes when you met her the other night. So my dear smart-ass cousin, you're a closet cunt man? [*He laughs and jumps off the bed like a*

wild man. Vinnie tries to sit up. He groans with pain.]

Jimmy
You always thought you were hot shit. Like you were too good for us.

Vinnie
I - I don't know what you mean.

Jimmy
You know exactly what I mean.

Vinnie
I really don't.

Jimmy
Cut the shit, Vinnie. You always acted aloof when you were with us guys. And you know it. I hated the way you used to stay in the background as us guys talked about fucking or balling some cunt. Always acting like some self-righteous bitch.

Vinnie
I never meant it to be taken that way. Are you sure Angie is all right?

Jimmy
I'm sure. Worry about yourself, man. You never meant it that way. That's a fucking joke. Is that why you corrected us guys when we didn't say the th's in length or fucked up the nt sound in couldn't or shouldn't? See, you asshole, how well I say those fucking words now. Of course, maybe not as well as you, the Harvard graduate, and shit, you're probably thinking that right now. So please don't give me that crap about you not meaning it that way. You knew exactly what you meant.

Vinnie
I don't know what you're saying. Look, Jimmy, if the real reason you're saying all of this is because you're worried about what I know, forget it. I figure it this way. If you're stupid enough to do such a thing to your father, then you're stupid enough to live with it. Another reason. You're my cousin. My God! Jimmy! You know I wouldn't do anything to hurt my relative.

Jimmy
Cousin! Shit! You would still screw me, cousin or no cousin. I knew I was telling you too much the other night. I guess I just got fucking carried away with trying to impress you. I always hated the way my mother threw you up as the perfect model of what an Italian boy should turn out to be. It makes me sick. This relative shit you're giving me also makes me sick. Everyone in this world is out to fuck over the other guy.

Vinnie
Oh, wow, you really have been hurt to feel that way. God, if relatives can't trust each other, then it's a sad state of affairs.

Jimmy
Yeah, maybe so. I just wish I could believe you.

Alter Ego
[*Sticks his head out from underneath the bed.*]
I can't believe this. Just can't, people. Shithead is actually conning Jimmy into believing him. Unbelieveable! Listen to shithead as he trys to protect his ass. He's now playing the game just like anyone else. Boy, I tell you, this just doesn't look good for me, not at all... Come on, Jimmy baby, don't fall for it, give him another good fucking twist of the nose. Scare the shit out of him. Please don't be fooled by his smooth talking, for Christ's sake, don't be fooled. I know for a fact beneath the surface of shithead lies a trembling child in confusion and fear. So go after him with everything you've got. Words, twisting, violence, whatever. I need help... I think I'm getting afraid...

Vinnie
You could believe me, Jimmy. There's too much of the same blood in us for me to be lieing. If you need help, I'm ready to help. And I mean it. No bullshitting..

Jimmy
Help is really not what I need. [*He starts to nervously pace in front of the bed.*] I just need someone to talk to about him. That's all.

Vinnie
Well, I'm ready to listen.

Jimmy
I'll tell you, Vinnie, I don't think I'll ever forget that simple-ass grin on his face while he was choking and gasping for his last breath. Sometimes I think the son of a bitch worked on getting me to hate him over the years so that I would be his executor. Always making fun of me with those screwball stories of his. Once I remember this time when after beating the shit out of me, he told me he should've killed me as soon as I was born for I was no good. Do you believe that shit? Telling this to a kid about seven or eight. [*He shakes his head in disgust.*] Then when I was about fourteen, he started to tell everybody that he didn't have a son named Jimmy, the devil took him in death. The hurt from those things was unbearable. A father saying those kinds of things to a young kid. God, I had no other choice but to hate him....

Vinnie
I understand, Jimmy, I really understand. I can't tell you how my father has hurt me.

Jimmy
[*Stops pacing and laughs weirdly.*]
    We Serranos just didn't make it in getting loving and accepting fathers, did we?

Vinnie
    I guess not.

Jimmy
[*Words now come out, strained and choked.*]
    I just wish I could describe to people how it is to live with someone who never uses your name. It was always you bitch, bastard, cocksucker, lazy-no-good-for-nothing. His best words in English, you know. Vin, it's so so hard to live with someone that tells you from the moment you wake up until you go to bed that he hates you? Just a smile, just a nice word, just something, but all I got was his hate, misery, and ignorant peasant ways... [*His voice is no longer audible as he fights to hold back his tears.*]

Vinnie
    It must've been really frustrating for you.

Jimmy
[*Braces up as if someone reminded him to do so.*]
    Yeah, that's why, Vinnie, you have to be strong. [*All traces of his tear-filled emotion of a second ago is gone. He points to his head.*] It's all in here. That's why I'm so passionate about Ziegler's theory of noses. It's getting me though. Very few people in this world have strong convictions about anything. And that's the problem. The great American ideals went down the tube when the WASP's got kicked in the balls in the sixties. And now it's a battle for people's minds. I remember once someone saying that the greatest calling for all men is to lead and I'll tell you, Vinnie, I hope to lead and gain support for my beliefs about noses. Serious scientists and philosophers like Ziegler feel there may be a key to the study of noses that may explain why we feel what we feel about certain people. I'll tell you man, I'm really excited about the whole area. I'm getting out of the fucking acting business. I decided, man, sitting around twenty hours a day to film just five minutes is crazy. I've been wasting my time. I just have never felt so high in my life as I do when I think about the possibilities of studying noses. Don't you think it sounds exciting?

Vinnie
[*Forces enthusiasm.*]
    Yeah, I sure do.

Jimmy
    Damn, Vin, I just wish we had spent more time together when we were younger.

Vinnie
[*Nods.*]
I know.

Jimmy
I should've listened to my mother. She always said you could've been a good influence on me. Maybe I would be some famous scientist now. [*He laughs.*] Still there's one good thing, I've got free of him! And my mother doesn't have to take his shit anymore. Hell, man, enough depressing thoughts, I'm going out and get drunk. Want to join me?

Vinnie
Maybe later, I can't leave Angie right now. Your friend wouldn't hurt her, would he?

Jimmy
Hell, no, unless I told him to do so. But, man, don't worry, I just told him to keep her down there until I was finished. Hey, man, I don't blame you for wanting to be with her. She's really a good-looking cunt. I just hate the way she goes around thinking she's better than everyone else. I've never liked broads like that. [*He starts toward the stage right doorframe, then turns, and in a colder tone.*] Listen carefully, my dear cousin, I believed you when you said you wouldn't say anything, but if that changes, if that changes at all... Well, I don't think a cock in the nose would feel very good. [*He laughs, turns, and goes out.*]

Alter Ego
Hey, people, I got to do something quickly or I'm done. I could see that now. No more fucking around. Watch out, shithead, I'm getting ready to give you my best shot. Hell, I got a reputation to protect. I just could see the other Alter Egos laughing their asses off if they knew I blew it with someone like you. I would be nothing, nothing, you know that, shithead? Jesus Christ, I just could see myself being reassigned to some fucking idiot who's in prison because he ate his mother and father. No, sir, that's not for me. I'm not going down without a fight. Oh, hell, here comes his beauty, she's not helping, either. In fact, I get this feeling that everyone he meets is against me now... I wonder how many Alter Egos attach themselves to other Alter Egos... Hell, I might be the first one...

[*Angie enters, goes over to Vinnie and puts her arms around him.*]

Angie
Are you okay:

Vinnie
Yes. [*He strokes her hair.*] Please hold me tight, please.
[*He kisses her as his alter ego starts to bang his head on the floor.*

The lights and curtain come down.]

ACT II - SCENE IV

[*Mario and Theresa Serrano's Apartment. Everything is the same, except this time Mario Serrano, fully dressed in shirt, pants and shoes, is lying on a small bed behind the stage left doorframe which is nearest the audience.*

When the lights and curtain come up, Concetta and Theresa are sitting around the table. Concetta is facing the audience and Theresa is facing stage left.

Wearing only an undershirt and pants, Vinnie slowly enters from the other stage left doorframe. He has just been awakened from a deep sleep. His Alter Ego also enters and goes over and sits in a cross-legged position on the stove and sink unit.]

Mother
You look so washed out, Vinnie, I bet you didn't sleep good?

[*Vinnie takes a seat opposite his mother.*]

Vinnie
Oh, no, mom, I slept wonderfully. I mean it. It's the best sleep I've had in months. What time is it?

Mother
You have about an hour before the funeral starts. That's why I woke you. Concetta also wanted to see you. I told her some other time but she said no. Concetta, you should be getting all the rest you need. Today is going to be so hard for you.

Concetta
Don't worry, Three, everything will be okay. I've finished my mourning, funeral or no funeral, I now must do what I must do.

Mother
Oh, but I don't know. [*She shakes her head and sniffs as if she's ready to cry.*] I just don't know. It's not the right time. Any other time but now, please, Concetta, don't put yourself through this, please, listen to me.

Vinnie
I don't understand. What's wrong, mom?

Mother
Nothing. Nothing! How about some nice eggs and bacon, Vinnie?

Vinnie
No, mom, please tell me, what's wrong

Mother
Do you want me to make you some sandwiches so you'll have them for your trip back to West Virginia?

Vinnie
No, never mind the damn food, mom. Just, For Christ's sake, will someone tell me what the hell is going on?

[*His mother bends her head and starts to cry.*]

Concetta
Vinnie, you must understand your mother has been under a great deal of strain of late. Little by little, your father is destroying her. That's why I'm here. I'm scared he's getting as miserable as Louie was all his life. And, Vinnie, I'll tell you this, I won't have my sister go through the same hell I went through. Vinnie, I was able over the years to push his hatred for me and my family out of my mind. I got hard. But your mother is too sensitive, it will eventually kill her. We must protect her, Vinnie. I love her too much to see her torn apart by him.

Vinnie
Yeah, but maybe after the funeral is over and time has passed, he'll get better. Grieving is always worse at the beginning.

Concetta
He'll never get any better. I've seen it happen in my husband. Their misery is like a cancer. They feed on it and on everyone else's. No, Vinnie, he'll never change. He, like my husband, is an ignorant peasant just like the peasants that still live in the small village they came from in Italy... They hate life and wait for death as a relief!

[*His mother's crying gets louder.*]

Vinnie
Mom, are you okay?

Mother
Oh, why did God make it so difficult? I pray to him every night that he'll change. Bring back the Mario I know, I pray... We had so much, Vinnie,... why? [*She cries some more as she now nervously twists a handkerchief around her fingers.*] Please, Concetta, don't say anymore. I don't think I could stand to hear you talk about it in front of Vinnie... I'm so ashamed...

Concetta
I'm sorry, my dear sister, Vinnie must know. You can't go on like this.

Vinnie
Please, I feel like I'm on the edge of hysteria. What is it,

what must I know?

Concetta
Okay, Vinnie, you know I'm not very tactful. So here it is. Your father has always liked boys better than girls. Everyone in the North End knows about it.

Alter Ego
[*Leaps off the sink and stove unit.*]
Now, shithead, it's out. Let's see you deal with this without my help. Your old man is queer. Why are you trembling? Do you feel like puking? You better not. I don't think your mother would appreciate it on her clean floors. Do you need me, huh? Well, suffer for a while, kiddo.

Concetta
Now there is one thing I must admit, Vinnie, my husband was always good to your father. He loved him as a brother should. At least, thank God, there was some good in him. Anyway, I heard from a friend that Louie would follow your father to a bar on Beacon Street and once there he would make sure the guy your father met was not one of those gay kooks who was into chains, whips, and crazy stuff like that. You know what I mean. I can't go on about that, it's too disgusting. Anyway, Vinnie, you just don't know how much your mother loved your father and how she pleaded with him to get help. But he was too proud. He thinks he has been cursed...

Mother
[*Crying.*]
Please, Concetta, that's enough. I feel like it's my fault. That I failed him. Oh, God, I tried so hard, but he still went out those nights... Oh, please, Concetta, no more.

[*Vinnie sits there with a dazed look on his face.*]

Concetta
[*Reaches over and comforts her sister by patting her hand.*]
Three, these are difficult times for all of us. [*She looks over to Vinnie.*] Vinnie, my dear, you must do what you have to do. Jimmy had to do it. If you love your mother and don't want to see her suffer anymore, there's no other choice.

Vinnie
[*Frightened.*]
My God! I can't... no, I can't...

Concetta
Don't speak too loudly, he's sleeping in the other room. Vinnie, I do believe this when I say it, and that is I think he'll be happier. I think Louie is. Really. We sometimes must help God.

Vinnie
[*Shaking his head and pressing his hands against his ears.*]
No, no, no. I won't listen. Oh, my head is pounding, pounding... please stop...

Concetta
Everyone deserves a little happiness in their life. You'll see how happy we'll all be afterwards. We could be close as a family again. You and Jimmy could work for me. You could get that great book of yours published. I know my publishing company will do wonderful things with it. You ask for it, Vinnie, and we'll do it. It's right. I feel it in my soul. Everything is going to be okay afterwards. Yes, it is. I know it....

Vinnie
Mom, mom, do you expect me to do this, do you? Please, mom, say something. [*His mother keeps staring down at the table while still nervously twisting the handkerchief around her fingers.*]

Concetta
Vinnie, we'd better go. Even though I give the appearance of being strong, this has been hard on me, too. Now I must get myself ready so I can get myself through the funeral. [*She gets up, goes over to Theresa and pats her on the shoulder.*] I know, Three, everything will work out. It's God's will. [*She then takes out from a dark leather purse a glass tube curved at one end and a napkin which she opens. She lays these things down on the table in front of Vinnie. Three pieces of chewed meat are visible on the napkin.*] Everything you need is here. I know everything will work out. [*She goes over and kisses Vinnie on the cheek. Then she helps Theresa up. They leave through the stage right doorframe with his mother never looking up and still crying.*]

Alter Ego
[*Comes over and sits on the table next to the glass tube and chewed pieces of meat.*]
And so my dear friend, the devil has many faces. I can't stand to see you suffer anymore. Want some advice? Do it. Kill the son of a bitch. It doesn't matter. It's over. Forget him. He'll never come back to you. Stop looking for things to be the same. Shit, you were only twelve. That was a hell of a long time ago. Like sweet-ass Concetta said, he'll be better off dead. They were miserable in this world. They were still living as Italian peasants. Screw them, man, if they couldn't grow with the times, they deserve it. Why should he suffer anymore... Better yet, shithead, why should you? Come on, shithead, give the old fart a good blow in the nose, come on...

[*Vinnie gets up and goes to the doorframe where his father is lying. He looks in and speaks out loud.*]

Vinnie
Oh, dad, how my heart burns with love for you. No matter what you did to me, I couldn't ever hate you. You were so gentle and kind that night. And all the time before you treated me as if I was a Roman God... Oh, my father, how I would love to watch you as you concentrated on your work. The smell of leather all around us. You bending your broad shoulders over an overturned shoe which would be laying on a worn shining black steel form...

Remember, dad, before that night, I would sometimes after school perch myself on one of your elevated shoe shining chairs and listen to you tell people stories about Italy... Oh, I really loved it when you used to get into an argument with one of your friends. Your face would flush beet red and your eyes would pop open like an owl's. Then while gesturing with your shoemaker's cutting knife in one hand and with your black apron flapping around your solid legs, I remember how you would destroy your opponent, one, two, three, with language that would sing. I'll never be able to speak Italian like you. It was so much a part of you... I also remember at these times how you would look out of the corner of your eye to see if I was looking. God, dad, was I so proud of you then. Why did you have to change? Why?... I love you even more after that night.,,

Alter Ego
Why, you ask, shithead, I'll tell you why! You happen to have a father who likes men's rooms better than you.

Vinnie
[*Turns around quickly.*]
Fuck off!

Alter Ego
I don't believe it. What did you say, shithead?

Vinnie
I said fuck off! Jesus, I'm tired of you following me around and telling me what I should do and what I shouldn't do. I've had it with you. [*He moves closer to his Alter Ego.*]

Alter Ego
Oh, come on, shithead, you need me more than ever now. Those memories are flooding your mind as if a dam has burst. Remember, kiddo, I'm your mask and that's the only way you can discover truth. We all need some shield in order to discover who we really are.

Vinnie
No! That's false. The more I depended on you, the harder it was for me to cry out for help. I could never be fully me until I rid myself of you. Yeah, you held out your damn hand to me, only so you control me and feed off me. I want to live again with only myself in control. Hell, you're the one that kept telling me that I needed to accept all my parts. Well, I can't, if you keep playing one part against the other. I think I'm ready now to say I still want my father, even if it means in a forbidden kind of way. I don't care anymore. I'm my own judge. Another gem I've learned from you... Now I want my own space and time. And I want it without any fear. Always with you around I had this fear of displeasing you. No more. I want to act because I decide to act, not because you said it's okay. I also know now that all truth is personal. We have seen this truth before we were born. And it's our job in this world to see it as clearly as before. But you like morality are unhealthy for my soul. I can't see pure truth unless you, my judge, my censor, my conscience are gone. I must let go of you if I'm to get closer to my inner and personal truth. I must.

Alter Ego
Pure intellectual shit.

Vinnie
Can't you see that I'm ready to accept him, that night, all of it? I don't need you anymore.

Alter Ego
I still don't care, shithead. Your cross is too heavy to bear without my support... Hey, come on, let's stop arguing. Listen, once you take care of old fart face, you'll never know I'm around. We can be like co-disciples exploring your world of truth together.

Vinnie
No! No! No! You fucker, you'll never understand. [*He leaps onto the table, sits on his Alter Ego and violently twists his nose. Then quickly, he sticks the glass tube up one of the Alter Ego's nostrils. Then powerfully he blows the chewed-up meat through.*] As the worn bloodstone loses its quartz to the ravaging sea, so too will this ugly thought be lost amidst the artifacts and events of the thousands of days that have passed me by. [*Moaning with pleasure, he blows into the tube again and again. Now the song that was being played at Longo's is in the background and it increases in volume.*]

I talk, babe, you listen
You talk, babe, I listen
Hoping each time
It will glisten,
But like the unending
Circle of time,
It goes on and on
And it's not
Worth a time
I talk, babe...

Vinnie
[*Smiling to himself, he jumps off the table. The song stops playing.*]
Finally, I'm free! Free! Free! Thank you, God. [*He goes over and leans against the doorframe where his father is lying. He stands there staring at his father for a very long moment.*

Now the lights come down. Two figures are silhouetted. A small figure is lying in bed, the other, a large figure is standing over him.]

Small figure
Daddy, what's wrong, please...

Large figure
Don't be scared, daddy won't hurt you. [*He gets into bed with the small figure.*] I love you, Vinnie. I need you. Daddy has no one else... [*He embraces the small figure as the lights get dimmer.*]

Small figure
Oh, no, daddy, no, I don't think...

Large figure
Does it hurt?

[*A long pause.*]

Small figure
[*Moaning.*]
Oh, no, daddy, it feels good now, so warm...

[*A long pause again. Then suddenly, the large figure leaps off the bed.*]

Small figure
Please, daddy, don't leave, I love you, don't...

Large figure
Oh, God, God, what have I done, my own son... [*He runs into the darkness.*]

[*After another long pause, the lights come up on Vinnie still standing there looking at his father.*]

Vinnie
   Oh, dad, why did you leave me, I needed you so much more... so much more... [*He rushes over, throws his arm around his father's chest and kneels down beside him.*]

Father
[*Startled, he opens his eyes and looks at Vinnie. Gently, he starts to stroke his head - apologetically now.*] I'm so sorry, my son, it hurts me every time I look at you. I feel so ashamed... I love you so much.

Vinnie
   Dad, it's okay now, I love you, too.

Father
[*Shaking his head sadly, as he now sits up in bed.*] Vinnie, I can't tell you the shame I feel inside. I don't understand, I tried to do everything that was right in this country. I worked hard, saved money and put you through school. I know I'm a good shoemaker. I don't owe anyone any money. I pay all my bills. I've tried to be a good person, Vinnie. I really have...

Vinnie
   I know, I know, dad. [*He gets up and sits beside him on the bed.*]

Father
[*Trembling and fighting hard to hold back tears.*] What do I say? It's too hard. How can I tell you about this animal that is crawling around inside of me? How can I tell you how it's eating away, chewing and chewing at my brain?

Vinnie
   Stop, dad, I can't bear to see you like this. Please, I understand, I want to help you. I love you. [*He hugs his father.*] Everything is going to be all right.

Father
   All these years, Vinnie, I've been wanting to tell you I was sorry. There's nothing I could do. It has me. Nothing. [*He cries against Vinnie's shoulders.*]

Vinnie
   Dad, you didn't do anything bad, it was one of the few times I've ever felt loved. You must understand that, dad, you must. [*He rocks his father in his arms.*]

Father
[*He suddenly breaks away from Vinnie.*] I do, but Vinnie, what a burden

you had to live with all these years. A father to do that to his own son. No punishment could ever wipe that memory away.

> Vinnie
> Please, dad, don't talk anymore about it. Let it be, please.

> Father
> I know people in the North End think Mario Serrano looks healthy on the outside. A good strong man. Sure, but, Vinnie, they don't see the animal chewing away at me. They don't see it killing me, possessing me day and night. They don't...

> Vinnie
> Dad, please stop it, don't talk like that. I can't stand all this self-hatred. I love you too much to have you do this to yourself. Please, stop...

> Father
> Let me finish, Vinnie, I must talk about it. Can't you see that my life would've been nothing if it wasn't for you and my brother. God, I miss him. No one will ever know the way those bastards treated him. No one, and you, my dear son, will never know the hate your mother had for me because of this thing inside of me. When I told her about it, she just said that she always knew the Serranos were impure and that she felt sorry for you because you had my blood in you. I was destroyed and if it wasn't for Louie, they would be probably still looking for me in the Boston harbor. He gave me the courage to go on living with it. My dear brother understood while she only mocked me...

> Vinnie
> I can't believe that. I often wondered about you and mom. I knew you two didn't like each other, but you seemed to exist with each other. But I hated it when you two fought, I always thought it was because you resented having me.

> Father
> Oh, how little you know, Vinnie, she was always fighting with me because she despised me. And you know why she despised me? Because I left her cunt empty.

> Vinnie
> That's enough, dad, I don't like having mom called that, please.

> Father
> Let me finish, Vinnie. My dear wife and her sister are both the same. They're whores, my son. You know how Concetta would always take your mother along on her business trips. The excuse was always she needed company. Well, she kept her company all right. She kept her company while they both fucked anything that had a prick between its legs. I know. I met someone by accident who fucked both of them

in one night. They wore him out, he said. Louie hadn't fucked Concetta for years. He hated her so much. That's why they both despised us, they couldn't get fucked.

Vinnie
Stop, dad, no more, I don't care about them. Talk about you, you and me. My life always seemed to be split up between the time before that night and the time after. Do you remember how we treated each other? That's what I want to talk about. I was just twelve, it seems so far away, but so close. I still feel everything that happened that night, I'll never forget it.

Father
[*Crying a little.*]
I was drunk, son. I was so unfair to do that to you. It was like someone else doing it. I'll never get it straight. I don't want to either. I have so much to make up to you. I've saved up a little money which your mother doesn't know about. I want you to have it.

Vinnie
I don't care about money. I care about you because I need you and want to love you.

Father
No, Vinnie, it could never be. Do you understand?

Vinnie
Yes, it could be. I'm going to take care of you. I want you to come live with me. We're going to get away from this hell. I've always dreamed of going away to an island in the Caribbean and we're going to do it. I've met this wonderful person, dad, I want her to come, too. I know you'll like her, dad, she's Italian.

Father
That's nice. Remember I always told you that the Irish are like all the WASPs, they always make you feel that you don't belong. I'm happy that you want me, but it cannot be, can't you see. It will always be an illicit act in my mind. Nothing can change that. Maybe someday, I'll come see you. [*He stands up.*] Vinnie, he needs me there at his funeral, I can't leave him now. I must go.

Vinnie
No, dad, please come with me. This world here will eventually kill you. I want to make up some of those years we lost...

Father
We can't, my dear son, we can't. Do you understand that? It's best for the both of us. There're my friends. I need them. There's nothing I could do about that. You have your ideas, your books. They're different worlds. I have to live with the curse that I need men and their pricks, son. I can't ever forgive myself for that night.

Someday maybe I would be a good father to you. But it's not to be now. My brother Louie would always say that once a tree has been cut and shaped, it could never be what it was before. And so, I think, my son, the same is true for us. [*Crying, he bends over and rushes out.*]

        Vinnie
[*Crying also, then after a long pause, he goes out and dials the phone, still crying.*] Angie, Vinnie. I love you and need you more than ever. Let's go to our island in the sea... Yes, thanks... nothing is here for me anymore... only a dream that was not to be. [*He sobs into the phone as the lights and curtain come down.*]

RECOVERY
A PLAY

Recovery, which opens energetically with Chuck Mangione's "Tarantella," takes place in the late 1970s in the Boston apartment of Mario and Theresa Serrano. The storyline revolves around their son Vinnie, a confused poet and professor who suffers from an overwhelming, unaccountable depression and from a nervous breakdown. His inability to cope with his marriage, job, and life in general is the constant concern of his mother and father. In short, the play is about far more than just Vinnie and his struggles. More broadly, it depicts the intertwining lives and dynamics of an Italian American family from the old country, hard-working parents, and their modern-day children with their own distinct problems.

Recovery was presented at the Pittsburgh Playhouse on March 25–27, 1982. In addition, it was presented at the F. Scott Fitzgerald Theatre in Rockville, Maryland, on April 6–10, 1983.

CAST

Vinnie Serrano, early forties

Jimmy Serrano, mid-forties

Toni Serrano, mid-twenties

Mario Serrano, father, mid-sixties

Theresa Serrano, mother, early sixties

Jenny, dancer, mid-twenties

Glenn, Chairman, mid-forties

All the scenes take place in and around Mario and Theresa Serrano's apartment. Also all entrances and exits are made stage left or right.

ACT I

(The "Tarantella" dance music plays as the lights come up at stage center on a set representing Mario and Theresa Serrano's apartment. The set has a large, oval-shaped table with five chairs placed around it. At stage right there is a bookcase with few books on its shelves but with lots of pictures of Vinnie, Toni, and Jimmy. And yes, also figurines - loads of figurines meticulously placed on the bookcase's shelves.

Upstage and almost directly behind the oval-shaped table there is a kitchen with a refrigerator, stove, and sink.

Vinnie's mother, Theresa, is placing a plate on the table with a sandwich on it. His father, Mario, is looking out the kitchen window.)

Theresa
Mario, come and eat now. I'll watch.
(Mario comes out and sits down.)
How many did you have this morning?

Mario
(Starts to eat)
Two. Five dollars for five hours work. It's nothing when I think about what I used to make.

Theresa
(Goes to kitchen window)
Maybe this afternoon'll be better.

Mario
I don't know. We'll see how many come. The problem is that the damn people today are too cheap to pay for a haircut. They go and make eight dollars an hour for themselves but still want to pay only twenty-five cents for a haircut...
(Chews on his sandwich)
Well at least I had time to wash the floors. Now tomorrow I won't have to do them.

Theresa
Why don't you bring Jimmy and Vinnie over to help you? Well maybe, just Jimmy.

Mario
Hell he's just like him too. Both of them always cause me more work when they help. Your kids are not workers Tree. They just know how to have a good time and get sick.

Theresa
(Comes out of the kitchen)
Jimmy can at least help you wash those front windows of yours. They look like they haven't been washed in years. Put a little Spic and Span in hot water and you'll see how nice they come out. That's not hard.

Mario
We'll see if I have time.

Theresa
(Goes to window again)
Concetta wants us to come over tonight for some dessert. After we have supper.

Mario
I don't want to go over there with those big-mouth brothers of yours sitting around and eating like pigs. We have our family here now. Why should we go over there? I'm sick of them.

Theresa
(Comes out)
We'll just stay a little while. And don't talk stupid, my brothers treat you like a king. You know that.

Mario
I just don't want to go tonight Tree. Jesus, can't they leave us alone just for one night? They're so damn nosey those people. They want to know all your problems, but they won't tell you anything about theirs. And you big mouth have to tell them everything about us.

Theresa
I don't. I just can't lie when they ask like with Vinnie.

Mario
Why not?! They lie all the time about their kids. Look at Concetta's son Anthony. He was separated six months from his wife before we found out.

Theresa
I know, but Concetta said she promised Anthony not to tell anyone.

Mario
See what I mean? You do the same thing too to them. Don't tell them nothing.

Theresa
I won't anymore. I see that now.

Mario
Just think if you didn't marry me what kind of life you woulda had with those brothers and sister of yours. You woulda been cleaning and cooking for them all the time.

Theresa
(Laughing a little)
You forget how Joe Longo wanted to marry me. Look at all the money he makes now. I coulda had anything I wanted he said, if I would marry him. I still remember that big Cadillac roadster he had. Remember?

                        Mario
Yeah, but it was you who would come out and sweep the stoop everytime
I went to work. You and your family from Milan thinking you're
better than all of us poor people from Naples.
            (Affectionately laughs)
You son of a gun, you know you had a good thing when you saw it.
Longo or no Longo.

                        Theresa
I don't know about that. I bet if I married him I would be living
now in that house I liked so much in Cohasset. Remember Mario all
those big trees and how roomy it was?

                        Mario
That's in the past Tree. No more dreaming, we got too many problems now.

                        Theresa
But it was beautiful Mario, you must admit it.

                        Mario
I know, but we had everything here. If we lived there I would have
to drive to work every day and the taxes are double there. We could
never afford it.

                        Theresa
Could we at least take a drive this Sunday and see who's living
there now? Maybe all the kids will come too and we'll buy ice cream
like we used to.

                        Mario
We'll see. I gotta paint that hallway Sunday. Tree when you own
buildings and rent out to people you always got something to do.
There's no time for Sunday drives and ice cream. I wouldn't have
anything now if it wasn't for the rent I get from those apartments.

                        Theresa
But Mario you got to relax a little. All work is no good either.

            (Jimmy, Vinnie's brother, enters from downstage left.
            He's wearing a jogging suit and is zipping up the top.)

                        Mario
I've been up since five working and he gets up at noon. You've
already wasted half the day Mister Sunshine.

                        Theresa
Mario leave him alone. Jimmy, whataya want for breakfast?

                        Jimmy
            (Sitting down at the table)
Nothing just a glass of carrot juice Mom. Look are you people
drinking it like I told you?

RECOVERY | 95

Theresa
(Takes out the carrot juice from underneath the sink and stove unit and pours him a glass)
I want to but it gives me gas.

Mario
Listen to your mother talk. Hell everything gives her gas now, even water. Your mother is just getting old, that's all.

Jimmy
Okay people get cancer, I don't care. I've never felt better.

Mario
You look terrible. Everyone says it.

Jimmy
That's okay, let them die with their cancers and heart attacks. It's their life if they want to treat their bodies like garbage disposals, it's okay with me.

Mario
(Gets up, goes to the kitchen window and looks out)
We'll see who lives the longest. Your Uncle Nick says now all you have to do is shave your head, get a dress and some earrings and you'll look just like one of those Hare Krishnas on the Boston Commons.

Jimmy
Good.

Theresa
(Sets the glass of carrot juice in front of him)
Now don't spill it like you always do. Really Jimmy your father is right. You're too thin now. You even look worse than your brother in there.
(She looks downstage left. Mario is looking out the window again.)

Jimmy
(Gulps down his carrot juice)
Hell Mom, have you looked at yourself of late? You're really no Dolly Parton.

Theresa
Be quiet, I'm just saying put a little weight on. That's all.

Jimmy
I know. But God you people never stop nagging, do you?

Theresa
We just don't want you to get sick. One is enough.

(Mario comes back, sits down and starts eating again.)

Jimmy
Tell me, does he ever come out? I've been home two days now and I've only seen him once. What does he do in there all day?

Theresa
I don't know. Sometimes I hear him playing his Harry James records but he keeps the door locked all the time. I can't even get in there to clean anymore.

Jimmy
(Smiles affectionately)
That must be killing you, Mom. Theresa Serrano not able to do her daily cleaning. Jesus I guess Good Housekeeping won't be able to give you their seal of approval this year.

Theresa
Be quiet. I just wonder what I'mm gonna find when I finally get in there.

Jimmy
Probably a lot of drugs and dirty books. I always told you Mom when he was small he needed more fresh air.

Theresa
I don't know maybe when Toni gets home today and everyone's here, he'll come out more. The doctor says it's gonna take time.

(Mario gets up, goes over to the kitchen window and looks out again.)

Jimmy
But Mom that's the damn problem really. I don't have a lot of time. I mean Vinnie could go on for months like this.

Theresa
(Angrily, she picks up his empty glass and wipes the place in front of him.)
Oh I'm sorry! Do you want me to walk in there and say Vinnie you have one day to get better because your brother is a very busy man?! Now hurry up Vinnie and get it over wit! Your brother doesn't have much time!

Jimmy
Come on Mom, you know I don't mean that.

Theresa
(Shaking her head)
You kids are always thinking of yourselves first.

Jimmy
No I'm not. It's just so many things are going on in my life now. You know that Mom. I told you about the movie I had in production and about Marjorie now wanting me to go to England with her.

                        Theresa
I don't care about your movie, your Marjorie! All I care about now is
your brother getting better!

                        Jimmy
            (Feeling guilty)
I know. Okay then just tell me one thing, was it a nervous breakdown?
I mean he has more than just a bad ulcer, right? You never really said
nervous breakdown. It was a nervous breakdown. Wasn't it?

                        Theresa
Yes. But don't make it sound so awful.

                        Jimmy
I'm not. But Mom you know this was bound to happen to him. He's
always been nervous. Remember how he would bite his nails all the time
and the time he swallowed one and almost choked to death?

            (Mario comes back, sits down and starts eating again.)

                        Theresa
I know. That's why he needs his family around now. We have to help
him get better.

                        Jimmy
I agree but how long will it take Mom, six months, a year, two
years? I mean it's not that I'm not concerned about Vinnie. It's
just right now I'm into so many damn different things. Maybe too many
Mom.

                        Theresa
I don't know how long it will take. That's the problem. The doctor
said you never know wit nervous breakdowns.

                        Jimmy
But you really don't expect me to stay around until he's completely
cured, do you?

                        Mario
Our kids Tree only think of themselves. Nobody but themselves. And
that's the only thing they're good at besides complaining.
            (In mocking tone of voice)
how tired they are, how sick they are, how busy they are. Our kids
are selfish people! Selfish selfish people!
            (He shakes his head in disgust.)

                        Theresa
Mario don't start!
            (Looking at Jimmy)
I just want you to talk to him. Tell him he's got to get his mind
off himself. He listens to you. Maybe you two could go over and play
basketball at the center.

                        Jimmy
Jesus Mom I'm almost forty-five!

Theresa

Well damn it just do something with him! I think the more he stays in that room the more depressed he gets. You know just be wit him a few days. Then I don't care you could leave and go back to your precious movie and Marjorie!

Jimmy

Com on Mom, you know I've scratched and clawed for almost twenty years to get where I am now. Jesus how the hell did I know Vinnie was gonna have a breakdown at the same time Marjorie and I are "hot" items?! You think we planned it that way. Hell in my business you have to take advantage of being "hot" or you're done Mom. You saw that piece in the "Star."

Theresa

Yes and I didn't like it.

Jimmy

Why? I thought you liked it.

Theresa

I just don't like it how they made it seem that you're after her money.
(She goes into the kitchen and starts to wash dishes.)

Jimmy

(Yelling to her)
Well I'm not! I love her!

Mario

(Sarcastically)
You also said that about your other two wives.

Jimmy

Well this is different! I mean it's just something very special. Almost spiritual!

Mario

Spiritual my ass! You love her money! That's what you love! Tree when are you gonna see that! I know him! I know him like a book! She's got all that money from that TV series, and now he's gonna spend it for her. I know you buddy!

Jimmy

Hey I was doing okay before I met her.

Mario

Hell what are you talking about?! You didn't have a pot to piss in! You were selling goat's milk and seaweed when you met her!

Jimmy

That's not true! I was managing a health food store. And because of me it was making a lot of money!

Mario

I don't care what you were doing, selling or managing! You still didn't have anything when you met her!

Jimmy
Hey I don't care what you say I still say I was making it okay before I met Marjorie!

Mario
Hell the only thing son you were making all these years was girls who have names like Bambi or Wilma! God your mother and I will never forget that girl you brought home last year! Remember Tree? It was disgusting! Wearing all that cheap makeup and that tight silver suit. I thought she was a TV antenna!

Theresa
(Comes out of the kitchen)
Mario stop! And you too Jimmy! Let's at least pretend we're happy. The doctor said he needs to learn how to relax and how could he relax with you two yelling at each other out here?

(Mario gets up, goes to the kitchen window, looks out and then turns around.)

Jimmy
(Gets up also)
Fine with me. I gotta get going anyway. But just one more thing, I don't have to prove anything to you or anyone Dad! I really don't! I know what I've done and I don't have to apologize to anyone for those things!

Mario
(Comes back and faces Jimmy)
Is that right?! Well then buddy how about the thousands of dollars I've given to you over the years. You just want me to forget about that?! Huh?!

Jimmy
No I don't mean that.

Mario
Well what do you mean Mister Big Shot?!

Jimmy
I'm talking about other things.

Mario
Hell you don't know what other things you're talking about! All that money and for what?! I ask myself that every day. For what?! For a damn part in A movie wit Robert Redford! And you know what my big shot son actor did in that movie?!

Theresa
Please Mario!

Jimmy
No Mom let him go on. I don't care anymore.

Mario
Well my big shot son actor was Robert Redford's punching bag for three minutes! And that's all buddy except the time you played a monkey in a Jerry Lewis movie!

Jimmy
Hell that's a lie and you know it! Why do you do this to me all the time?! You know I've played hundreds of other parts!

Mario
(Sarcastically)
Oh so you played hundreds of parts. You're right son, really right. I almost forgot. Your mother and I went to all of them. But I think you mean you played hundreds of walk-ons.

Jimmy
To hell with it! You always win! I don't know why I argue with you! Jesus. Did you forget that last year I played Richard the Third here in Boston?!

Mario
No I haven't forgotten. Hell how could I forget? Finally, your mother and I said we could really be proud of you, you were doing serious drama. Shakespeare. Remember, we brought Grandmother Serrano, my sister Concetta, almost the whole damn Serrano family came? And what do you do but play Richard the Third as a homo! A damn homo! I'll never forget that look on Grandmother Serrano's face. Never!

Jimmy
Hey I don't care. I forced people to see Richard the Third as a real person with real problems. I really don't care what people say. I'm above all of that now.
(Almost in tears)
I really am.

Mario
You're above nothing buddy! You think you are! But that's your problem! You always—

Theresa
Mario stop, please!

Mario
(Backs off)
I'm just talking Tree. Can't I even talk to my son? I haven't had a chance to talk to him since he's been home. I just don't want him to be taken advantage of by other people, like he was in that play.

Theresa
But you could say things nice. You don't have to yell.

Mario
I wasn't, you're just too sensitive Tree. You think I say those things because I don't like him. I say those things because I don't want my

kids to be hurt. I hear every day in the barbershop how people screw the other guy.

(As he goes over to the kitchen window, Vinnie comes out from downstage left. He's dressed in an old flannel shirt and wrinkled khaki pants. He's unshaven.)

                Jimmy
Hi Vin.
            (Sings kiddingly)
Happy times are here again! Happy times are here again!

                Vinnie
Right. I could hear some of it.

                Theresa
How about some breakfast Vinnie?

                Vinnie
I'm not hungry Mom.

                Jimmy
Mom give him some of that carrot juice.

                Vinnie
No thank you. Maybe in a little while.

                Theresa
What are you gonna do today?

                Vinnie
            (Seems preoccupied)
What?

                Theresa
I said what are you gonna do today?

                Vinnie
I don't know.

                Mario
Well if you don't have anything else to do, come over and help me wash windows. Good hard work will make you forget everything.

                Vinnie
I wish it was that easy.

                Theresa
Why don't you also go over and see Grandmother Serrano today and maybe later you can go over and see Aunt Concetta too? I know they would love to see you.

                Vinnie
I'll see. I just wish I could gain control over this hand...
            (He looks at his right hand shaking.)
If I could only control it.

                    Jimmy
Vin, you gotta get the hell out of here for a while. Come on with
me over to Beacon Street while I talk to this guy about co-producing a
movie with Marjorie and me. It'll be a good change of pace for you.
The guy is sort of a jerk, but funny as hell. What do you say?

                    Vinnie
Maybe tomorrow Jimmy, but today I just can't.

                    Jimmy
Hell where's the old curious Vinnie I knew who used to follow me around
always wanting to know this and that. You were such a pain in the ass.
Remember quiet Marie? I had to teach you everything.

                    Vinnie
I remember.

                    Jimmy
You were so damn shy around girls.

                    Vinnie
I know and still am.

                    Jimmy
Hey what's happened to that old smart-ass Vinnie Serrano I knew?
What's the problem Vin?

                    Vinnie
I don't know. That's the problem.

                    Theresa
Vinnie go with your brother. It will do you good to get out. Go.

                    Vinnie
Okay maybe later, but not now, I just can't get go—

                    Mario
        (Looking out the window)
There's a customer. I better go. He looks well dressed.
        (Looks back at them)
You see what I have to do just for a couple dollars so youse kids
could be happy?
        (Looks out again)
He's trying the doorknob. What's wrong with that guy does he think I'm
stupid enough to leave it open?
        (Yells out)
Hey, hey I'll be right there!
        (Looks back)
Tree did I tell you what happened to Louie Rossi last week?

                    Theresa
No.

                    Mario
Someone broke into his apartment and took everything, even his hypertension
pills.

                    Theresa
That's too bad. I like him.

                    Mario
This section is going to pot Tree. Once those big shot lawyers
started to move in and those niggers on Salem Street all the crime
started. All the Italians are moving out. Remember how the North
End used to be the safest in Boston? Now it's getting as bad as Roxbury.

                    Theresa
Some of the people moving in are nice. Those two lawyers we rent to
in Apartment 6B always talk to me and say hello when I see them.
They're nice people.

                    Mario
They're not nice, they're pigs. I went to fix the faucet in their
apartment and the place stunk of cat shit. Hell you could even smell
it in the other apartments. I don't know how people live like that,
just like animals.

                    Theresa
Stop talking and go before the customer goes.

                    Mario
Your mother never likes hearing the truth.
          (Starts to leave)
Come on Jimmy after I finish the guy I'll give you a trim. You look
like a bum.

                    Jimmy
I just got a haircut. I'm doing fine Dad.

                    Mario
They didn't touch you. What did they soak you this time, twenty dollars?

                    Jimmy
Forty.

                    Mario
You're throwing away your money buddy. Those Hollywood barbers don't
know how to cut hair.
          (Brushes up the hair on the back of his head)
You should see the back of your head, it's all chopped up. At least
let me fix it up so you look halfway decent.

                    Jimmy
          (Starts to follow him)
Okay but please don't take too much off. I got an image to protect.

                    Mario
          (Now affectionately kidding)
I'll give you an image. Come on.

          (Mario and Jimmy pick up their shoes near the bookcase and
          put them on.)

Theresa
How about Vinnie, he needs one too?

Mario
(Coldly)
I asked him yesterday. He said he doesn't want one. You see why college kids are what they are today, look at their professors. I don't care Tree, if he wants to look like a bum let him look like a bum. Come on Mister John Travolta.
(He begins to go off stage right with Jimmy following.)

Theresa
Don't forget to wipe when you come in. I found dog crap all over the stairs yesterday. Now go.

Mario
(He stops)
Your mother, what would she do without dog crap and dust?
(He laughs along with Jimmy as they now leave. The phone rings and Theresa goes and answers it. Vinnie lights up a cigarette. She speaks with controlled anger.)

Theresa
Oh hi... yes... okay... yes... Toni this is costing money... I can't talk anymore. An insurance man is here... Toni Bye. Bye.
(Quickly she hangs up and nervously starts washing dishes.)
She's called three times this week to tell us what time she'll be here. And always that girl calls at the most expensive times. Couldn't she call before eight or after eleven? You know your father sometimes talks stupid but this time he's right. She doesn't have any conception of money. He's right.

Vinnie
Then don't give her any more. She's on her own now.

Theresa
We've tried to stop but she still keeps asking. Sometimes she doesn't have enough to pay her electric bill, her car payments, it's always something. You know every time she comes here we have to pay for the plane. And that's not right. A girl wit her position should be able to pay for it. She's gotta learn how to budget her money. She can't keep buying four hundred dollar outfits and drinking expensive wine every night. I was there last month, I saw how she spends her money. I didn't say anything because I didn't want to start. But I would never think of spending money like that.

Vinnie
Look if you don't give it to her, after a while she won't ask.

Theresa
Well that's what we're gonna do because your father is getting tired of her spending money like water. We have to think of ourselves now.

Vinnie
Good you should. You and Dad should travel now and enjoy yourselves. Never mind us, we'll make out okay. I'm getting better.

Theresa
What about the hand?

Vinnie
Don't worry Mom, it still bothers me like now but it's really nothing like it used to be. Really Mom, I'm getting better.

Theresa
I hope so. Then maybe everything around here will be settled again.

Vinnie
Mom, you gotta stop worrying. Jesus look how tired you look. Do you ever sleep? You know I heard you roaming last night.

Theresa
Maybe I'll sleep better tonight. I was worrying about having enough sauce for tonight. Then I was ascared I wouldn't get up in time to start it.

Vinnie
Did your worrying about it really help the sauce?

Theresa
(Smiles a little)
Yes. It's almost ready for tonight.

Vinnie
Why don't you take a valium Mom? I've got some.

Theresa
No they make me too tired.
(She moves to the stove and starts to stir something in a pot.)
How about some nice homemade soup? It's already near twelve.

Vinnie
No, not now. Maybe later Mom.

Theresa
(Pleading)
Just a little bowl.

Vinnie
Okay I'll have a little. But just a little.

Theresa
(She spoons some soup from the pot into a small bowl.)
This is nice and hot. I just made it this morning.
(Brings the bowl and a spoon over to where he's sitting)
You want a glass of milk?

Vinnie
(He puts his cigarette out in an ashtray on the table.)
Okay. Just a little glass.

Theresa
(Goes back to the kitchen, takes the milk out of the refrigerator and pours him a glass)
You know you shouldn't smoke so much. The doctor said it's just as bad as alcohol.

Vinnie
I know.

Theresa
(Brings the glass of milk over)
You know I found ashes all over the bathroom floor this morning.

Vinnie
(Seems preoccupied again)
I'm sorry.

Theresa
The bathroom was also a mess yesterday. Hair all over. I know you've been sick, but there's no excuse for not cleaning up after yourself.
(Goes back to the kitchen and starts to wash some dishes.)
Vinnie please try to get over to see Grandmother Serrano today. She's always been so good to you. Sick and all, look what she did, she goes and makes you a loaf of egg bread. Do you want me to toast a slice now? It's good.

Vinnie
Not now Mom.

Theresa
Are you sure? I could put one in now.

Vinnie
(Getting upset)
Really Mom, I don't want any.

Theresa
Well it's here if you want it.

Vinnie
Okay.

Theresa
(Now stirring another pot on the stove)
God I got so much to do today I don't know where to start. I want to have a nice supper for tonight. You know it will be the first time in years that the family has been together? You know also I can't remember because it's been so long ago when all of you were together like this and sleeping overnight in the apartment? It'll be nice.

                    Vinnie
I know. I just hope my hand doesn't start shaking.
          (Holds up his shaking hand)

                    Theresa
Don't worry, just don't think about it.

                    Vinnie
I wish I could do that. It would be so great.

                    Theresa
You watch tonight with everyone here you'll forget all about it. You
think too much.

                    Vinnie
Look who's talking.

                    Theresa
          (Comes out of the kitchen)
I know.

                    Vinnie
          (Nervously rubs his face with his hands and then lights
          up another cigarette)
I don't know Mom sometimes I wish I could shut off my mind and never
turn it on again.

                    Theresa
Don't say that. I still think it was <u>her</u> that put you in the hospital.
<u>Her</u> running around being good to everyone except her own family.

                    Vinnie
          (Gets up now and slowly paces)
Mom I really don't feel like talking about it now.

                    Theresa
          (Bitterly)
Okay but remember when I first met her and I told you that I didn't like
that sweet and innocent smile of hers? Remember when I said that?

                    Vinnie
Yes. I know.

                    Theresa
Well even then there was just something about her. She was always
smiling but inside you knew she was thinking she was better than you.
Her parents were the same way Vinnie.

                    Vinnie
I don't know Mom. They always treated me good and they loved having the
kids around.

                    Theresa
That's because they didn't have to worry about cleaning up after you
people left. Her mother had a woman that came in each week. But I
had no one to help me. You know it always took me two weeks to get the
house back in shape after you and your kids left.

                    Vinnie
         (Stops pacing)
Damn it Mom! That's why we didn't come here very much! We always
had to worry about the kids breaking one of your precious figurines
or forgetting to flush the toilet or dirtying your floors! I mean it
was just too much pressure for the kids, for all of us.

                    Theresa
What are you talking about?! It was you who put the kids under pressure,
not me! They would listen to me and your father when you and her
were not around! You people spoiled them, not us!

                    Vinnie
         (Fighting back tears)
Okay we spoiled them... We spoiled them... Please Mom, no more.
         (Sits back down and rubs his face with his hands again)

                    Theresa
         (Goes back into the kitchen)
How about some more soup? I got a lot here.

                    Vinnie
         (Works hard at being friendly again)
Maybe after I finish this.
         (He takes a couple of spoons of soup.)
It's good Mom.

                    Theresa
         (Brings the pot of soup to him)
Here have a little to warm it up.
         (Spoons some soup into his bowl)

                    Vinnie
Mom that's enough.
         (Puts his hand up in a halting fashion)

                    Theresa
         (Goes back to the kitchen)
Look Vinnie, I gotta go to the store and get some lettuce. How's
homemade spaghetti sound for tonight?

                    Vinnie
Fine. Anything. Just rest Mom. You're doing too much.

Theresa
(Comes back out)
Be quiet, this is nothing. Listen if you're not going to be doing anything this afternoon, would you vacuum for me?

Vinnie
Okay, but why do you have to clean every day? Every day. Hell this place doesn't have a chance to get dirty.

Theresa
What else is there to do?

Vinnie
I don't know but there's got to be more to living than cleaning.

Theresa
I don't mind. I gotta go.

Vinnie
(Gets up)
Okay. Where's the vacuum cleaner?

Theresa
You don't have to do it now. Finish eating first.

Vinnie
That's okay. Just get the vacuum cleaner for me.

Theresa
(Goes back into the kitchen, on the upstage side of the sink and stove unit, and picks up the vacuum cleaner. Then brings it to him.)
Make sure you do a good job. And when you're finished with the soup, don't forget to wash the bowl and clean up. Don't leave a mess like you know how.

Vinnie
Don't worry, I won't.

Theresa
Okay I'll be back in awhile.
(She leaves stage right.)

Vinnie
Bye.
(He plugs in the vacuum cleaner near the window. Then he turns it on and begins to vacuum the floor. The phone rings. At first he doesn't hear it, but after the fourth ring he hears it. He shuts off the vacuum cleaner and goes over to answer it.)
Hello... yes, hi Bob... yeah... Oh, I'm doing okay now... I see... Well listen, you know my mother sometimes exaggerates things... I know... It's hard... Well I'm glad to hear you got over your divorce... No I have my own analyst. He's back in West Virginia if I need him... No

I don't think so. I have problems with singles bars. You know what
I mean? Sure... right... there are other fish in the pond... yes,
let's do that... Okay, bye.
> (He slams the receiver down.)

Asshole!
> (He sticks his head out the window. He yells.)

Yes world I had a nervous breakdown! You hear Vinnie Serrano had
a nervous breakdown! Now get off my back!
> (Almost in tears, he buries his head in his hands as the lights dim.)

> (Glenn, the chairman of the English Department at Vinnie's
> university, enters. He's dressed in a three-piece suit and
> has an air of authority about him. He's carrying some
> papers in one hand and in the other he has two narrow boxes
> stacked together and marked "IN" and "OUT." He sits down
> at the table, facing the audience. He then places the
> papers and boxes in front of him as if he's sitting at a
> desk. The lights come up as Vinnie still remains near the
> window.)

Glenn
Come on in Vince. Sit down.

Vinnie
> (Moves away from the window)

I can't.

Glenn
Why?

Vinnie
> (Starts to pace)

I got too many things going on inside.

Glenn
Well sit down and relax then. What's wrong?

Vinnie
Glenn I know why you called me in. It's the same old shit again. You
want me to fill out that damn peer review form, don't you?

Glenn
> (Nervously playing with the papers in front of him)

Yes. Jesus Vince what does it take to fill it out? An hour? Two
hours at the most?

Vinnie
I'm tired Glenn. I'm tired of playing fucking games with the bureaucracy.
If the damn university wants to know how I'm doing then let them take
the time to ask my students, read my books. Hell Glenn remember when
we first came here ten years ago and the dreams we had about making
this department the best in the country? Remember we wanted to do
more than lecture to students about writing and literature? We wanted

to have an open and free exchange with students about their thoughts on literature and their own styles of writing.
    (Choking with emotion)
What happened Glenn to those dreams? Collaboration between students and professors was to be the key word of our program. Jesus Glenn, remember? Was it all an illusion?

                  Glenn
It's just how it is now Vince. Your humanism and mine of a few years ago is no longer relevant.

                  Vinnie
    (Pacing)
So you're saying unless we get the hell out of the university we're stuck with playing nit-picking games about filling out forms and more forms. And questions of truth, beauty and goodness are also no longer relevant here in the university. Is that it Glenn?

                  Glenn
Look Vince. I understand what you're saying. And hell deep down I know you're probably right. But I don't make the rules.

                  Vinnie
    (Facing Glenn)
Then who does?

                  Glenn
    (Pointing up)
They do.

                  Vinnie
    (Explodes)
They, they! It's the they who are destroying us Glenn! Can't you see?!

                  Glenn
Please Vince don't put me in a position of pulling rank. We've been good friends for a long time. And I'm tired of arguing with you over this. Fill the damn forms out and then forget it! It's not worth it Vince.

                  Vinnie
    (Choking with emotion again)
Yes it is! Yes it is Glenn! Can't you see that once you start giving in here and there to them, before you know it they got your soul?! Can't you?!

                  Glenn
Really Vince, I have to see some other people. Just do it, and get some rest. You look like shit.

                  Vinnie
    (Suddenly apologetic)
I know... I'm sorry for blowing up Glenn. Jesus it's just —

                  Glenn
       Why don't you take some leave time Vince? I'll

get someone to cover for you. I'll even fill out the damn forms for you.
(He laughs)

                        Vinnie
I'll see. But maybe I will go home today.

                        Glenn
Good.
            (Vinnie starts to leave in the direction of stage right.)
Call me some weekend Vince and we'll have a couple brews
together. Hell we never get together any more.
            (Vinnie stops, turns and looks at him.)
And don't forget I need those damn old peer review forms by tomorrow
so I can finish my report. Take care buddy.
            (Vinnie shakes his head in disbelief and leaves. The
            lights fade out.)

ACT II

(The lights come up on Vinnie sitting at the table. The table is set for five people. Vinnie has a half-filled glass of milk and a plate of cookies in front of him. His mother is cooking in the kitchen.)

                    Theresa
You want some more cookies?

                    Vinnie
No Mom.

                    Theresa
I wish you would've gotten out today. You can't stay in all the time.

                    Vinnie
I know. Maybe tomorrow Mom I'll get out. I just didn't feel like it today.

        (Jimmy enters from stage right)

                    Theresa
Did you get to see that man?

                    Jimmy
Yes.
        (Goes to the refrigerator, takes out the carrot juice and pours himself a glass.)
I think he's interested in the project. You never know with movie deals. Here I send him a script two years ago and I never hear from him. Then two weeks ago he writes and tells me when I'm in Boston the next time he wants to talk to me about it. You just never know in this business. It's crazy.

                    Theresa
You want some cookies?

                    Jimmy
No, I told you how that sugar will eventually kill you. Okay, keep killing yourself.
        (Goes off at stage left and comes out with a towel around his neck.)
I think I'm gonna run for a few miles. Vin, you wanna come?

                    Vinnie
I don't think so.

                    Jimmy
Come on, you stay around here and all you'll get is more depressed, especially if he's in one of his mocking moods.

                    Theresa
He's just tired. He's really been looking forward to all of you being here.

Jimmy
I bet he has.
(Moving towards stage right)
You sure Vin, you don't wanna come?

Vinnie
I'm sure.

Jimmy
(Starts going off)
Okay. I'll be right back.

Theresa
Don't stay too long. We'll be eating pretty soon.

Jimmy
I won't. I'll knock off five miles in about four minutes.
(He laughs to himself as he leaves. Mario enters almost at the same time.)

Vinnie
Hi.

Mario
Hello. I don't know why he has to run when I got all this work around here to do. If he would just do half of what I have to do he would never have to worry about exercising.

Theresa
He enjoys it Mario. Not everyone is like you who is working all the time. And why are you home so early? It's only four.

Mario
(Takes off his shoes and puts them near the bookcase)
I only had three customers and after two-thirty nobody came. Why stay? Remember Tree when they would come all the way from Webster to get a haircut from me? They liked me because I gave them their money's worth. I wasn't like these young barbers today who take nothing off so you'll come back quicker for a haircut.

Theresa
You watch, tomorrow it will be busier. I hope you wiped before you came up. I had to wash the stairs again this afternoon. Someone came up with black cinders on their shoes.

Mario
Who?

Theresa
I don't know. I was out shopping. It was probably your brother Joe, coming to visit. He never wipes.

Mario
It couldn't be one of your brothers because they're so clean.
(He laughs)

Hell your brother Nick stinks worse than a pig.

      Theresa
Stop it, of all my brothers he's the cleanest.

      Vinnie
Are you really not doing the business like before?

      Mario
   (Nods yes without looking at him)
Tree, bring me the bottle underneath the sink.
   (Sits down at the table)

      Vinnie
Maybe once school starts and people get back from their vacations, it will get better.

      Theresa
Do you need it now? Why don't you wait until we eat?

      Mario
   (Sternly)
I want it now.

      Theresa
   (Comes back out)
But you know about Vinnie.

      Mario
He's not gonna be drinking it! I am!

      Theresa
It's not –

      Mario
Just bring it! Damn it! Hell a little glass might even help him!

      Theresa
Never mind that's all we need is for him to get started again.
   (She goes back into the kitchen, reaches down underneath the sink and stove unit, gets the bottle of wine and brings it to him.)
Mario I don't want him to have any. You understand?

      Vinnie
Will you stop Mom. I'm not going to have any.

   (Mario pours himself a drink and gulps it down.)

      Theresa
I just don't want to go through this again. That's all. You don't know the worry you have put us through.
   (Presses her hand against her heart)
And my heart is starting to hurt again.

                    Vinnie
I told you don't worry anymore Mom. I'm going to be okay. Really
I am.

                    Theresa
Well just don't start drinking again and I won't worry.

                    Vinnie
I won't. You think I also want to go through that again?

                    Theresa
I hope not.
          (She goes back to the kitchen as Mario pours himself
          another drink and gulps half of it down.)

                    Vinnie
Maybe Dad, if it doesn't get business you should think seriously of
cutting down on the days you go in. I told mom this morning you and
her should relax a little and enjoy life.

                    Mario
Listen to him! How the hell could I enjoy life with your sister
trying to buy up New York City and you staying in that room all day
counting how many times your hand shakes?! Only Jimmy is doing okay
now. And he was the one I thought I would have the worst problems wit.

                    Theresa
          (Shaking her head)
Mario how easy you forget. Do you forget the time we were sending all
that money to him in Florida thinking he was using it for his tuition
at Miami University? Do you? And then we find out he's spending it
on whores and dog races?

                    Mario
          (Looking at Vinnie)
I don't care! I remember telling him wait, wait a couple years before
you get married. You got your Ph.D. from a good school, now work for
awhile and put some money in the bank and invest some. A family will
drag you down I said, didn't I?! Look at Dom Petro's son, the doctor.
He never married and now he has close to two hundred thousand dollars
in the bank. But no, my son Mister Hot Pants has to get married to
that Irish whore!

                    Vinnie
          (Angrily he gets up and starts shaking.)
Mom I'm getting out of here! I can't take him! I can't! Does he
also know that Dom Petro's son also hangs around men's rooms looking
for dates?!

                    Theresa
Mario stop! Whatsamatter wit you?! This morning it was wit Jimmy and
now Vinnie! Now stop or go lay down until supper! Maybe you'll be
in a better mood then!

Mario
Goddamn it Tree stop interfering! You know I don't get a chance to talk to my kids very much. So I have to tell them things when I think of them. I'm their father and I worry about them. It just hurts me to see him like this. He coulda become a doctor, a lawyer. That's what you shoulda become, not a teacher. There's millions of them. You'll never make any money working in the university. Everyone knows what you make there. You need a profession like Dom's son where you work for yourself. And I don't care what he does in men's rooms. At least nobody knows what he makes. You understand what I'm saying? I say these things because I don't want you to be broke all your life.

Vinnie
(Stops pacing and tries to become friendlier)
I know. But Dad I make enough. Really I'm not interested in making a lot of money. As long as I got enough to be comfortable, that's all I need.

Mario
But you'll never have enough. You gotta learn how to save. Banks and now divorce lawyers own you buddy.

Vinnie
(Blows up)
Hell Dad what do you want from me?! One of the reasons I'm so screwed up now is because I always worked my ass off in school! I never had any fun! I had to make sure you got your money's worth! And still you're not satisfied! What the hell else do you want from me?! Tell me! What else?!

Mario
(Backs off)
You know Tree I don't know what's wrong with my kids. They're all so sensitive.
(Looking at Vinnie)
I'm just trying to tell you these things so you won't have to suffer like I did. I say these things because I love you kids and want you to do good in this world. I don't care for myself anymore. My life is almost finished. But I want you kids to be secure. You understand?

Vinnie
(Feeling guilty, he sits down)
Yes, but think of yourself now Dad. Forget us, we'll be okay. Really.

Mario
(Almost in tears, takes a sip from his drink)
I can't forget you kids. I want to help you kids as long as I'm able.

Theresa
(Goes to kitchen)
Mario, Toni is gonna be here pretty soon. Go over to Julio's and get a loaf of fresh Italian bread. I forgot it today.

Mario
(Gets up)
You want me to get two?

Theresa
I don't care.

Mario
Well why don't I? Do you want anything else? How about some prosciutto?

Theresa
No I got some. Just the bread.

Mario
See everything we do is for youse kids. That's why I say the things I do.
(Goes over and puts on his shoes. Looks at Vinnie)
You want me to get you a big T-bone steak for tonight? I worry you're gonna get sick again.

Vinnie
I'll eat the spaghetti tonight Dad, thanks anyway.

Theresa
Don't forget to wipe.

Mario
Yes okay.
(He goes off stage right)

Theresa
He's got too much time on his hands now. That's his problem. You got to keep him busy. First he can't wait until
(The phone rings and she goes over to it)
you kids get home and then when you get home he becomes moodier than hell. I don't know.
(She answers the phone)
Oh yes Father, he's right here.
(She puts her hand over the receiver)
Vinnie, it's for you. It's Father Charles, now be nice.

Vinnie
(Whispers)
Mom I don't feel like talking to anyone now.

Theresa
(Whispering also)
You have to. He's always been good to us.
(She holds out the receiver to him and puts her hand over it.)
Here tell him you appreciate him calling.

Vinnie
(Gets up and goes over and takes the receiver from her)
Hello... yes Father, I'm doing fine... Thank you... Yes it feels good to be home... Oh I don't think I could get up that early in the morning.

But thanks for offering... Well I'm sorry to say I haven't been that active in the church of late... You see Father I'm into Satan now. I attend three black masses a week and I'm in charge of music. Thanks for calling Father.
(He slams the receiver down.)

Theresa
Vinnie why did you do that?!

Vinnie
(Leaves the kitchen)
Because I'm sick and tired of people calling me up and trying to tell me how to get over a nervous breakdown! Mom, I'm really not interested in being a lay minister at this time!

Theresa
(She follows)
Okay but you shoulda been nicer.

(Toni now enters. She puts her luggage down and goes over and kisses her mother and then Vinnie. She affectionately holds him for a while.)

Toni
Hi.

Vinnie
Hi.

Theresa
How did you get here?

Toni
Taxi.

Theresa
Why didn't you call? One of us coulda picked you up. How much was it?

Toni
Ten. Mom will you stop. Damn I just got home!
(Lets go of Vinnie)

Theresa
But why didn't you take the limo or bus? It's cheaper.

Toni
Do you want me to go back?! I mean I'll go back right now if you want me to! I'm not gonna start off this way! I'm not!

Theresa
Oh stop feeling sorry for yourself! It's just that youse kids never learned the meaning of money. The problem is we gave youse kids too much.

Vinnie
(Sits down)
Welcome Toni to Serrficial Finance Company. Or should I way superficial? Anyway we give you all the money you want only if you give us your soul.
(Laughs a little)

Toni
Yeah right. Look I gotta go to the bathroom. I don't know what's wrong. I've been going all morning.
(Goes in the direction of stage left)

Theresa
One is worse than the other in this house.

Toni
I don't know I think maybe it's the chili I ate last night. I really feel awful. I can't hold it anymore.
(Goes off)

Theresa
(Goes near where Toni left)
Listen Toni when you come out look at the sauce and stir it if it needs it, okay? I gotta run over to Concetta's. She made those small Italian cookies you like. I'll-

Toni
(Yells back)
Shit Mom here I want to go and I can't now because you're talking tomato sauce while I'm trying to concentrate on going! Oh God it's hurting!

Theresa
I don't want the sauce to burn so we could have a nice dinner tonight. It gets too thick if you don't stir it enough.

Toni
Mom nothing is coming out! Oh shit no my hemorrhoids are up now!

Theresa
Listen Tone lower the fire if it starts to boil. Just don't push so hard. That's why you have hemorrhoids. I gotta go.
(Comes out to Vinnie)
Vinnie maybe you should go in and rest for a while. You look white.

Vinnie
I'll see.

Theresa
(Picks up her shoes near the bookcase, puts them on and leaves stage right.)
I'll be back.

(Vinnie now stares at the bottle of wine left on the table. Then quickly he picks it up and guzzles some down. He does this twice. The lights dim and after a moment a spotlight shines on Jenny stage center. She is dressed in a black leotard and white leg warmers. She's doing some dance warmups while holding onto a chair.)

                          Vinnie
            (Speaks from his seat)
Hi.

                          Jenny
            (Acts coolly as she continues to do her warmups)
Hi. This is interesting.

                          Vinnie
            (Gets up and walks over to her. The lights come up.)
Are you still too mad to talk to me?

                          Jenny
No, I don't care anymore. But damn it you're unreal walking in here like nothing happened.

                          Vinnie
I thought maybe we'd get together again.

                          Jenny
Why?

                          Vinnie
I want to be with you. I've been thinking about you a lot of late, especially these last four weeks.

                          Jenny
            (She does a couple of pirouettes.)
What happened? Has Chris found a new lover?

                          Vinnie
Yes.

                          Jenny
Who? You're kidding.

                          Vinnie
Jesus Christ. She's joined a group called "The Eyes of Christ." And now we both know how to hide from each other. She goes to her prayer meetings nightly and I go to the study and write. And when we are together we bore each other to death.

                          Jenny
Well that's too bad. Maybe Chris will convince you to be the poet laureate for the group and you too will have meaning in your life.

                          Vinnie
Come on Jen, I'm down and I need someone to talk to. Stop being such a ball-buster.

                          Jenny
            (Stops dancing)
So you turn to old Jenny. That's right good old Jenny will be there. She'll be waiting like a nice obedient kept woman. Jesus for seven months, we have a tremendous time together and then one night you're

not there, no call, no letter, nothing. But now you expect me to take you back with open arms. Bullshit!

                       Vinnie
        (Moves toward her)
I know. I'm sorry.

                       Jenny
Did you ever care how I was doing, how my dancing was going? It was never my work, always you, your work. That's how our relationship worked.

                       Vinnie
Come on, you know that's not true. I cared about your work, Jen.

                       Jenny
Well damn it why don't you ask me about it now?

                       Vinnie
Okay shit I'll play your game. How's your dancing going Jen?

                       Jenny
Gee I'm glad you asked Professor Serrano because it's going shitty right now. I auditioned for the touring company "Dancing," and for the one hundred thousandth time they gave me that shit about being good but not good enough. When Professor do you get good enough? Can you tell me? When?
        (Almost in tears)

                     Vinnie
        (Moves closer)
I'm sorry Jen. I really am.

                     Jenny
        (Moves away and does some more warmups)
I bet you are. Here I am finally getting some of my shit together minus the dancing part of course and you had to come back into my life again. Why?

                     Vinnie
        (Moves closer to her)
Look Jen I didn't know how to deal with what was happening between us. I mean it. Really I felt guilty falling in love with you and also still being in love with Chris. I just couldn't deal with those confused feelings.

                     Jenny
        (Crying changes to anger now)
Well how about me and my feelings?! Huh, Vinnie?! Did you know I was mute for weeks after you left? I couldn't sleep. I couldn't dance. I didn't want to talk to anyone. I even tried killing myself one night with some pills because of you. Then one morning, I woke up and I said the hell with it. It's over with that bastard. And I promised myself never to let myself get so screwed up over a man again, especially a damn married one!

                    Vinnie
I get the feeling you're really pissed off at me.

                    Jenny
Right.
          (She turns away from him and starts her dance warmups again.)

                    Vinnie
I just can't believe you're being like this.

                    Jenny
          (Stops the warmups)
Come on Vin, don't start trying to get me to feel sorry for you. I
did that for seven months. I should've charged you a hundred dollars
an hour just like any other therapist.

                    Vinnie
Listen Jenny, can't we just talk for a few moments? I want you to
know I really need you now. I needed distance before Jen. That's
really why I left.

                    Jenny
          (Starts the warmups again)
You got it. Please go Vinnie.

                    Vinnie
What the hell do you want from me?! I said I was sorry. Hell do you
want me to get a bushy whiskbroom and start flagellating myself like
they do in Iran?

                    Jenny
          (Smiles a little)
Not a bad idea.
          (Stops the warmups)
I'll tell you one thing Vinnie, our relationship has forced me to
seek some clarity in my life. That was the other problem I had with
our relationship. I was never sure what you wanted from me.

                    Vinnie
I don't understand.

                    Jenny
Come on Vin, you know exactly what I mean. The whole sexual thing.

                    Vinnie
I know, but what can I do I still have this thing about being loyal to Chris?

                    Jenny
But can't you see, even though I loved the times we were together, you
were not being fair to me? You got the sympathy and sometimes a little
love-making which frustrated the hell out of me, especially when you
used to get up and leave after you had me all worked up. But what about me?

                    Vinnie
I'm sorry.

Jenny

Listen Vin, I just need you to tell me what you want me to be to you. If you want me to be your friend, I'll be your friend. If you want me to just hold your hand when you come over, I'll do that. But I just need to be clear on what you want from me Vin. I've got to have some clarity in my life. You understand?

Vinnie
(Moves closer to her)

Yes.

Jenny

I lied Vinnie. I'm really not getting any of my shit together. My ex is still shitting all over me. Every time I see him, he's got a new girlfriend. Now it's a fifteen-year-old girl who greets me at the door when I go to pick up my son with a stoned grin and a bongo drum. Then my son comes home after a weekend with him acting like a little Adolf Hitler because he spoils him rotten. I think his father bribes him all weekend so that he'll stay out of the way while he and his Pocahontas make rain music together... Vin you're really getting me at a time when I'm holding myself together with a lot of nerve pills and fake courage...
(Almost in tears)

Vinnie

God I missed you.
(He brings her close to him and kisses her for a long while. He breaks the kiss.)
You know I thought about you all the time I was away. I really did.

Jenny
(Kiddingly)

You son of a bitch then why didn't you do something about it.
(They kiss again for a long while. She breaks the kiss this time.)
Oh God, I love you.

Vinnie

I do too...
(They kiss again. He breaks the kiss.)
But shit, I better get out of here before I get you frustrated again. I promise Jen I'm going to get it straightened out with Chris. I mean it even though now I want to stay here so bad. But I must get it straightened out. We can't go on like this.
(He starts to go off stage left.)

Jenny

Vinnie you're not playing games with me, are you? You'll come back this time, won't you?

Vinnie
(Comes back and kisses her again. He breaks the kiss.)
God I want you so bad, but I gotta go. Really I gotta go.
(Moves away)

                    Jenny
Vinnie how come you always have to be in control of yourself?

                    Vinnie
        (Comes back and embraces her again)
I don't know. I think maybe I'm scared if I completely let myself go I'll never gain control again. I don't know. It's all so crazy.
        (He kisses her)
Look I'll see you.
        (The spotlight fades out on Jenny and after a moment the
        lights come up on Vinnie still sitting at the table.)

                    Vinnie
        (Talking out loud to himself)
Forget it forget it. Concentrate, concentrate now. Concentrate Vinnie. Concentrate... Please God help me. Please...
        (Toni comes out from stage left)

                    Toni
I can't go now I'm constipated. I probably got a blockage or something.

                    Vinnie
        (Forces a smile)
No.

                    Toni
        (Comes over and sits down)
How about you? How are you doing?

                    Vinnie
I think I'll be okay once I get the hell out of here.

                    Toni
Why?

                    Vinnie
Because getting over a nervous breakdown in this house is like trying to whistle a tune while you're being mugged. You know what I mean?

                    Toni
Well they're gonna be even worse after I tell them that I'm marrying Neil.

                    Vinnie
You mean that guy who's divorced?

                    Toni
Yes.

                    Vinnie
Oh wonderful.

                    Toni
We're getting married next week.

Vinnie
Lovely. Happy valley will really be happy then. Jesus I don't know if I'll be able to handle all the joy that will be soon filling this house after you tell them.

Toni
Look Vin I'm tired of playing games with myself and them. Hell I almost blew it before with Neil because of them and I'm not gonna let that happen again.

Vinnie
(Smiles)
Well I guess now you'll be out of the will and Jimmy and I will get everything.

Toni
Aren't you lucky.

Vinnie
Yeah I'm overjoyed. I don't know Tone is it all worth it?

Toni
Yes this time for me it is. Last year I couldn't deal with their shit. But now after being in analysis for a year I know I don't need their approval anymore. I mean I'm not scared of myself Vinnie like they want me to be. Hell look at today. I couldn't believe it..
(Almost in tears)
God here I'm calling to tell them when I'm coming home and she almost hangs up on me because she thinks I'm spending too much money on the phone call.

Vinnie
Oh the hell with it Tone let's have a little party. You want some of dad's wine?
(He picks up the wine bottle.)

Toni
I thought you couldn't drink?

Vinnie
One little tumbler of wine isn't going to hurt.
(He pours her a drink and then one for himself.)

Toni
Vinnie I don't think you should, really.

Vinnie
(He takes a sip of his drink. Being an alcoholic, it doesn't take much to have an effect.)
Look don't worry. I'm not going to blow it Tone. Old Vinnie has everything under control.
(He holds up his glass.)
And now to a happy prenuptial affair and to the happiness your parents will bestow upon you once they know the good news of your forthcoming wedding.
(He finishes his drink and laughs.)

Toni
Yeah thanks a lot. Look, what about you? What are you going to do with your life now?

Vinnie
I don't know. Maybe I'll run for President of the Universe.

Toni
Come on be serious, you gotta do something. Are you going back to the university?

Vinnie
I don't know. I could do an ethnography on the Navajos, or go on relief.
(He pours himself another drink.)

Toni
Really Vinnie, aren't you going to teach anymore?

Vinnie
I don't know. Really I don't. How can I do anything with my hand like this?
(He raises his shaking hand.)

Toni
You can. Just give yourself some time.

Vinnie
(His voice is a bit sluggish.)
I don't know maybe I'll go back to the nuthouse. No one there gave a shit if I wrote two novels or fifteen novels. They were just happy because I was getting up each day. I was being... I don't know, does that make any sense?

Toni
No, but you know I really feel bad because I didn't come to visit you in the hospital. But I can't stand them, they all smell of death and Lysol.

Vinnie
I wasn't in a hospital. I said I was in a <u>nuthouse</u> Tone. Hell at least you could've sent me a book on how to communicate with hand puppets.

Toni
I wrote every week, didn't I?

Vinnie
The trials, loves and tribulations of a manic depressive. It wasn't really what I was looking for.

Toni
I'm sorry. Next time I'll just send you a get-sane quick card.

Vinnie
Hell I'm getting depressed.
(He finishes his drink, picks up the bottle and gets up.)
I think I'll go in my room and get myself good and stiff. Tone, did I ever tell you you know shit about having parties?!

Toni
Thanks. Listen sit down. I got something serious to ask you.

Vinnie
Ah seriousness, the hemlock of Socrates, Hemingway and that poor old drunk Fitzgerald, I would do anything to have a couple minutes of conversation with them now. I mean I would even say twenty rosaries a day, do charity work with female impersonators, anything if God would just grant me this wish. Anything.

Toni
Vinnie, will you please stop with that mad hatter's world of yours and listen to me?! Please!

Vinnie
Okay okay, what is so damn serious?

Toni
Did mom ever say I love you to you?

(A long pause)

Vinnie
I don't know. I just never thought about it... I don't think she did. Hell I don't know.
(Sobering up)

Toni
Well I never remember her saying it to me and maybe that's your problem too. Maybe you're like me you just never got enough warmth from her. My analyst and I decided that it was part of my problem. She's such a cold bitch and I think I saw myself becoming just like her in my relationships.

Vinnie
You know, hell it's funny. I just can't remember now ever being hugged by her. Maybe I never expected it from her. I don't know I think I just accepted the way she was. Always cleaning, cooking, worrying. That was just her. But there is something which I finally figured out about her this year.

Toni
What?

Vinnie
(Takes a swig from the wine bottle)
I don't know but I think because she was on the verge of having a nervous breakdown I was sent off to prep school at age fifteen.

Toni
Why do you say that?

Vinnie
Look, Jimmy was off in Florida trying to sign up eighty-year-old prostitutes for his health club, and it wasn't bad with only me home. I was like an only child. Then you came along and I think unplanned. So here she has a kid hitting puberty and asking her questions about pubic hair around his penis and you being born with a hundred and fifteen allergies.

Toni
It makes sense. Hell I don't know Vin.

Vinnie
Did you know mom reads a lot?

Toni
Yes. She always has.

Vinnie
Jesus how come I never knew it?

Toni
She hid them when we were small. I'm always exchanging books with her now. I guess she figures now I'm old enough to read Harold Robbins or just plain trash. How did you find out about our mother's favorite pastime?

Vinnie
I discovered in my room a drawer full of paperbacks like "Peyton Place" that date back to the early fifties. She probably put them there after I left the last time and forgot to take them out.

Toni
You know Vin she worries about you. Really. That's all she talked about when she came to visit me last month.

Vinnie
There've got to be other things worrying her too. Hell like I just said she's always been a worrier.

Toni
I know, but right now you're her number one worry. And I'm worried about you too Vin. You know because of our age difference and because you were always off to prep schools and universities we never got close. And I want us Vinnie to get close as a brother and sister should.

Vinnie
I don't know if I'm up to the brother part Tone. I blew my parts as father and husband. I see red cherries on crosses in my dreams and I say I love you when I walk into bathrooms. The odds Tone are not good. You know what I mean? I'm definitely not on a good roll.
   (Takes another swig from the wine bottle)

                    Toni
I don't care. Let's at least try. And please Vin don't drink any
more. I need you to be sober tonight so you could stick up for me
when I tell them about Neil and me.

                    Vinnie
I'll be sober, don't worry. When Mario the Great performs those of
us interested in social pathological behavior become fully alert.
Listen I just had a thought — why don't you and I, Jimmy, mom and
dad get our licenses and do family counseling? I mean it. We'll be
great. Really especially dad with his warm and accepting ways. What
do you say Tone?

                    Toni
I say you're getting drunk.

                    Vinnie
No I'm not. I'm already there.
          (He heads now for the kitchen, goes to the window and sticks
          his head out. He yells.)
Listen out there, tonight our fine family counseling service will be
demonstrating how a family deals with a daughter who wants love and
happiness! You'll see true sensitivity and empathy! Apartment 4C,
that's the address! Home of family unity and understanding! Perverts
are especially welcome!

                    Toni
          (Quickly she gets up, goes over and pulls him away from
          the window. She takes the wine bottle away from him.)
Jesus Vinnie will you stop! There just might be a bunch of perverts
out there who'll come! And that's all we need!

                    Vinnie
Good, then maybe we could charge admissions. Our good father will see
that he's really mistaken about us. He'll see dear sister that deep in
our hearts we have always been unfeeling greedy bastards!
          (He sticks his head out of the window again.)
You hear that America?! Toni and Vinnie Serrano are greedy bastards,
just like all of you!

                    Voice
          (A man's voice offstage)
Shut up goofball! You damn Serranos are all crazy!

                    Vinnie
          (He leans further out and yells up)
That's only because we had to put up with assholes like you all our
lives. Is that you Frankie?! I bet it is! You still washing your
mother's underwear?! You big asshole!

                    Voice
You people are animals down there!

                    Vinnie
Animals?! If we're animals, then you asshole you're
          (Stammers)
existential waste! A zero! Doomed to eternal nothingness! You
hear? Doomed!

(Suddenly he gets hit with flying garbage, probably a basket-full.)
Son of a bitch!
(Stunned and dazed, he brings his head in. Slowly, he starts to wipe the garbage off his face.)

                    Toni
Oh shit Vinnie, that's disgusting!

                    Vinnie
I don't believe that asshole did that... I don't. What a thing to do to someone...
(He shakes his head in disgust and is almost in tears.)
They're winning Tone, and we're losing. The Frankies of the world are winning Tone... They're winning...
(He cries)

                    Toni
(She flicks off some garbage that is still in his hair, then Vinnie starts walking towards the table.)
Don't say that. People like him Vinnie will get theirs. It all balances out in the end Vinnie.
(She sticks her head half out of the window.)
You'll get yours pissant! Wait and see Frankie!

                    Vinnie
(Sits down and places the bottle in front of him)
Jesus Tone there's only so much drowning one can take. Only so much... God I don't know.

                    Toni
(Sits down also)
I know about the drowning feeling Vinnie. You just gotta learn how to relax and not let everything bother you. I know I should talk, Miss Hypochondriac of the World, but I'm learning. I really am. We have to Vinnie or we're going to blow it, we have to...
(Pours herself a drink)
And we also got to stick together Vinnie. I mean we have no one else Vinnie, except us. Jimmy only has deals on his mind, and to them, we're just a bother.

                    Vinnie
(Half crying)
I don't know Tone... I really don't...

            (The lights now dim as a spotlight shines on Jenny at
            downstage left. She's dancing to Harry James' "You Made
            Me Love You.")
And why the hell did she have to kill herself?!

                    Toni
Who?

                    Vinnie
Someone I cared about a great deal. Her name was Jenny.

(Jenny keeps dancing. Her voice is heard over the music.)

Jenny's Voice
Dear Vinnie, I knew after waiting for two months and you didn't come back it just would never be for us...

Vinnie
(Gets up and moves towards Jenny)
No that's not true. It could've worked. Please believe me. I really wanted it to work Jen.

Toni
(Follows)
What did you want to work?

Vinnie
Us.

Jenny's Voice
I just wish you would've been more honest with me that night.

Vinnie
But I was. It's just that I didn't have the courage to tell Chris. I just couldn't. Please understand that Jen. I just couldn't.

Toni
Vinnie what is it? Jesus Christ don't do this to me Vinnie. I'm scared.

Jenny's Voice
I hope Vinnie when you get this letter you'll understand I'm leaving this world not only because I can't have you but because I can't stand being <u>rejected</u> any more... The pain is too much. I want out... I will always love you Vinnie. Jenny.
(She brings her hand up to her mouth, swallows, dances some more and fades into the darkness.)

Vinnie
(Rushes over to where Jenny was dancing)
Jenny no! Goddamn it no!... I love you! I love you!

(He stares at the spotlight fading out. Numb, Toni stands in the background. Then lights and spotlight fade out.)

ACT III

(Evening meal. As the lights come up, Theresa is in the kitchen stirring something on the stove and Toni is setting plates around the table.)

Toni
Mom have you read "This Towering Passion?"

Theresa
No, is it good?

Toni
Yes, you'll like it. It's full of a lot of good sex and mushy stuff.

Theresa
(Embarrassed a bit)
Good. Did you bring it wit you?

Toni
Yes it's in my suitcase. I'll give it to you later. I'm reading another good one now called "Stolen Rapture."

Theresa
Don't forget when you're done, save it for me.

Toni
(Goes to the kitchen)
Okay. Mom I wonder do you ever want to be like those characters you read about?

Theresa
No. I just do it to pass the time.

Toni
Maybe you need some other hobbies.

Theresa
I sew and knit. And don't worry with your father I got enough to do.

Toni
I know but you need some other -

(Jimmy enters from stage right, wiping his face with the towel.)

Jimmy
Hi Tone.
(Gives her a perfunctory-type of kiss)
How's the New York girl?
(Goes over to the refrigerator, takes out the carrot juice and pours himself a glass)

Toni
Okay. How's the Hollywood boy?

Jimmy
(Comes out and sits down)
Gorgeous, and after a good run I always feel great. You gotta get that

blood pumping hard for a few minutes each day Tone or your body starts
to die on you. You should jog Tone.

        Toni
   (Places some glasses around the table)
I tried but because I have scoliosis it throws my back out.

        Jimmy
What is it with you and Vinnie? Am I the only healthy one in this family?

        Toni
Must be. Right now, it's not my back that's hurting but it's not being
able to go good. Just a couple black pebbles came out the last time I went.

        Jimmy
Listen get started on my health food diet and you won't have
any problems going. I go once a day in the morning like clockwork and
it's always nice and loose.

        Toni
You're lucky, sometimes it's weeks before I have a good one.

        Jimmy
Look I got some tofu in the refrigerator. One meal of that Tone and
you'll go with an explosion that you'll never forget.

        Toni
Yeah, but I know with my luck afterwards I'll probably end up with
diarrhea for months.

        Jimmy
No you won't. You'll feel great.

        Toni
I just don't like any of that health food stuff. It tastes so awful.
In fact, a couple months ago I went to a health food restaurant with
a friend and I don't know the stuff tasted like pieces of leather sprayed
with Raid.

        Jimmy
That's because you have ruined most of your taste buds with spicy foods.
It takes a while for them to come alive again.

        Toni
Jimmy how much of this new interest in health foods is just a passing
fad for you? I mean last year it was est. The year before it was human
encounter groups and this year it's health foods. Hell for all I know
next year you could be into light bulbs.

        Jimmy
Hey I've always looked after my body. I've been studying foods for
years and I probably know more now than any food expert in the country.
I also wouldn't own two health food stores if I didn't believe in it,
right?

        Toni
   (Sits down)
I guess.

           Jimmy
Jesus look at the people in Hollywood that come to me for advice about
their bodies and what they should eat.

           Toni
I know I read about it.

           Jimmy
Well it's all true. Burt Reynolds used to invite me over every Sunday
to cook up some tofu soup. In fact next year I think Burt and I are
gonna be doing something together. You know I even told him one day
that he's wasting his time playing all those comedy parts. I said you
gotta do serious drama Burt. You're too talented to waste your time
in movies where all you do is get chased by fat-assed cops. And you
know I think the son of a bitch listened to me because next year he
told me he's gonna do something serious that I know will do for him
what "Gone with the Wind" did for Clark Gable.

           Toni
That's the other thing that pisses me off about you. Why the hell do
you always have to try to impress everyone by talking about all those
big Hollywood stars you know? I really am not impressed Jimmy. Maybe
other people are, but I'm not. Shit I think I'm getting a headache now.
           (Pressing her forehead with the tips of her fingers)

           Jimmy
Good. Serves you right after making fun of me and my friends.

           Toni
           (Leans over toward Jimmy)
I'm just saying here you and I are talking about tofu soup and Burt
Reynolds' career when we should be talking about how we can help Vinnie.
And something else which really is gonna make mom and dad go bonkers tonight.

           Jimmy
What?

           Toni
           (Lowering her voice)
Next week I'm getting married to a divorced man that they happen to hate.
Don't talk loud, I don't want mom to know yet.

           Jimmy
Old Mario is gonna love to hear that.

           Toni
I know. Why do you think I'm so upset? I'm also worried about Vinnie.
I wish we could help him Jimmy.

           Jimmy
I've tried but he doesn't want any help. I still say he's a nervous
wreck because of all that time he used to spend in his room reading
books on astrology, philosophy and all that shit. Hell when he was ten
he talked and acted like fifty. He's too fucking smart, that's his
problem.

                    Toni
I don't know. But what can we do?

                    Jimmy
Hell I don't know either. Maybe we should send him back to the psych ward and tell them this one they sent out is still not functioning properly.

                    Toni
Don't say that.

                    Jimmy
Well it's true, isn't it? Our brother is a true-blue wacko.

                    Toni
No, he's just had a tough time and needs our help like I need yours tonight. Listen Jimmy, mom and dad didn't say a damn thing to you when you got divorced twice and I want you to remind them of that.

                    Jimmy
Don't worry I will.

                    Toni
I just wish I could believe you.

                    Jimmy
You can. Don't worry, you worry too much Tone. Old Jimmy will have everything under control tonight. Tell me what does this guy do for a living anyway?

                    Toni
He's a stock broker.

                    Jimmy
How much does he make?

                    Toni
I don't know, I guess he makes a pretty good salary. Look you son of a bitch
         (She grabs his arm and talks through clenched teeth)
I don't expect the third degree from you. I said I want your help. You understand?

                    Jimmy
Okay okay don't worry. I said I would take care of things. Hell I know they're still living in the stone age. I would love just once to bring them to a Hollywood party. They would really go bullshit then. Last week I was at one where the hostess greeted me at the door with only rhinestone-framed glasses on, nothing else, I mean it. Then she handed me a baggie full of red pills, green pills, purple pills, coke, whatever you wanted it was there. You do dope Tone?

                    Toni
Sometimes grass, but I have to take two shots of Maalox before I do it or it kills my stomach.

                    Jimmy
I'll tell you there's nothing like a great high. I mean I don't do hard stuff but a little pot really helps me see things so much better and it's so so relaxing. I got some Tone. You want some?
                    Toni
No Jesus that's all we need is to have mom and dad think we're dopers.
          (Looks at Theresa)
Jesus I think mom is sleeping and cooking at the same time. She's unreal.
          (She gets up and starts heading for the kitchen. Jimmy laughs as Mario enters from stage right with two loaves of Italian bread in a grocery bag. He is seething with anger. Toni comes back out.)
                  Mario
          (Looking at Jimmy and then Toni)
What the hell did you do with my keys this morning?! And so the Queen of Sheba has arrived.
                  Toni
          (Gives him a perfunctory kiss)
Hi Dad.
                  Jimmy
What keys?
                  Mario
The keys to the shop stupid!
                  Jimmy
I gave them back to you after you went in.
                  Mario
No you didn't!
          (Squeezing the Italian loaves in the grocery bag he starts to poke Jimmy as he talks)
I don't have them! I looked all over for them!
          (Jimmy gets up and trys to avoid Mario's piercing stabs with the Italian bread)
Jesus Christ why, why do you kids always do things half-ass?! Good thing I thought to check the doors to the barbershop. Something just told me to check. Then I remember I never locked them and then no keys. I looked all over the damn place! You son of a bitch what did you do with them?!
          (Keeps fiercely stabbing Jimmy as Jimmy backs around the table)
                  Jimmy
          (Defensively)
Dad I gave them back to you. Remember you gave them to me while you went around front and checked the mail? I let the cutomer in and when you came back I remember handing them to you. Remember?
                  Mario
Will you stop trying to blame someone else like you always do!
          (Mocking tone of voice and still stabbing with the grocery bag)
Not me Dad. I never do anything wrong. No sirree. You big bullshitter! I wish the hell I had the razor strap, I would beat the shit out of you now! That's the problem I didn't give you kids enough beatings!
          (Frustrated, he throws the grocery bag at Jimmy.)

                    Theresa
          (Comes out of the kitchen)
Did you look in your pockets?

                    Mario
          (Patting his pockets)
Yes I looked all over for them! Damn kids! I wish we never had them Tree!

                    Theresa
Stop talking crazy Mario! How about in the door? Did you look there?
I remember once you left them in there.

                    Mario
No they're not there. I told you I looked all over. He lost them! I
know he did. He probably took them wit him and left them in some
whore's apartment!

                    Jimmy
Shit I didn't go to any whore's apartment! I went to see someone about
backing a picture! I told you I gave them back to you!

                    Mario
Goddamn it, I had the keys to everything on it! The key to the shop, to
the safety deposit box, to the house, to the apartment, to the cellar!
What the hell am I gonna do now?! It will take me months to get them
made again! All because my kids are lazy bastards! They don't know
how to take care of property!
          (He shakes his head in disgust)
Will there ever be a time when I don't have to worry about something?
Always something. Always.

                    Toni
Dad you'll find them. Don't worry.

                    Jimmy
          (Acts friendlier)
Let's go over to the shop Dad. I'll help you find them. Really I gave
them back to you. At least I think I did.

                    Mario
          (His anger kicks off again)
Son of a bitch I knew it! I knew it! See you did lose them!
          (Mocking tone of voice again)
Oh Dad I didn't lose them. I gave them back to you. You must be crazy
Dad. I don't know anything about them.
          (Angry voice again)
Whataya think I'm stupid or something?! Come on I know we won't find
them, but at least you could stay there while I see if I could get a
lock for the shop tonight!
          (He walks off stage right. Jimmy follows, stumbling as he
          picks up his shoes and tries at the same time to put them on.)

                    Theresa
          (Goes back to the kitchen)
Toni go in and get your brother. We're gonna eat pretty soon. It
isn't right for him to stay in that room like that.

Toni
It's called avoidance behavior Mom.

Theresa
(Stirring something on the stove)
What?

Toni
(Shakes her head)
Nothing.

(She goes off stage left. The lights come down and then come up partially. Vinnie is sitting on the edge of a small bed downstage left. There is a half-emptied wine bottle near the bed. Glenn, his chairman, enters from stage right. His vest and suitcoat are off. As before, he's carrying IN and OUT boxes in one hand and some papers in the other. And also as before, he sets the table up as a desk. The lights come up.)

Vinnie
(Speaks from the bed)
I'm sorry for the outburst. I just couldn't stand it any more.

Glenn
(Harshly)
I want you to know right now Vince that your outbursts in my staff meetings are something I will no longer tolerate.

Vinnie
(Get up and moves toward the table)
I know. I'm sorry but you must understand that –

Glenn
I can only guess that you upset my staff meetings because you have some compulsion for self-aggrandizement.

Vinnie
No you know me Glenn. I'm not like that. I'm just tired of talking about policy bulletin number one hundred and fifty-four and what this committee found out and that committee found out and how to fill out the new peer review forms and so on and so on. Jesus Glenn there's go to be something more than the shit we usually talk about, especially in a university where we're supposed to be dealing with the great questions of the world.

Glenn
Sorry that's how it is. The university is a business now and forget all that other idealistic crap. Save it for another book or lecture.

Vinnie
(Angrily)
Jesus Glenn then what the hell have I been educated and assimilated for?! Tell me Glenn, for what?! To play nit-picking games... My God Glenn, I'll tell you it's getting so bad

that at night I'm dreaming how to cut nit-pick the nit-pickers. You know what I mean? I just want the other faculty to damn question what we're doing. They just don't seem to care any more.

                            Glenn
Look Vince, I don't want to talk about it any more. I gotta go to another meeting. I just don't want any more of your idealistic sermons at my staff meetings. You understand?!

                            Vinnie
Yes I understand, but please Glenn why don't you let me try out that collaboration program we designed. I need some new ideas to keep me going.

                            Glenn
The faculty would never accept that program Vince.

                            Vinnie
I don't know I think they would if they could see it working. Remember when we first shared the idea with them and all the support we got?

                            Glenn
Come on Vince, you know that's not exactly true. They were -

                            Vinnie
I remember even the dean coming over to me afterwards and shaking my hand. He was quite impressed with my presentation. He couldn't believe how much thought I had given to the program design.

                            Glenn
Damn it Vince bury the dream, the program! It just can't be done here. Forget it!

                            Vinnie
              (Leans over and grabs his arm)
Please Glenn let me try it. I'll even do it on top of my normal load of classes. Glenn I'm falling into a rut. I don't want to be like Bill Thomas and John Pirsig who are just sitting around and waiting to retire. They act so damn noble and scholarly but Glenn they're dead like so much of the university. Please Glenn let me try it! Please!
              (Grabs his arm again)

                            Glenn
              (Pulls away and works hard at controlling his anger)
I <u>don't</u> want the program Vince. Period. And there's something else I might as well talk to you about.

                            Vinnie
What?

                            Glenn
I've gotten reports about you showing up to class drunk and unprepared.

                            Vinnie
That's not true. I was sick a couple times Glenn, but never drunk.

Glenn
Let me be as honest as I can with you Vince, if you need help get it. Because I'm becoming terribly disappointed in you of late. Friend or no friend, get your act together or it's going to become touchy between you and me.
    (Vinnie sits down)
Maybe a year's sabbatical is really what you need now.

Vinnie
    (Shaken)
Jesus Glenn, I'm not that bad.

Glenn
    (Gets up)
Really I gotta get going to this other meeting.
    (Picks up his papers and the IN and OUT boxes.)
Why don't you stay here for a few minutes and think about what I said.
    (Goes out stage right)

Vinnie
God I can't believe I was begging! But damn it the dean, everyone that day was impressed with the program. I don't care what he says. I know they would go for it again.
    (Gets up and starts to go in the direction of stage right. Lights dim.)
Glenn! Glenn!
    (Off stage)
Where did Glenn go Shelly? I got something to tell him.
    (The lights come down and then come up. At downstage left Vinnie is lying down on a small bed. Toni enters from stage left. She walks over to the bed and shakes Vinnie.)

Toni
Vin, Vinnie. It's Toni.

Vinnie
    (Slowly he turns over, opens his eyes and looks at Toni for a long while.)
Hi.

Toni
Hi. Mom wants you to stop playing hermit and come out to supper.

Vinnie
I really don't feel like eating.

Toni
Well at least come out and show your face for a little while. I need you.
    (She touches his forehead)
You realize you're sweating like hell?

Vinnie
I know.

Toni
What is it Vin? Is it related to that girl Jenny and that whole crazy scene this afternoon?

                    Vinnie
        (Sits up)
Some of it is.

                    Toni
Is she the reason Chris divorced you?

                    Vinnie
        (Lights up a cigarette)
Yes, but the sad thing is that I never told her until they found Jenny's
body. But being the good Christian she is, she could care less about
Jenny's death. Her primary concern was with how much whoring around I
had been doing during our marriage. She didn't believe me when I told
her that Jenny was the first one. In fact, I couldn't even complete
anything with Jenny because of my love for Chris. Anyway all Saintly
Chris was able to do was scream and yell like a crazy woman and beat
me with her fists. She was really understanding... Shit I don't know...
        (Gets up and starts nervously pacing)
You know I almost killed the chairman of my department.

                    Toni
        (Sits on the bed)
You're kidding?!

                    Vinnie
I wish the hell I was. That's the scariest thing of all this shit
that's been happening to me the past year.

                    Toni
God Vin what happened? I can't believe it.

                    Vinnie
I know. I can't believe it either when I think about it. I thought
for a while it was because so many things were happening to me at the
same time: Jenny's death. The divorce. My writing was going nowhere.
But now I know it was none of those things. It's me Tone. It's in me!
And like everything else now I can't damn control it!

                    Toni
Do mom and dad know all about this?

                    Vinnie
Hell no. They know I was fired but they think it was for drinking too much.

                    Toni
It's still so hard to believe. Really Vin.

                    Vinnie
        (Stops pacing)
I know I know.
        (He begins to choke up with emotion)
But damn it Tone I just couldn't stand to sit there at those staff
meetings any more and not say anything. I'm too intense... I just am...
        (He begins to cry a little)
They all thought I was trying to be a mean son of a bitch when I questioned
him time after time. I knew that's what they were saying behind my back...
I'm not Tone. I was just trying...

>（He cries some more)

You see... I can't talk about these things any more... because I always start crying... They wanted me to be Doctor Serrano, Professor of English Literature... A heartless mannequin, like all of them! No emotions allowed. They could care less that someone I loved very much was dead! Just fakery and lies! And more lies! This is what the university is about Tone!

>(He tries hard to gain control of himself as he puffs on his cigarette.)

Toni

I know what you're saying. It's even like that in my job. If it wasn't for New York and Neil, I would quit in a minute. Anyway I'm sorry, go on Vin.

Vinnie

Well I don't know it's crazy. I mean here is this asshole supposedly my good friend, and he calls me in and says because I refuse to fill out this stupid-ass peer review form I was being charged with insubordination. Which meant in so many words I was being fired. And the next thing I remember is feeling his fat flesh against my squeezing hands! I still remember his eyes rolling back into his head as I squeezed as hard as I could! Harder Vinnie! Harder Vinnie! He was going! Going! Har - I don't know. I don't know... God Tone, what's happening to me? What's happening? Remember how I used to always run away from fights when I was little?... I can't believe it. I would've been a murderer if they didn't stop me.

>(Toni gets up)

Oh God I can't think about it... I'm scared. What does this all mean Tone?! Who's taking over my body?! Who?!... Oh God Tone I'm tired... I wanna go to sleep now...

>(He lies down. Toni puts a blanket over him and gently touches his head as the lights fade. Then after a short moment, the lights come up as Mario and Jimmy now enter from stage right. Theresa is sitting at the table, sleeping.)

                    Mario
          (Holding up the keys)
I found them Tree.

                    Theresa
          (Startled, wakes up)
Good.

                    Mario
Look at her she doesn't sleep all night, so she sleeps all day. I
don't know what I'm going to do with her.
          (Smiles affectionately at her)

                    Theresa
I was resting not sleeping.
          (Gets up)
Where were they?

                    Mario
Near the back door.
          (Looks at Jimmy)
Where Mister Francis Ford Coppola dropped them.

                    Jimmy
I did? You mean you did when I handed them to you.

                    Theresa
Get your shoes off, both of you.

          (They obey her command as they place their shoes near the
          bookcase. Theresa heads toward the kitchen. Mario sits
          down. Jimmy goes in the direction of stage left.)

                    Jimmy
Mom do I still have time to get a shower in? I feel all sweaty from
my run.

                    Theresa
Go ahead, but wipe down the walls afterwards and also pick up your hair.
Vinnie left hair all over this morning.

                    Jimmy
Jesus here I am supposedly a big producer in Hollywood and I'm cleaning
shower walls. Thank God Marjorie isn't around, she would laugh her
ass off at me.

                    Theresa
Be quiet, I bet you and that girlfriend of yours live in a pig pen.

                    Jimmy
Right, Marjorie only has two cleaning ladies and a full-time cook. Our
house is dirtier than sin.

                    Theresa
Stop Jimmy, just go and clean up after you finish.

                    Mario
You want me to come and wash your back, Mister Big Shot?

                    Jimmy
          (Laughs a little)
No I think I can handle it.
          (He leaves stage left.)

                    Theresa
          (Comes out of the kitchen with a large salad bowl and a couple
          of bottles. She places these things in front of Mario.)
Here fix the salad for the kids, they always complain I put too much
vinegar in it.

                    Mario
          (Gets up and starts fixing the salad)
Give me some salt.
          (She goes back to the kitchen.)
And bring some wine.
          (She gets the salt from the sink and stove unit top and the
          wine from underneath. Then she comes back out and gives the
          salt and bottle of wine to him.)
What the hell happened to all the wine in this bottle?
          (Looks at the half-emptied bottle)

                    Theresa
I don't know. Maybe someone came over while I was out. Toni and Vinnie
coulda given it to them.

                    Mario
          (Pours some wine in his glass)
What did I spend that three thousand dollars for, huh? So that my son
could come home from the hospital and become a drunk again?

                    Theresa
Stop Mario, you don't know if he drank it. Fix the salad and be quiet.
Don't start now.

                    Mario
          (Continues to fix the salad)
You make me laugh. I never start.

                    Theresa
          (Sits down)
No you never do. How's it taste?

                    Mario
          (Takes out a leaf of lettuce and chews it)
Good. Here taste.
          (Puts a leaf in her mouth)

                    Theresa
          (Chews)
Put a little more salt on.

                    Mario
You heard Jimmy last night. Too much salt is bad for you.

Theresa
I know, but put just a little more.

Mario
(Shakes a little salt in)
Do you have enough food for tonight?

Theresa
I think so. I'm just waiting for the water to boil so I could throw the spaghetti in.

Mario
Where's Toni?

Theresa
She's with Vinnie.

Mario
You know it makes me feel good to see how close they are. Our kids are really good kids Tree.

Theresa
But Mario you got to learn how to talk to them. Think before you talk.

Mario
I do. They understand, don't worry. They know I do everything for their own good.

Theresa
Okay just for now while they're all home, talk nice.

Mario
Don't worry, everything is gonna be okay. You worry too much. Look at how you're falling asleep all the time.

Theresa
Never mind. Listen, I need some money. Patsy's son Mike is getting married next week.

Mario
I'll tell you I wish the hell we never lived around here with all your family around. We give out and give out and we get nothing in return because our kids live away.

Theresa
Listen Mario, Patsy has always been good to me and also to you. His wife sends stuff here all the time.

Mario
(Sits down and pours himself a glass of wine. He drinks some.)
Sometimes I get so disgusted from giving to this one and that one. Everyone always wants something in this world for nothing.

Theresa
I know, but someday you'll get it back.

Mario
I'll never get it back. I'll tell you one thing when I retire I'm not giving anyone a damn thing except my own family.
(Gets up and starts shaking the salad in the bowl)

Theresa
I don't blame you.

Mario
We're going to spend it on us and our kids.
(Takes a leaf of lettuce out of the bowl)
Here taste now.

Theresa
(She takes it and chews on it.)
Good. It's good.
(Gets up and goes to the kitchen)
I better check the water.

Mario
You got some roasted peppers? They all like that.

Theresa
There's some in the cellar, if you want some. Go and get some if you think they'll eat them.
(He wipes his hands on his pants and as he starts to go in the direction of stage right, Toni comes in.)

Mario
Did you get your brother straight in there?

Toni
I wish it was that easy.

Mario
How about the oil in your car? Did you change it last week like I said?

Toni
Yes.

Mario
It's sad how you let that car go. Your mother told me how it looked when she was there. If I had it here, I would keep it like new for you.

Theresa
Go Mario, and get the peppers. I'm ready to throw.
(She picks up the spaghetti from the sink's counter and throws it into a pot.)

                        Mario
            (Looking at Toni)
You want anything else to eat for tonight? How about some canned peaches?
I have some nice ones we canned this year.

                        Toni
No. I'm on a diet.

                        Mario
You and your diets. That's why you have problems with your stomach.

                        Theresa
Mario go, you could finish talking when you come back.

                        Mario
Your mother, she drives me crazy. But still I wouldn't trade her in.
She always worries about me. I think she's scared I'm gonna get sick
some day and—

                        Theresa
            (Comes out of the kitchen and kiddingly acts mad)
Mario, will you go. Go where you had to go now.
            (He laughs, picks up his shoes, puts them on and leaves stage right.

                        Toni
            (Sits down)
Did he find the keys?

                        Theresa
            (Goes back to kitchen and stirs the spaghetti on the stove)
Yes.

                        Toni
Will he ever change Mom? One minute he's going crazy because he lost
his keys, and the next minute he's trying to be sweet as anything. You
just never know how he's going to be. My whole life in this house was
always worrying about him and making sure I didn't upset him. Hell
Mom, how do you stand it?

                        Theresa
            (Comes out of the kitchen)
I've learned over the years not to argue with him when he gets mad because
he always gets over it. We do this every day. One minute we're killing
each other, the next we're throwing roses at each other. That's how it is.
Your father doesn't mean half of what he says when he gets mad. He's just
hot-headed Toni. Look how he brought youse kids to amusement parks,
swimming pools, basketball games. Some fathers couldn't care if their
kids live or die. He even took youse kids to Atlantic City. All over.
Remember?

                        Toni
            (Feeling guilty)
I know but of late every time I come home he seems to bitch about everything.

Theresa
(Sits down)
Try living with him everyday and listen to him bitch about this person, that person...
(Her voice is choked with emotion now)
Anytime I want to go to visit someone or go shopping wit them he bitches about it. They're no good, they're taking advantage of you, he always says. He just wants me to stay home and wait on him. But I won't or I'll end up bitching just like him. I want to live a little. That's why every time I get a chance I run over to Concetta's or over to my brothers. It gets me out. I know he gets mad but I don't care. All he wants to do now is just to stay here every night and watch TV. Then he falls asleep as soon as he sits down...
(Almost in tears)
Youse can't change him Toni.

Toni
But it's so depressing now to come home Mom. I don't look forward to it at all anymore.

Theresa
(Gaining her composure)
I don't know maybe after Vinnie gets better he'll get happier. Toni, sometimes you forget and I forget how tough your father's life has been. Remember he came over to this country when he was twelve with just five dollars in his pocket. I don't know maybe that's why he gets mad at youse kids. I think he thinks youse kids had it too easy.
(Goes to the kitchen)
I gotta see if the spaghetti is done.

Toni
But Mom you gotta start thinking of yourself. You can't live this way, always worrying about what you say so he won't blow up.

Theresa
We all have crosses to bear.

Toni
(Gets angry)
Bullshit! That's a bunch of Catholic church baloney! You don't have to bear crosses for anyone! You should be only responsible for yourself! You understand?! Yourself!

Theresa
That's not true. He's my husband and he's your father and we must live wit what God gives us. There's a lot of good in him. Look things will get better when everything gets settled around here.

Toni
Mom I don't think it's going to be settled for a while. I'm getting married to Neil next week.
(A long pause. Slowly Theresa comes out of the kitchen.)

Theresa
No Toni, no. We got enough trouble wit Vinnie now. Please don't do this now. My God that's all your father needs to hear. It'll destroy him.

Toni
I'm sorry Mom.

Theresa
You're not sorry! Your father's right! He's right! All youse kids just think of is yourselves!
(She runs back into the kitchen.)

Toni
(Runs after her)
Please Mom don't act like this! My God it's not like I want to murder someone Mom! I just want to get married! You people always make everything so awful, even something like marriage when people should be happy! But not in this family for Christ's sake, it's like I've committed the worst sin on earth!

Theresa
(Pleading)
All I'm saying Toni is to wait. Wait until Vinnie gets better. Your father will go crazy if you tell him now. He's got too much pressure on him. He worries about Jimmy putting up all that money for pictures. I don't care how much money his girlfriend has. What if he loses it than your father will have to come up wit the money. He worries about Vinnie and what he's gonna do wit his life now. And he worries about you the most because you're not settled yet.

Toni
Mom I don't want him or anyone to worry about me. I'm a big girl now.

Theresa
Listen to her she's a big girl now! You the Tinker Bell of toilet bowls! You who calls every time you have to take a shit! You who calls when your left toe itches because you think it's some new disease! Oh God I hate this arguing! I want out! Out God, you hear me!
(She sticks her head out the window.)
Out! Out! Out!

Voice
(A man's voice offstage)
Mom I thought you said the mother was the only sane one down there! Listen to her!

Toni
(Pulls Theresa in)
Mom please, I know you'll really like Neil once you get to know him. Really, give it a chance to work Mom. I still can't believe you're doing all of this because I'm getting married.

Theresa
(Getting a hold of herself, bitter now)
I met your Phil remember—

Toni
Neil Mom, Neil.
(They come out of the kitchen, facing each other)

Theresa
Whatever. I remember I didn't like him then and I won't like him now. Whatever happened to that lawyer you were going wit?

Toni
You mean Fagan?

Theresa
Yes, he seemed nice. What was wrong with him?

Toni
Everything. He had ulcers, colitis, high blood pressure, bad migraines. I know it's hard to believe but he was more neurotic than me.

Theresa
How about those others, the doctor and that Exxon salesman?

Toni
All bad. You know for a while I really thought seriously about living without men. I'm serious Mom, they were all such pains in the ass. For a couple moments of pleasure you spend the next several months paying for it. One time I even thought of going into the nunnery. Then I met Neil and things started to fall into place for me.

Theresa
But he's divorced. All he could give you is more troubles.

Toni
Look Mom, before I met Neil some of my dates ranged from guys who read pop-up porn books to others who sleep with pacifiers in their mouths.

Theresa
But what if it doesn't work out wit him? That's what I worry about. What then? He'll leave you like he left his wife.

Toni
Mom I'm sick of what if this or what if that! I don't care about the what ifs anymore! I want to live now and for once not think of the consequences of what I do! Remember you and my catholic education helped me major in guilt and what ifs. I feel good being with Neil and that's what I want Mom! And if it doesn't work out I'll join the Moonies and pray that my virginity returns!

Theresa
Stop talking stupid! I'm just trying to get you to see if you get married to him don't expect to see your father at the wedding or ever be allowed in this house again.

Toni
I don't care anymore. Jesus Mom I remember if dad just raised his eyebrows at me, I would go to pieces because I hated confrontations. But no more Mom. I mean it! I swear to God, I'm going to get through this!
　　　　(Vinnie comes out from stage left and walks over to the table.)
Well I told her. One down, one to go.

152 | VOICES ON THE EDGE

Vinnie
Huh? Oh good, good deal... God I really slept.
(Sits down and combs his hair with his hands. He smiles at Toni.)

Theresa
Do you know what she wants to do?

Vinnie
Listen Mom, there's nothing you could do. It's her life. Let her live it.

Theresa
But look at you, maybe if you had waited you woulda found someone different and not that little Miss Muffet you ended up wit.

Vinnie
I don't know. I doubt it.
(He reaches over for the wine bottle on the table.)
Mom I'm gonna have a little. For medicinal purposes, okay?

Theresa
You've already had enough of that medicine to last you a lifetime.

Vinnie
I just need one.
(He pours a drink and smiles at Toni)

Toni
Just cool it with that stuff Vinnie.

Vinnie
Don't worry Tone. Be calm and relaxed like me.
(He laughs and holds up his glass)
You want some?

Toni
No thank you.

Vinnie
Mom how about you?

Theresa
No. I just don't know what I'm gonna do. Please Toni don't do this to us. Please!
(She starts crying)
He'll make my life miserable. You don't have to live wit him after. Please Toni!

Toni
Mom I'm not giving in. I'm not gonna feel guilty this time. I'm not! I don't care what you say. I'm not!

(Theresa still crying rushes into the kitchen)

                    Vinnie
             (He drinks some wine from his glass)
Shit what a bunch of depressing people. I thought when I came home it
would be your typical fun-loving Italian family. Kisses, pinching
cheeks, bear hugs and all of that. You know what I mean?

                    Theresa
             (From the kitchen and still crying)
Shut up Vinnie!

                    Vinnie
             (Gets up)
Ah my dear sister what can I do for you now before our dear father
comes dancing in? I'm perplexed. Should I become your Friar Lawrence
or Tybalt, my dear sister?

                    Toni
Stop, Vinnie. Please don't drink anymore.

                    Vinnie
Hold, daughter Toni: I do spy a kind of hope,
Which craves as desperate an execution
As that is desperate which we would prevent.
If, rather than to marry Count Neil
Thou hast the strength of will to stay thyself,
Then it is likely thou wilt undertake a thing like death to chide away
This shame,
That cop'st with death himself to scape from it;
And, if thou dar'st, I'll give thee a remedy my dear sister.

                    Toni
I'm taking the damn bottle Vinnie!
             (She goes for the wine bottle but he gets to it first)

                    Vinnie
Sorry my dear sister. The old boy might be nutsy but he still has
some fairly good moves.
             (He sits down, holding onto the bottle)
Why, look at you now, how unworthy a thing you make of me my dear sister!
Call me what instrument you like dear sister, though you can fret me you
cannot play upon me, or upon my father.
             (He laughs to himself)

                    Toni
Vinnie really you've had enough! Give me the damn bottle!

                    Vinnie
When it's finished. Hey look I'm just having a little fun. Fun Tone
you know what that is. You just talked to me about it.
             (Yells in the direction of the kitchen)
Mom you know what fun is?!
             (Spells it out)
F-U-N!

Theresa
Vinnie I don't like you to talk to me like that. Please be nice. We got problems now.

Vinnie
(He holds up his glass)
To problems Tone and good luck, congratulations, whatever.
(He drinks some more as Mario enters from stage right. Quickly Vinnie puts his glass down. Mario has a can in his hand.)

Mario
We have some Tree.
(He sets the can on the table, takes off his shoes and puts them near the bookcase.)
Bring me a can opener.
(Looking at Toni)
You want some nice roast peppers?

Toni
No Dad, I'll have some when I eat.

Mario
Vinnie, you want some? They're good for you.

Vinnie
(Sobering up)
I'll wait too Dad.

(Jimmy enters now from stage left. He's bare-chested and wiping his wet hair with a towel.)

Mario
Jimmy, have a roast pepper? Tree come on, bring me that opener.

Jimmy
(Sits down)
Maybe just-

Theresa
(Comes out of the kitchen)
Forget the damn opener Mario! Your daughter has some wonderful news for you!

Mario
Now what?

Toni
(Forces a nervous laugh)
I'm getting married next week to Neil.

Mario
(Stunned)
You mean that guy who has the kids and is divorced? I thought that was over wit

Toni
No. It wasn't ever over with.

                    Mario
          (Full of anger, he moves toward her)
Last year you said it was all over wit! Saying you're going out with
this fellow and that fellow and all the time you're sneaking around
wit him! I knew that's what was gonna go on in that apartment!
          (He goes for her but Theresa pushes him away)
You whore! Lying whore!

                    Toni
          (Trying hard to control herself)
I don't care what you say Dad. I did want your approval but if I
can't get it, I'm sorry. I'm still getting married.

                    Theresa
Mario, maybe things will work out. Let her be.

                    Mario
Work out my ass! Nothing ever works out! Well lady you could forget
ever coming into this house again! You can get out now if you want to!
Get out! Get the hell out of this house you whore!

                    Toni
          (Crying now)
I will I will. Don't worry I will.

                    Mario
I told you before if you ever married him I didn't want to see you! Go!
Get out of here! Go to your divorced friend! He's probably a liar just
like you!

                    Theresa
Mario stop, this is only making it worse.

                    Toni
My head feels like it's gonna explode! Please help me God! Thanks
Jimmy and Vinnie for all your fucking support!
          (She runs off stage right, crying and screaming)

                    Mario
          (Sits down)
Bitch! After all I did for her, this is how she repays me!

                    Vinnie
          (Forgetting himself, he pours himself another drink. The bottle
          is empty now.)
Dad she'll be okay. Don't worry.
          (He drinks some.)
                    Mario
Yeah, sure, just like you. Look where youse kids end up when you get
sick or need money. Always here! In three months you watch she'll be
calling home because he took off wit all their money, and she'll be left
with his kids and won't know what to do. Your mother and me are the ones
who end up suffering not youse kids.
          (He shakes his head)
You watch. And why the hell are you drinking?!

                          Vinnie
I just needed a little to relax. I was tense.

                          Mario
Hell I don't know what from. You haven't done anything in three months
except lay in bed. All of youse kids just need a good kick in the ass.

                          Vinnie
So she's marrying a guy who has been married before. What's the big deal
Dad? The guy will probably treat her great because he failed the first
time around.

                          Mario
Shut up! You don't know what you're talking about. Look at your brother,
did he learn after two times? Huh? And you. You know how embarrassing
it is for your mother and me to say to people oh our son Jimmy has been
married two times, or our son Vinnie also just got divorced and yes people
now our daughter is marrying someone who's divorced and has two kids. Aren't
we lucky parents people, to have such wonderful children? And yes people one
of our sons thinks he's a blender. And the other is into mushroom soup. And
listen we're really proud because we have a daughter who shits twelve times a
day and knows every restroom in New York City. The motto of the Serrano
family is a nut a day keeps the doctor away!

                          Jimmy
Dad listen, what Vinnie says is true really, sometimes it takes people
like me a little longer to understand what marriage is about.

                          Mario
I don't want to hear anymore! It's finished! No more talking about it!
          (He takes the bottle of wine. Angrily he looks at Vinnie.)
Jesus have you drank all of this?

                          Vinnie
There wasn't much there.

                          Mario
          (He holds up the empty bottle.)
Tree get me another bottle before your son the <u>drunk</u> gets to it.

                          Theresa
Mario stop, he's just had a little.
          (She goes to the kitchen and from underneath the sink brings
          back to him a full bottle of wine.)

                          Mario
A little hell, he drank all of this. You know that!
          (He holds up the empty bottle)
You're a liar just like him! This whole family is full of liars!

                          Vinnie
          (He holds up his glass)
To lies and illusions Pop!
          (He drinks some more from his glass.)

                    Mario
Shut up or I'll take out the razor strap! You're never too old for that!
          (Goes to slap him but Theresa stops him)
                    Theresa
Mario sit there, and drink your wine, and be quiet! I've had it with your
mouth today!
                    Jimmy
I still say Vinnie if you get yourself on some B12 and Vitamin E most of
your problems would be licked. Mom get me some of that carrot juice and
bring that bottle of vitamins over here.
          (Theresa goes to the kitchen)
                    Vinnie
          (He finishes his glass)
Actually, I would prefer something in dark blue.
          (He lights up a ciagrette)
                    Jimmy
          (Theresa comes back, places a glass of carrot juice in front of
          Jimmy and hands him the bottle of vitamins. She sits down.)
Listen Vinnie these are made from organically-grown vegetables and fruits.
Your whole problem is that your body equilibrium is off. And when that's
off everything starts breaking down. I'm serious. If the poisons in your
body are not balanced or expelled then your thinking, your nervous system,
your bowels, everything is affected. Look I bet you even have bad breath.
                    Vinnie
Just what I needed. A Listerine commercial.
                    Jimmy
Listen to me Vinnie, really the reason you have bad breath is because you're
not getting enough of the grain millet in your body. I know, I used to have
bad breath but I don't anymore ever since I started eating millet.
                    Vinnie
I don't have fucking bad breath! I have a hand that shakes like hell and
I am seriously considering being a participant in Germany's Saint Vitus
Dance festival. But no bad breath. You understand?!

                    Jimmy
Well that's what I'm trying to say Vinnie. I'm trying to give some good
advice here so you won't have a shaking hand and be so damn screwed up.
Do you know all that sugar from the alcohol you drink, even from the cigarettes you smoke is depleting your mineral reserves and you need them to
keep a balance in your body? Really get some barley and whole grain Vinnie.
Mom could learn how to cook them and you'll see the difference.
          (Looks over to where Theresa is sitting. She's almost asleep.)
Mom, really you can cook those things. Use that health food cookbook I
gave you last year. You'll see after a while you'll start feeling better
too. Damn it! For Christ's sake, Mom go get some sleep!

Theresa
(Startled)
I'm listening to everything. I'm just resting.

Mario
(Impressed)
You know Tree, this kid of ours knows a lot. You listen to your brother Vinnie. You know sometimes we make fun of him but listen how well he talks. Just like a doctor.

Vinnie
(Confused)
I don't know. Maybe you're right Jimmy. Hell I know nothing about the body. I should but I don't. But give me a poem, a novel or whatever and I'll intellectualize it to death.
(He takes a couple puffs on his cigarette.)

Jimmy
I'll tell you what your other problem is brother. You gotta get the hell out of that shithole West Virginia. You're dying there man. Come with me to Hollywood where people will appreciate your talents. Shit that last book you wrote was so full of surreal stuff that no one will ever understand it. I showed it to a producer friend of mine, Ray Calacucci. He's got two series on TV. He said you have a lot of talent but he said you have to think of being commercial in your writing Vinnie. Really, forget all that artsy crap. Commercial man, that's where it's at.

Vinnie
But most of the movies or books today only deal with simple truths. There's nothing around that forces people to face difficult truths. The real questions of life. You know what I mean?

Jimmy
That's bullshit! People want to escape when they read books or go to the movies. So life sucks man! We all know that! But why should people be told that over and over again?!

Vinnie
I don't know. Shit maybe because I love dark holes.

Jimmy
Yeah sure. Listen I'm curious, tell me what you do in that big university of yours?

Vinnie
I teach a couple of classes in literature and one in composition.

Jimmy
And what are you working on now? Is it a novel?

Vinnie
Yes, but I don't think, Jimmy, you would understand it. In fact I don't even know if I fully understand it. I haven't looked at it in a long time

Jimmy
(Angry)
Look, I might not have a Ph.D. in English literature but I do have one in life. So try me, man.

Vinnie
Well I have this major character who responds but in a sense doesn't really respond to the life around him. There's other characters in the novel but for the most part they're all insignificant to him. What's important to this character is his thoughts about another civilization, a civilization that is separate from this civilization which he sees as one big exercise in fakery. He thinks you could reach this other civilization when you start getting closer to understanding the esoteric principles you could find in mathematics, philosophy, literature, science and in art. He believes this is the real center of humanity and that only through rigorous study can you get close to these esoteric principles. You see, he believes that prophets like Jesus Christ really wanted to help people understand that we're self-evolving beings and that our salvation is not to be found in worshipping prophets or gods but to be found in ourselves, in our inner circles which will connect us to higher forms of consciousness.

Jimmy
Have you ever read Gurdjieff?

Vinnie
No. I don't think so.

Jimmy
(Condescendingly)
Well you should because he said the same things. I can't believe you never read Gurdjieff.

Vinnie
I don't know, I just never heard of him.

Jimmy
He got a lot of his ideas from the priests and monks in the far east.

Vinnie
I read Ouspensky and he studied them too. In fact, I got a lot of my ideas from his books.

Jimmy
Hell man, where do you think Ouspensky got his ideas?

Vinnie
Where?

Jimmy
From Gurdjieff.

Vinnie
I didn't know that.

Jimmy
You know anything about Sufi?

Vinnie
Not really.

Jimmy
Well that's where Gurdjieff got most of his thoughts. Sufists have some interesting ideas how one should change his soul in accordance with the changes taking place around him. For the Sufists the soul and the future life are the one and the same. You really should read Gurdjieff. Hey Dad, ever hear about Gurdjieff?

Mario
No, but you're a smart kid Jimmy.

Jimmy
What do you think about your son with all those degrees not knowing about Gurdjieff?

Mario
I don't know maybe I wasted all that money on his education.

Vinnie
(Angrily, he jumps up.)
You son of a bitch Jimmy, I don't believe you're doing this! Do you need his love so bad?!

Jimmy
Whataya talking about?

Vinnie
Never mind, you know exactly what I'm talking about!

Jimmy
Really what the hell are you talking about?! I was just kidding you about that Gurdjieff stuff if that's why you're mad. I read books too you know.

Vinnie
You know bastards like you are all tricky! Always trying to manipulate people so that you come out looking good! Always wanting to win! Screw the other guy! Fuck him over! That's why I want to get people beyond this world so that they don't have to deal with assholes like you!

Jimmy
(Now he angrily jumps up)
Hey what the fuck is your problem?! I was just trying to have a nice intellectual discussion with you and you go bullshit. Shit you know what your whole problem is boy is that you have no guts! No guts man to face this world! Always hiding away in books so you don't have to face the fucking realities of this world! Chickenshit is what you're about brother!

                    Vinnie
          (Wildly, Vinnie goes after Jimmy. He gets Jimmy on the
          floor and begins to fiercely punch him.)
Talking! Talking! Talking!... And never saying anything!...
          (Chokes him now.)

                    Theresa
          (Gets up)
Mario stop them! Please! They'll hurt themselves! Jimmy stop!
Vinnie, please! Mario—

          (Toni enters from stage right and rushes over to the fight.)

                    Toni
Oh shit no Vinnie!
          (She jumps on Vinnie's back and tries to pull him off Jimmy,
          but Vinnie still continues to punch Jimmy unmercifully.)

                    Mario
          (Gets up)
Toni let them be! I waited for years to see him stand up and fight back.
My son is no sissy nomore! I'm proud of him, both of them.
          (He tries to get Toni off but she won't budge.)
Come on Toni, they'll be okay. Come on.

                    Jimmy
          (Finally pushes him off)
You crazy looney! You're lucky I didn't use the karate I know or I
would've killed you! They should have locked you up for good! Jesus
what a wacko you are!

          (Vinnie and Jimmy's clothes are torn and their faces are
          spattered with blood.)

                    Vinnie
          (Almost in tears)
Oh God Jimmy, I'm sorry...
          (He tries to help Jimmy up, but Jimmy refuses his help.)
I'm sorry...

                    Mario
          (Anger kicks off)
What the hell are you apologizing for?! Your brother teased and teased
you, and you did what any man would do. You knocked the shit out of him!

                    Vinnie
          (Shaking and looking at Mario)
Oh God help me, help me! What the hell are you trying to do to me?!
Don't you understand I've already done this before and I hate it?! I
hate it!

                    Mario
Where?

                    Vinnie
          (Holding back tears)
At the university. I almost killed my chairman.

Theresa

Oh Mother of God, help us!

Mario

So what Tree, it's good for him to get it out! He's been keeping it in too long. You can't be weak all your life. You got to be strong to face this world!

Theresa
(Sits down, crying)

Mario, no more.

Vinnie
(Pulling himself together now)

I don't care if I'm weak! But why don't you admit it and get it over with?! You hate me! Admit it! You give me that shit all the time about you doing all these things for me because you love me! Bullshit! Hell you don't know how to love! The only thing you know how to do is to destroy people by making them feel guilty for damn living!

(Jimmy gets up from the floor and with noticeable pain sits down.)

Theresa

Vinnie how could you say that? He doesn't hate you. Look at all he did for you. He does love you.

Vinnie

Bullshit, he hates me! I know he does! I know he does!

Theresa

Vinn—

Mario

Shut up Tree! Here I work my ass off all my life for youse kids! Here your mother and me buy our clothes at Goodwill so youse kids will have the best! The best education! The best clothes! And you say I'm destroying you! Youse kids don't appreciate nothing! Nothing!
(He goes after Vinnie and slaps his face hard. Vinnie stumbles backwards.)
I wish to hell you never came back from that hospital! I spent three thousand dollars and what for?! So my kid could come home and tell me I'm no good! I'll show you you stupid bastard who's destroying who!
(He gets ready to strike Vinnie again but Vinnie ducks and pulls Toni with him. Mario in frustration turns and sits down.)

Vinnie

Come on Tone, we're getting the hell out of here! Come on!
(Goes off stage left as Theresa sits down.)

Toni
(Starts to follow)

I never unpacked. I knew we would end up this way. Why is it every time I come home we end up fighting? Can't we ever be happy?! Just once?!

Mario

Is it my fault?

Toni
Damn it Dad, it's nobody's fault. It's just everything would be much happier in this house if you would just accept us for what we are and let us live our lives the way we want to. Stop trying to control us Dad! You hear me?! That's all!

Mario
I don't care any more. I wanted you kids to make people turn their heads when you passed them on the street. I wanted them to know you were a Serrano. But no more.

Toni
But we can't be anything more than we are. Vinnie is what Vinnie is. Jimmy is what Jimmy is. I'm what I am. And that's it. There's nothing you could do to change that!

Mario
   (As if he's having a conversation with himself, he shakes his
   head in disgust.)
Here I thought he would come home and we would sit around and talk and have a good time with each other.
   (Vinnie comes out carrying his luggage)
But no, all he does is lay around feeling sorry for himself and telling people what's wrong with them.

Vinnie
Come on, let's go Tone.

Mario
   (Sadly)
You can have him Tree. I don't want him anymore. I'm done wit him. Wit her. I'm done.

Toni
I give up Dad.
   (Goes off stage left)

Vinnie
Hurry up Tone!
   (He looks at his father, pauses, sits down and now speaks with
   compassion.)
I might feel sorry for myself Dad, but I also now feel sorry for you. You're carrying a <u>huge</u> <u>anger</u> in your heart, just like me, and there's nothing we can do about it. We're victims of our background. I understand that now.
   (Reaches out and touches his father's arm)
And that's what we're about Dad, nothing more and nothing-

Mario
   (Angrily he pushes his arm away and gets up)
You bastard! Get out of here! Get out of here!
   (Nervously Theresa gets up and tries coming in between them but
   he pushes her out of the way. Forcefully he knocks Vinnie over
   in the chair.)

Theresa
(Crying)
Please Mario, stop! Please! Enough is enough!

(Mario sits down as Toni now comes out with her luggage. Confident and relaxed now Vinnie stands up.)

Jimmy
(Gets up, pleading)
Listen, Vinnie, Toni, this family is all we got! We need it. Don't do this to mom and dad!

Vinnie
He goes over and kisses Theresa on the cheek.)
I'm sorry Mom. Take care.

(Toni also gives her a kiss on the cheek.)

Theresa
I still don't see why youse can't have anything to eat. Why do youse have to go now?

Vinnie
I can't stay here Mom, Really, take care Mom.
(He then goes over to Jimmy.)
I'm sorry...
(He hugs him.)
Take care of them.

Toni
(With detachment she kisses Jimmy on the cheek.)
I hope you're happy now.

Jimmy
I didn't start it. He did. Blame your precious Vinnie, not me.

Theresa
Vinnie what should I do with all the sauce I made?

Vinnie
I don't know freeze it I guess. I'll see you.

(Vinnie and Toni pick up their luggage and go off stage right) Theresa moves in the direction they went out.)

Theresa
(Yells to them)
Call Toni and ask for yourself when you get there! I'll be worried!

(The lights come down. Then after a long moment, the lights come up. Empty plates are still in front of places where Toni and Vinnie were to sit.)

Theresa
(To Jimmy)
Do you want some more?

                    Jimmy
No this is fine Mom. I've already had too much.

                    Theresa
          (Goes over to Mario)
How about you Mario, you want some more? I got a lot.

                    Mario
No this is enough.
          (She goes into the kitchen. He looks at Jimmy.)
You want some of this wine?
          (He holds up the bottle as he pours himself a glass.)
This is good stuff.
          (Theresa comes back, sits down and starts chewing on her spaghetti.)

                    Jimmy
No Dad, I got my carrot juice.
          (He holds up his glass of carrot juice.)

                    Mario
          (Now almost begging)
Come on, just a little. It will put hair on your chest.
          (He forces a laugh.)

                    Jimmy
Okay just a little.

                    Mario
          (He pours him a glass and hands it to him.)
You know I'll never forget what my father said to me just before he
died. Tolino che salta all albero del me lo e grida che e uno mela.
Quello e lo sbaglio. You know what that means?

                    Jimmy
No.

                    Mario
None of my kids speak Italian. I'll tell you son you'll be sorry some
day. Look at how well Concetta's kids speak it. You'll see everything
I say comes out true. It means that we Italians are strong like olives,
but the olive that jumps to the apple tree and shouts it's an apple
makes a terrible mistake. You see my father meant that Italians in
this country who want to become Americans get soft and rot like apples,
but not so with olives. Like a good Italian, they become firmer and
more beautiful with age.
          (Choking with emotion)
You know Tree the worst thing I did was to educate my children. Look
around, they all should be sitting here with me. We should be talking,
having fun, enjoying ourselves. But I have no one except for you and
Jimmy. I lost the other two Tree. I lost them...
          (He cries a little as he drinks from his glass.)

Theresa
Don't say that, you didn't lose them. You just don't know how to talk to them witout getting mad and blowing up like some crazy man.

Mario
I don't know. I'm tired Tree. I don't care anymore. Maybe we could go live wit Jimmy in California.

Jimmy
(Suddenly surprised)
Sure, that's okay.

Mario
I don't want to live in the same house wit you. I just want some little place like a trailer or a small bungalow.

Jimmy
There's a couple nice trailer places right near us. They're almost like homes with small little yards and all. They're really nice. But listen Dad why don't you just come and stay a few months just to see if you like it there. I would hate to see you sell everything here and then after a couple months decide you hate it there.

Mario
See even you don't want us.

Jimmy
No that's not it. It's just that California is really different Dad. I mean they're just some real weird people that's all I'm saying. And I was just thinking some of my good friends that come over to our house a lot are like that. So you would have to get used to guys who wear nail polish and sometimes even dresses. You got to understand Dad that a lot of creative people don't care what other people think. It's just how they are out there Dad.

Mario
So these people are your friends? People who wear nail polish and dresses.

Jimmy
Yes, some of them are.

Mario
(Shakes his head in disgust)
Jesus I don't know what's wrong with you kids. I thought that once you played a homo it was really just for money but I don't know. I'm starting to wonder about you and that Marjorie girl now.

Theresa
Mario stop, he can't help it if he works wit them. Be thankful at least he's working now. Anyway I don't want to live in California. We'll come and visit Jimmy but not stay.

Jimmy
Listen really I want you to stay. I just want you and Dad to see if you like it there before you sell everything here. That's all I was saying Dad.

                    Mario
          (Depressed)
I don't know anymore. We'll have to see. A lot of things could happen between now and then.
          (Theresa gets up and starts picking up the empty plates.)
Let him help Tree. I'm tired of you always having to wait on these damn kids!...
          (Jimmy gets up and starts to help. The lights start to fade.)
All we've done for these kids and they can't even pick up a dish for the mother. We did too much for these kids Tree.

                    Theresa
          (Goes to kitchen)
Mario, let him finish eating.

                    Jimmy
It's okay Mom, I'm finished.

                    Theresa
Maybe later Mario we could all take a ride to Cohasset to see that house we almost bought.

                    Mario
          (Hands Jimmy his plate)
We'll see. And get some of the crumbs that fell on the floor over here! There.
          (He points to a spot near where he's sitting. Jimmy comes
          over, gets on his knees.)
Good. And over here!
          (He points to another spot.)
Good.

          (The lights fade out as a spotlight now comes up on a small bed at
          stage center. Toni rushes in from stage right, crying
          uncontrollably. She throws herself on the bed. Vinnie also
          enters from stage right. He is clean-shaven and is wearing
          a dark blue turtleneck and khaki pants. He goes to Toni and
          sits next to her on the bed.)

                    Vinnie
          (Rubs her back)
It's over. He left.

                    Toni
          (Turns over, still half crying)
What did he say?

                    Vinnie
Nothing much, except he hopes you'll understand.

                    Toni
Understand hell! How do you understand catching your husband of three weeks in bed with a string bean? And Jesus, he wasn't even discreet enough to go to a sleazy motel in Newark. God I hate him!

Vinnie
Your swinging Neil just told me that he needs lots of women but he hates himself for it. He said he just can't help it.
(Gently touches her shoulder)
I guess according to jumping Neil that's what broke up his other marriage. Really forget him Tone, he's such an ass.

Toni
I can't believe it. I just can't. Jesus you were here. Didn't you hear them in there?

Vinnie
No I really didn't. Oh I was having a good day at writing and when that happens Tone I hear nothing outside of what's happening in my brain.

Toni
You weren't drinking, were you Vinnie?

Vinnie
No I told you I don't touch it until night.

Toni
Jesus why do these things happen to me?
(Looks up)
Why God?! Why?!

Vinnie
Look Tone it's probably best, guys like him can't change. Really think about it. What do you do? Give guys like him a pill or send him to jail because he can't be monogamous?

Toni
Shit I don't know. Of course mom and dad are going to love to hear this. Just once I would like something to go right in my life.

Vinnie
(Gently touches her arm again)
It will. Now just relax. Do you want a couple of valiums to help settle you down?

Toni
I've already taken three at the office. They didn't help. For days I've been too wound up. I knew something was wrong. People in the office were calling me raccoon-eyes because I haven't been sleeping. So here I was hoping to come home, have some nice wine and have a nice relaxing evening with my husband. That dirty bastard! Jesus, he stands there naked with that damn shitty grin on his face and says, "Sorry Tone, I don't know what to say." Damn! After three weeks of marriage I find out I'm married to a closet male nympho. I hope to hell when he and his acne-faced girlfriend kiss again they choke to death on their tongues...
(Almost crying)
Really Vinnie, what the hell am I going to do? Did he say anything about the kids?

Vinnie
No.

Toni
You know now what mom and dad are gonna say, "See, we told you so." Please Vinnie, tell me what to do.
 (She sits up and embraces Vinnie)
I need you Vinnie. You won't leave me, will you?

Vinnie
No. I'll take care of you. Don't worry, everything is going to be okay.

Toni
You know Vinnie, sometimes I wish I was back when I was making my first communion. Then everything felt right with the world.

Vinnie
But the world isn't right Tone.

Toni
I don't know any more.
 (Embraces him again)
Vinnie you sometimes seem so far away from me and I can't get close to you. It's like you see the world as a joke and you're just going about putting your time in while your mind has already escaped here.

Vinnie
I don't know Tone maybe you're right. Maybe I've already started to part this world. I don't know. Sometimes when I'm writing or working through a difficult thought I feel like I'm entering a higher consciousness where I feel things I never felt before and think thoughts that I think nobody else has had. That's what I'm trying to describe in my book. But maybe I can't. I don't know.

Toni
Vinnie you don't want me around. Here you are philosophizing about higher consciousnesses and new thoughts, and here I am worrying about what I'm going to do with two spoiled brats. And on top of that I'm worried about my stools because they were yellow this morning. The distance might be too large for us Vinnie.

Vinnie
You're wrong. I still need to feel useful in this world Tone and you help me to do that. And another thing is that I love you even though your stools are yellow.
 (Both laugh as they embrace)

Toni
Vinnie you don't think I have cancer of the colon, do you?

Vinnie
 (Laughs)
No you don't have cancer of the colon. Now lie down and I'll rub your back.
 (She obeys as he starts to rub)
We'll do okay. Don't worry, the King and Queen of neurosis will do okay. While one is parting, the other will be working on colons.
 (Both laugh.)

Toni
Vinnie.

Vinnie
What?

Toni
Should I call them later to see how they're doing?

Vinnie
Go ahead.

Toni
We still love old Mario, don't we Vin?

Vinnie
Yes. There's nothing we could do about it. We're all crazy. Now be quiet.
(Rubs her back)
How's that feel?

Toni
Wonderful. I could stay like this forever.

Vinnie
Oh no, ten minutes is all. Then it's my turn.
(Both laugh as the spotlight slowly fades out while the "Tarantella" plays in the background.)

THE END

THE GENE NETTI SHOW

A PLAY

The Gene Netti Show is a moving and forceful play about Dave, a Vietnam vet who decides to kill his stepfather, Gene. For years, Dave has been in and out of hospitals trying to cope with living the rest of his life without legs. He blames Gene for encouraging him to fight in Vietnam. Gene is a forty-eight-year-old disc jockey who was "King of the Rock 'n' Roll DJs" during the fifties and sixties, but in the mid-seventies finds himself on the way down in a small resort town in South Carolina. Some parts of the story are based on the Hall of Famer Dick Biondi who, through his mid-eighties, DJ'd on Chicago's WLS-FM. The play uses music from the sixties and seventies as background.

The Gene Netti Show was presented at the Monongalia Arts Center in Morgantown, West Virginia, on March 31 and April 1, 5, 6, 7, and 19, 1984.

Cast

Gene Netti	A disc jockey who is forty-eight years old
Dave	Gene's stepson, he's in his mid-twenties and has no legs
Pat	A policeman in his early fifties and friend of Gene's
Burt	A black gas station owner in his early fifties and also a friend of Gene's
Alice	A seventeen-year-old girl who works as Gene's secretary
Telephone Voice	Gene's wife

Note: All the characters except for Gene have a southern accent. Gene's accent sounds like a New York accent which has been mid-westernized.

At times in the script, the normal English formulations are changed in order to guide the actors in interpreting the voice of the characters.

THE SCENE

WNAB's radio studio

TIME

Latter part of September, early morning, 1975

Act I

(The lights come up on a set representing a small radio studio, WNAB, North Atlantic Beach, South Carolina. At stage right, there is an entrance door and a small reception area. It's separated from the studio by a counter which has a coffee urn on it along with a phone, paper, and magazines. One stool is near the studio side of the counter. There are also three chairs scattered around the reception area. Upstage and on the studio side, there is a door with the sign "Employees Only." Against a stage left wall is a large desk-controll unit. Gene Netti, who is wearing a checkered red and white shirt and matching pants, is sitting on a small swivel chair in front of the desk. The desk is cluttered with styrofoam cups, papers, records, a typewriter, and a built-in dial phone which is used by speaking into a microphone extending out from the control panel. There is also a series of extension buttons on the control panel which flash when a caller is on. Above the desk-control panel is a large clock which reads four-thirty. Pat is drinking coffee while leaning against the counter on the studio side. He is dressed in a wrinkled white shirt with a loosely knotted black tie. His police officer's cap is lying on the counter.)

                Pat
(Sipping from his cup)
So you're leaving us poor peasants again.

                Gene
(Turning some knobs and placing a record on the turntable)
Right.

                Pat
Aren't you gonna miss us?

                Gene
(Cynically)
Terribly.

                Pat
How long will you be gone this time?

                Gene
Forever.

                Pat
Come on.

                Gene
Really I don't know. A week, two weeks, a year. We'll just have to see how things go.

Pat
You know it must be nice to take off anytime you want to. Hell it seems just last month you were off for two weeks.

Gene
(Smiles)
That's how it is when you're a star and dying.

Pat
Jesus Christ do you have to say it like that?

Gene
How do you want me to say it?

Pat
I don't know, but you don't have to be so, so I guess honest about it.

Gene
Why not? Bullshit will not rain on my dying parade. Truth is my way. You know what I mean?

Pat
Bullshit.

Gene
You got it, my friend.

Pat
(Shakes his head)
You're too much.

Gene
I'm also thinking about having my dying as a topic for one of my shows.

Pat
Shit, you crazy. You want some more coffee?
(Looking at the clock)
You still got twenty minutes before you go on.

Gene
(Handing Pat his empty cup)
Put more cream in it. I don't want to be pissing every five minutes.

Pat
(Pours coffee and then cream in Gene's cup)
Something has to clean out all that bad guinea blood in you.

Gene
(Smiles)
Yeah, especially if it's been contaminated by cancer and Pluto the clown cop.

Pat
(Shakes his head and laughs)
You damn little guinea wop, really how are you feeling?

Gene
(Serious)
I'm doing okay. It isn't spreading anymore. Or I don't think it is. In fact, that's why I have to go to Richmond tomorrow to see how it's doing.
(Looks at clock)
Look Captain Midnight, I don't have time to fuck around with you. I gotta get to work.
(Nervously he stacks some papers and records in front of him.)

Pat
You know one of these mornings you son of a bitch I'm gonna let you come over to the studio by yourself. And if someone sticks a gun up your ass, don't call us, we'll call you. Tell me how many DJ's in South Carolina have their own private chauffeur?

Gene
(Looks at clock. Puts the earphones on and adjusts the microphone)
I told you I can't screw around with you all morning, anything happen of interest last night for the local news?

Pat
Nothing really, a fender bender on Pacific Avenue and a couple drunks who got carried away at the Holiday House. But that's about it. You know how it is at this time of the year.

Gene
Boring and Boring.

Pat
I like it that way.

Gene
Not me.

Pat
Why?

Gene
Because I like a charged environment, especially now.

Pat
Well come around with me some night and I'll get you a charged environment.

Gene
How?

                        Pat
I'll introduce you to Rosie over there at the Ramada.

                        Gene
That's not what I'm talking about. I'm tired of routine. I mean
cancer is not the only thing I'm fighting.

                        Pat
I know. I sometimes wish I could say the hell with it and get the
hell out of this hole. You want some more coffee?

                        Gene
    (Looking over the papers in front of him)
You know I played golf with Burt yesterday, and that son of a bee
won a hundred from me.

                        Pat
You gotta watch out for those middle class nig—I mean blacks. Sorry
I almost forgot how you don't like the word nigger.

                        Gene
Be quiet. That son of a bitch has a knack of knowing what people
want. You watch in five more years Burt will own half of North
Atlantic Beach.

                        Pat
I always said give a nigger a slice of watermelon, and before you
know it he'll want the whole thing.

                        Gene
No different than you or me. And come on with that shit about
niggers.

                        Pat
    (Laughs)
Okay, but I wouldn't want the whole thing, maybe just ninety-nine
point nine percent of it. Oh shit, I almost forgot to tell you. It
concerns you.

                        Gene
What? Hurry I got to get on.

                    Pat
Well I met this kid in a wheelchair last night on the beach. I remember
I was gonna to tell you earlier when I picked you up this morning, but
I forgot. Anyway he said he used to listen to you in Chicago.

                    Gene
     (Pretending disinterest)
That's nice.

                    Pat
He told me he was a Viet Nam vet. And he sort of looked stoned. So
I thought I better check him for drugs but then I said the hell with
it, those poor son of a bitches have been dumped on enough. I also
figured if I didn't get assigned to the MP's in the states during the
Korean War, I could've ended up just like him. Gene, I think he
didn't have any legs. I'm not sure because it was dark. But it
seemed empty there. Anyway he said he might be over to see you
today. I told him how you were leaving tomorrow.

                    Gene
Wonderful Pat, what do you think it is—a Jerry Lewis Telethon? I
got enough problems.

                    Pat
Hell the kid Gene is probably on drugs, so he won't come over. Those
types are always half in and half out.

                    Gene
Like us, right?
     (Looks at clock)
Hey really, it's time to go to work. Stick around, I just got to
introduce the national news feed.

                    Pat
     (Finishes his coffee)
I can't. I gotta couple reports to make out. Maybe I'll stop over
before I go home.

                    Gene
Okay, just don't go catching any muggers and spoiling your image.
You know, while the North Atlantic Beach Police sleep muggers and
rapers feast.

                    Pat
Okay guinea wop, but you just make sure you don't slide out of that
chair. If you know what I mean.
     (Laughs)

                                    Gene
          (Turns around and throws an empty styrofoam cup at him as Pat
          leaves. He then turns back, faces the microphone, puts on the
          earphones, looks at the clock and begins talking as the
          clock reads five o'clock. The actor playing Gene should deliver
          the DJ lines warmly, fast-paced, and at times wildly.)
Good morning, this is Gene Netti on WNAB, Twelve Fifty, FM. It's
five o'clock this Thursday morning. The North Atlantic Beach forecast
for today looks like it's going to be sunny and mild. The temperature
will range from highs in the mid-seventies to lows in the mid-fifties.
I hope you'll enjoy today with me where we'll have some music for you,
national and local news, and of course talk. I'm still curious about
what we're going to do with those two hundred condos going up and our
infamous city council unwilling to debate it. True democracy, huh?
Anyway, God, I feel great today even at five in the morning. You
know last night I went out to eat at Henry's, and believe me people,
Henry Sobel, if possible, has food at his restaurant that is better
than ever before. I had lobster that was really out of this world.
I mean people the taste of that wonderful meal is still with me.
I'll tell you for reasonable prices and exquisite and unforgettable
meals, Henry's Twenty-Twenty Shore Drive is the place to go. Really,
there is no finer restaurant in the North Atlantic Beach area. Try it.
Remember, Henry's at Twenty-Twenty Shore Drive. God, I'm getting
hungry all over again.

          (Places a record on the turntable and a rock and roll chorus
          sings: "Twelve fifty FM WNAB, WNAB. Twelve fifty is the
          place to beeee. With Gene Netti on WNAB. News and weather.
          The place to be on WNAB, WNAB. Gene Netti, WNAB, WWW, NNN,
          AAA, BBB." Lights fade out for a moment and then come up with
          the clock reading seven ten. Burt, a black man, is drinking
          coffee on the studio side of the room while Gene is talking
          into the mcirophone.)
Listen, if any of you out there think you could beat this goodlooking
Italian, get yourself over to Merlin's Water Slide today. Old Merlin
is really cutting prices. Merlin says that if anyone beats me on the
banana slide, they'll win a month of free rides next season. So as
they say, "Come on down, come on down." For those brave ones that
will challenge me they're in for the worst water slide beating of
their lives. Really people, I'm good. You won't believe how good
this skinny Italian is! I mean really people, they're even thinking
of taking me around the county like they did with boxers in the olden
days, and challenge all comers at any water slide.. Come see me
slip and slide to greatness! Don't miss it because one day you can
tell your kids I saw Gene Netti right here in North Atlantic Beach
slide at Merlin's on his you know what to the thrill of victory
and to the anguis of others defeats! Not good English but what the
heck, great water sliders don't need anything but their you know what
and a great water slide like at Merlin's on Nineteen-Nineteen
Pacific Avenue!

(Places a record on the turntable, takes off the earphones, gets up and looks at Burt)
Did you get that resonator for my car?

Burt
Not yet, maybe later this morning it'll come in.

Gene
I don't know Burt, didn't you order it three weeks agp? Shit I need it I'm leaving tomorrow, you know.

Burt
I know, but how much more Gene do you think you can get out of a 15-year-old Mercedes?

Gene
Not very long, for you see the owner doesn't have much time either. Or haven't you noticed of late that the owner's skin is turning into what painters call deathly pale.

Burt
Listen, you got a lot of time left. When I looked in the paper this morning I didn't see your name in the obituary column.

Gene
Yes that's true, but yesterday did you notice in the obituaries that there were two heart attacks and that four died after a long serious illness which usually means cancer. So Burt, if I was you I wouldn't place any money on me to win. To be shown yes, but to win, no.

Burt
Well I don't know about that. You're looking pretty good to me today.

Gene
On the outside, but on the inside there is someone who keeps opening up flood gates one and nine, unleashing a wild river of black curd, specked with red, and sometimes wiping out my lunch, dinner and what feels like a small town in Boone County, West Virginia.

Burt
Really, are you not feeling good today?

Gene
No, in fact I'm feeling pretty good today. I feel a little tired but that's about it.

Burt
Good. Say who's that skinny looking kid in the wheelchair out front?

                        Gene
How the hell should I know? What's he doing?

                        Burt
He's got a transistor and he's listening to you. I told him to come
in and meet you.

                        Gene
     (Sitting down and turning some knobs)
What did he say?

                    Burt
He said maybe later.

                    Gene
I can't wait. Hey el cheapo, did you put any money in for coffee?
    (Puts on his earphones)

                    Burt
    (Drops a coin in a cup on the counter which has written on it,
    "Free Coffee")
I'm sorry Boss.

                    Gene
Well I just wanted you to understand that I didn't come here to help
out you people. You know what I mean?

                    Burt
Yes sir Boss.

                    Gene
Hey really Burt, make sure that car is ready by tomorrow morning.

                    Burt
Are you going to that hospital in Richmond again?

                    Gene
Yes, but I'm also thinking of taking a little vacation afterwards.
Right now, I think Connie and I both need it.

                    Burt
I don't blame you.

                    Gene
You know I started working in this business at seventeen and now
I'm forty-eight. Thirty-one years man is almost too long in any
business. And really I had it all Burt. I had close to seven million
listeners in Chicago. I've had the big house in the suburbs and all
that shit. So what? It means nothing now. Well I shouldn't say
that. Last week, the Chicago Times called because they were doing
an article on where the DJ's of the sixties are. And then yesterday
I got a call from WMNS in Chicago and they say that the article
created so much interest in me that they wanted me back. Do you
believe that? Here's the station where I told the former manager on
the air to go shove it and now they want me back. Do you believe
that shit?

                    Burt
Would you go back?

                           Gene
I don't know. Maybe if I didn't have this thing, I might. I don't
know. I's tempting, but also scary. I would have to take on a lot
of young hot shot DJ's from the other stations.

                           Burt
You would beat their asses.

                           Gene
I don't know.
       (Looks at clock, takes off the record, puts on the earphones
       and flips on a switch)
That was just a little Mozart for all you country-western fans.
Remember Merlin's Water Slide today. I don't care how good you are.
I am good. There is no doubt about it. Ask God?
       (Laughs)
Listen people, I got an idea let's get old Merlin out of bed and see
what he thinks aboug giving away two months of free passes instead of
one. Don't you think it's a good idea? Anyone that beats me,
deserves more than one month. Sure.
       (Looks back at Burt)
Burt Johnson who's here drinking all my coffee up also thinks it's
a good idea.
       (Dials the phone)
Old Merlin is gonna to love this, he sleeps until noon.
       (The phone rings. A southern female voice answers it on the
       third ring.)

                           Voice
Hello.

                           Gene
       (Nervously tapping a pencil on the desk)
Betty this is Gene, is Merl awake?

                           Betty
You know Gene he's never awake at this time.

                           Gene
Well tell him to get up because Gene Netti has been making bucks for
him since five this morning.

                           Betty
Gene, come on you know dear he'll get mad at me if I wake him.

                           Gene
Well I know you Betty, and with that precious smile of yours and
that sweet little voice of yours, he won't stay mad for very long.
Please wake him, the people of North Atlantic Beach anxiously await
his lovely voice.

                              Betty
Okay Gene I'll try but only because it's you.

                              Gene
Thanks, you are a lovely, beautiful woman Betty.

                              Betty
     (Yells in background)
Merl, Merl it's Gene Netti from WNAB. He wants to talk to you... Merl,
it's Gene Netti from WNAB...
                              Merlin
     (In background)
Will you please tell that crazy Italian to shove a stick of pepperoni
up his as—

                              Gene
     (Quickly turns some knobs)
Ooops people, sorry FCC. Why don't we listen to this from Stevie
Wonder. I just don't know how that wonderful and beautiful Betty puts
up with such an old grouch like Merl. It must be true love.
     (Turns some knobs, puts on a record, takes off the earphones,
     and turns around. Alice enters. She's wearing jeans and a
     t-shirt with the call letters "WNAB" on it. Sleepily she nods hello
     as Gene looks up at the clock.)

                              Gene
You know Burt, it has to be nice to come in to work at any time you feel
like it.

                              Burt
Yeah, today's kids really have it tough.

                              Alice
     (Walking into studio part)
Hey I'm only ten minutes late, I had a lot of homework last night.

                              Gene
Right.

                              Burt
Right.

                              Alice
Okay okay, you need any commercial scripts typed Gene?

                              Gene
I got most of them ready. But I do need one you typed yesterday for
Harry's Tire Shop. I can't find it.

THE GENE NETTI SHOW | 187

Burt
(Starts to leave)
I'll see you later, and I'll see about that resonater.

Gene
Good, take care.
   (Burt leaves.)

Alice
   (Sits down on a stool near the counter and shuffles some papers)
How you doing?

Gene
Fine, except for a little headache. Thanks for last night.

Alice
Thank you.

Gene
Can you get me a glass of water. I better take these pills.
   (Picks up a rusty-colored tube and takes a couple
   pills out. Alice goes to the "Employees Only" room and
   brings out a glass of water to him)
Thanks.
   (Swallows the pills and gently touches Alice's arm)
Last night meant a lot to me.

Alice
I'm glad. It meant a lot to me also.

Gene
You're a very special person to me, you know.

Alice
   (Touches his arm)
I know Gene.
   (Gives him a little kiss on the lips)
Okay, time for work. Alice get working, get working, concentrate, concentrate.
   (She goes over and starts shuffling papers on the counter)

Gene
   (Sits down and puts on the earphones)
Right, we must work. It is in work that we become happy. That's the American way. Too much pleasure warps the mind, and it is in doing that we are born to eternal life—

Alice
Stop it, Gene.

                        Gene
Okay my love, grant that I may not be so sad that I may be happy in
my dying.
        (Laughs)

                        Alice
Please Gene, I don't like it when you talk like that. It gets me
scared.

                        Gene
I'm sorry. Look why don't you go out to Mister Doughnut and get a
dozen glazed.
        (Takes some money out of his pocket and hands it to her)
I'm starved.

                        Alice
Okay.
        (Touches him and leaves)

                        Gene
        (looks at clock, turns some knobs and adjusts the microphone)
Slide! Slide! Slide, Gene baby, slide!
Gene Netti here on WNAB, Twelve fifty, FM. The lines are now open so if
you want to talk, we're here at 621-8156. Any subject except sex,
drugs, and politics.
        (Laughs)
Not really, just call 621-8156 and we'll talk for a while about anything
you want.
        (Hums and nervously taps a pencil)
De De De Da De Da Da. Let's see while we're waiting for someone to
call why don't we call Joe Logan at Star Grocery. I know you're listening
Joe while you work all those poor people to death.
        (Dials the phone and listens to it ring)
Come on, old Joe or I'll get my Uncle Carballi to blow up your watermelons.

        (A male voice answers)

                        Voice
Hello.

                        Gene
Hello Joe.

                        Joe
Hi Gene, I heard you dialing. What can I do for you, my very Italian
friend?
                        Gene
Do you have any fresh lettuce?

                        Joe
Yes.

THE GENE NETTI SHOW | 189

                                    Gene
Good. That's all.
    (Hangs up)
People that's what the world is about—lettuce. If you don't have lettuce in this world people you're done. Lettuce is the glue that holds this country together. The more lettuce you have the more together you'll be.
    (Starts to sing in an operatic voice. He's terrible)
Lettuce! Lettuce! Lettuce! Lettuce my love! It's all in the name of the game called lettuce! Lettuce!
    (Alice enters with a bag of dougnuts and points to a flashing button on the countrol panel.)
It works all the time. There's just something magical in how my voice attracts people. We have our first caller.
    (Presses in the flashing button)
Hello, you're on the air. The caller is male.

                                    Caller
Gene?

                                    Gene
Yes.

                                    Caller
Are you still teaching people how to kill little babies?

                                    Gene
    (Shocked)
What?

                                    Caller
You know, babies, Gene, small little innocent babies.

                                    Gene
    (Angrily Gene presses in another button.)
Damn kook! Remember people we're on a seven second delay because of kooks like I just had on. Well anyway here's something by Willie Nelson and when I get back we'll open the lines again. The number is 621-8156. Remember 621-8156. And please all you kooks out there get lost, or get a job or whatever.
    (Places record on the turntable, takes off the earphones, lights up a cigarette and gets up)

                                    Alice
God that caller really sounded sick.

                                    Gene
He is.
    (Nervously pacing)

                    Alice
(Places the doughnuts on the counter and hands Gene a piece of
paper)
Gene, settle down. Here's the Harry's Tire Shop spot.

                    Gene
Don't worry, I'll be okay. Sometimes, it just all gets to me.
        (She gives him a quick kiss on the check as he sits down and
        takes off the record.)
Enough of Willie today, I wanna talk baby, talk. The time is
        (Looks at clock)
eight o five on Twelve fifty, FM, in North Atlantic Beach, South
Carolina. The weather people at the Cape tell us that it's going to
be a beautiful day today. Mild and sunny and in the mid seventies.
A great day for golfing.
        (A button on the control panel begins to flash)
Okay let's go to the lines again, we have a caller.
        (Presses in the button)

                    Caller
        (Same voice as before)
Gene?

                    Gene
Please don't do this.

                    Caller
Gene?

                    Gene
Listen, I wanna be fair. Really—

                    Caller
Fair?
        (Forces a laugh)
I like that Gene. Fair. You're horseshit Gene, never stops, does
it. Should I—

                    Gene
        (Angrily pushes in another button but works hard at
        controlling himself)
Well today just must be kook day in River City people. This day has
to get better. I think I need a Barry Manilow, or maybe two
Barry Manilows and a glass of water.
        (Looking through the stack of records, he takes out an album.)
Okay Barry do your stuff, fiss fiss and plop me to relief.
        (Places the album on, takes off the earphones and lights up
        another cigarette. Pat enters)

                    Pat
That kid in the wheelchair is gone.

                              Gene
That's good. God I'm tired.

                              Pat
Can I get you anything?

                              Gene
No, that's the worst thing about this thing I have. Sometimes it
just wipes you out.

     (Burt enters)

                              Gene
Well, what's the story about my car?

                              Burt
It'll be ready later this afternoon. The part came in this morning.

                              Gene
Good I can't wait to get the hell out of here.
     (Picks up a paper from the desk)
So Harry's having a sale? Big deal. He sells retreads and tells
people they're new. Would you do that Burt?
     (Getting his energy back again)

                              Burt
Honesty is the best policy I always say.
     (Smiles a little)

                              Pat
Bullshit. Action speaks louder than words. What you charge for a
brake job is a rip-off.

                              Burt
     (Slyly laughs)
Overheard, man.

                              Pat
Overheard my ass, you mean that new swimming pool in your backyard
is the overhead.

                              Burt
Oh that, I almost forgot about that little old swimming hole. You see
I need it for health reasons. The chlorine helps clean out my sinuses.

     (A button on the control starts to flash.)

                              Alice
Someone's calling in again. You want to take it on the air or just
in here? You still got a good two or three minutes left of
Manilow.

                        Gene
Let me take it in here first.
        (Alice goes over and turns some knobs. Gene leans over and
        talks into the microphone.)
Hello, this is Gene Netti.

                        Caller
        (Same as before)
How you doing Geno?

                        Gene
How come you're here?

                        Caller
For your death. And listen Geno don't hang up because I'll just keep
calling and calling and calling. See old Geno if you understand this?
"When a tree is polled, it will sprout new shoots near its
roots. A soul that is ruined in the bud will frequently return to the
springtime of its beginning and its promise-filled childhood, as
though it could discover new hopes there and retire the broken
threads of life. The shoots grow rapidly and eagerly but it is only
a sham life that will never be genuine." You understand that Geno?!
Do you?! Do—

                        Gene
        (Angrily slams the flashing button in and looks at the clock,
        puts on the earphones and takes off the album.)
It's now eight fifteen, on WNAB, Twelve fifty, FM. Gene Netti here
until eleven. And if you're looking for fast and reliable tire
service go to Harry's Tire Shop on One Sixteen Fifth Street. He
cares about you and that's why his tires are of the highest quality.
Caring and quality service is why Harry has been in the business for
over thirty years. No finer tire shop exists in this area. Harry's
Tire Shop, One Sixteen Fifth Street. Remember Harry cares. Okay
people, the lines are open again at 621-8156. We'll talk about anything
you want. I especially want to talk about what our esteemed city
council approved last night, giving Lakco Corporation permission to
build two hundred condos on the beach. I ask you where will the
sewer lines be hooked up to our already overused treatment plant?
I'll tell you people one of these days we're going to find ourselves
without clean water and no beach to walk on. You know there's only
so much development we can take before we lose out to the sea. We
can't beat out Mother Nature. Like it or not the sea will eventually
win, people. So call if you have an opinion pro or con. I don't
care. We must do something quickly or we'll be buried in a few
years underneath our own garbage and you know what. Toilet water.
The number is 621-8156, 621-8156. And while we wait for our lines
to stack up, let's listen to Frank Sinatra sing "September Song." He
does things with words that nobody else can.
        (Places a record on the turntable and stares at the control
        panel)

Alice
Anything wrong Gene?

Gene
No, I'm fine.

Alice
Who was that person on the phone? It sounds like you know him.

Gene
Look you guys dig into the doughnuts. I gotta call Connie. Don.!t worry, I'm doing okay.
(He dials the phone as Burt and Pat start to eat the doughnuts. Gene speaks into the microphone.)
Hi... He's here, did you   What did they say?... Okay... But— Okay... We'll just see what happens... Okay I'll see you... Don't worry... No, I'm feeling fine... Just don't worry.
(Presses in a button and takes off the earphones)

Pat
(Worried)
Gene, you sure I can't help?

Gene
No, but you can get me another cup of coffee, buddie.

Pat
(Goes over and pours him a cup of coffee)
How about some fishing later today? Charlie Santi won't charge us anything. His boats had a good year with the tourists.

Gene
I'll see. Right now every bone in my body aches. Hey Pat get Burt another cup. I say it's about time the police started to wait on the blacks around here.

Burt
Not a bad idea.

Pat
(Pouring Burt a cup of coffee)
Don't get cocky Burt or I'll have to call out Charles Walen and his little old KKK organization. You know they're getting started again.

Burt
I know.

                    Pat
    (Laughing)
They're just trying to keep you people in your right place.

                    Burt
I guess so.

                    Gene
    (Full of anger)
Hey Pat, cut it out! For Christ's sake,—Burt why do you let Pat
dump on you like that? Remember this is Nineteen seventy-five.

                    Burt
Because I know he doesn't mean it.

                    Pat
    (Handling Burt a cup of coffee)
That's right Burt tell that yankee. We understand ourselves down here
better than all those do-gooders that came here in the sixties. Hell
they never looked at their own communities where the real problems
were.

                    Gene
Yeah, and that's why the blacks here in North Atlantic Beach have to
go to Salina Beach to swim. That's because you people have it all
worked out. Everyone knows their role. Shit,
    (Looks at the clock)
I gotta get back to work. The bullshit in here is getting dangerously
high.
    (Turns some knobs, puts on the earphones and takes off the
    record. A button on the control panel is flashing)
Eight forty-five on WNAB, Twelve fifty, FM. And we have a caller.
    (Presses in the flashing button)
Hi, this is Gene Netti.

                    Caller
    (Older female voice)
Gene I want to say something about those condos being built.

                    Gene
Okay.

                    Caller
I have lived here for almost all my life and people like the Lakco
Corporation have been destroying this fine little town of ours so
that it's nothing but ugly hotels and cheap bars. All these companies
that come in here to North Atlantic Beach only care about making
money, nothing else. Gene I don't know what's happening to this
country. Nobody cares about human beings anymore, only making money
and more money. There will be a time when
    (Suddenly the entrance door swings open and a young man in
    his mid-twenties enters in a wheelchair. He's wearing a

fatigue jacket with a navy blue t-shirt underneath. He has no legs, only stumps covered by pants tucked underneath him. The wheelchair has sticks of dynamite attached all over it. He wheels into the reception area. Everyone freezes.)

                            Gene

Listen Madam, sorry but we're having some problems hearing you. Please call back in a few minutes and keep thinking about that condo problem. Now here's a Simon and Garfunkel song. Hopefully when we get back I'll be able to hear you better.
    (Places a record on, turns around and takes off the earphones)
They already called home and said you had left without permission.

                          Stranger

Five years is enough.

                          Pat

    (Starts moving toward him)
You're not serious, are you?

                          Stranger

If you get any closer, this whole place goes up in a million pieces. See this button?
    (He has his hand on a huge red button which is on the
    right arm of the wheelchair.)
It will ignite with the slightest of pressure.

                          Gene

Pat let him be.

                          Pat

But Gene why? I want him to understand that I know where he's coming from.

                          Stranger

Nobody knows where I am coming from!

                          Pat

I know, but I had a nephew over there in 68, and I watched him go through hell when he came home.

                          Stranger

I don't care about your nephew. Now listen, I want all of you to sit down on the floor here.
    (Pointing to an area in front of counter on the studio side)
And you Geno you stay in that chair. We got some work to do...
Sit! Please.
    (They obey)

                          Gene

What do you want?

                    Stranger
To tell the world what a wonderful father you were.

                    Gene
Dave, come on, let's go home and talk. These people are not interested in your problems with me.

                    Dave
They might be interested in your death.

                    Gene
You know you don't mean that.

                    Dave
How wrong you are Geno.

                    Alice
    (Frightened)
Gene, is he really your son?

    (A long pause)

                    Gene
Stepson.

                    Alice
I didn't know that.

                    Gene
Connie was married before.

                    Dave
And you see I came along as part of the package. My real father is somewhere out there in nowhere world.

                    Burt
    (Raises his hand)
Can I call my gas station and check in? I told them I would be back in five minutes.

                    Stranger
They will soon know where you are. All of you.

                    Gene
Please Dave, let them go. We'll work it out.

                    Dave
I doubt that. No one works out anything with you.

                    Gene
    (Anger building)
Godamn it Dave, why are you doing this? Why?! What do you want from me?!

Dave

Revenge.

Gene

You're sick, that's what's talking, not the real you. It's your depression.
(Looks over at the turntable)
Oh shit, there's gonna be dead air on if I don't get back on.

Dave

Okay you just get on and tell them that you're still having problems with the phones. Then I want you to tell them you'll be back on with a news bulletin about Gene Netti.

Gene

I can't do that.

Dave

You will or we all go up in a puff of smoke.
(Taps the red button)

Gene

I really can't.

Dave

(Wheels closer to him)
Do it! And stop fucking around, Geno!

Gene

(Slowly he turns some knobs and speaks into the microphone)
People we're still having some technical difficulties with the phones so for the next five minutes you'll be listening to a new album by Neil Diamond. This is WNAB, Gene
(Dave wheels even closer to him)
Netti. It's nine fourteen and it's going to be a nice sunny fall day, somewhere in the 70's. Oh, also I'll have some important news about me when you come back. You might want to listen or you might not.
(Places the album and turns around)
Dave stop this, please. You're pushing just a little too much.

Dave

(Wheels back)
Tough. Are you getting worried old Geno?

Gene

(Coldly)
Never.

Dave

Well we'll see.

                        Gene
     (Warmly)
Look Dave, let the others go. I'll call your mother and we'll get
things worked out.

                        Dave
     (Coldly)
Never.

                        Gene
But why do you need the others here, if it's me you want?

                        Dave
Because I want it that way. I want a live audience for the Gene Netti
Truth Show.

                        Alice
     (Raises her hand)
Can I go to the bathroom?

                        Dave
Where is it?
     (She points to the door marked "Employees Only.")
Let me take a look first.
     (He wheels over to the door and looks in.)
Okay, but hurry up.
     (She gets up and goes in. The phone on the counter begins
     to ring. He looks at Burt.)
Answer it.

                        Burt
     (Gets up and answers it)
Hello... yes... he's here...
     (Placing hand over receiver)
It's for Pat, it's his boss. He wants to know if Pat is coming by to
sign last night's reports.

     (A long pause)

Okay, get over there and tell him I don't want to be bothered until
the Gene Netti Truth Show is finished. If we are, we blow.

                        Pat
     (Gets up and takes the receiver from Burt)
Are you sure you want me to tell him that? Once it's out about what's
happening here, I won't be able to pretend that it never happened.
I mean once my boss knows, it becomes a major offence. You understand?
Because you're Gene's son, I can forget all of this if you stop now.

                        Dave
I'm not his son! I'm not anyone's son! I'm an orphan, fellow!

                          Pat
I'm sorry, but just think about it. Nobody likes to put Vietnam
vets in jail.

                          Dave
Bull, and more bull! You cannot sail on light rays if you're
blinded by the evil all around you.

                          Pat
What?

                          Dave
Never mind, just tell your boss he better be in the know or we blow.
Tell him!

                          Pat
        (Takes hand away from the receiver)
Brad, this is for real what I'm about to tell you. Gene, Burt, and
a girl that works here are all being held hostage by Gene's stepson.
He's in a wheelchair that's all wired up with dynamite. He says he'll
blow us up if you try to come in... I don't know... I'll ask.
        (Looks at Dave)
He wants to know what your demands are.

                          Dave
Only to be left alone.

                          Pat
Just to be left alone, he says... Okay, I'll see.
        (Looks at Dave)
He says you must have other demands because people like you always
have more demands...
        (Listening to his boss on the phone)
I mean he wants to know if there is a political message involved here...

                          Dave
        (Unbelieveably, shakes his head)
Hang up!
        (Pat hesitates)
Hang up I said!
        (He obeys)
Good, now both of you sit down again.
        (Burt and Pat obey.)

                          Gene
What happen Dave? They said in Richmond it would be just a few more
months and finally things would be good with you.

Dave
Geno, things were never good with me. I just pretended to be what they wanted me to be. A nice obedient paraplegic who accepted his condition. Then they were happy because they had won. And now I was like all the paraplegics and quads on my floor. They could twist and turn my stumps, giving me pain that was unreal. But they felt good because they thought I no longer wanted to kill myself. Then you see they would lose if I did. I had to pretend that I would be happy the rest of my life in a squatting position. You know I've discovered Geno that the hardest thing in the world is to be what someone else wants you to be. And the easiest thing I discovered is to be myself. And you know now I feel more human than ever before, especially now I know I have control over my life. And I will be completely in control when I decide on the right moment to die.

Gene
But you have no right to die especially not after the progress you made these last few years.

Dave
In what? To be able to take a shit without making a mess? Or to make children with my nose?

Gene
What happened to you wanting to be a sports announcer? You were good. Remember the high school games you used to do with me?

Dave
But that's when I could dream about being like those football players running swiftly in front of me. But you old Geno and a minefield in Mi Lac took those dreams away.

Gene
You must really hate me.

Dave
I do, oh do I hate you Geno. God do I hate you. And that's why I'm here. To direct the Gene Netti Truth Show.

Gene
I won't do it.

Dave
Oh yes you will. Just pretend you're going to confession except this time your priest is your audience. And for once in your life you won't be bullshitting them.

Gene
(Full of anger, he gets up and swings at Dave but Dave wheels out of the way. Gene falls to his knees.)

Even though you were not my real son, I treated you just like you were mine. Damn it. Dave, how the hell did I know that war was a no win situation!
  (Exhausted and with great effort, he gets up and sits down.)

        Dave
Because it was on the signs of protesters and in the mouths of your fans.

        Gene
 (Sits down)
But I didn't know that until after you went. Before I just thought it was a bunch of spoiled brats trying to chicken out of the war.

        Dave
I don't care what you thought. Let's go, get on the air Geno.

        Gene
But what should I say?

        Dave
Why don't you tell them about the night I came home and told you I was drafted. Yeah, let's get started there. A good place, a good dramatic place to start the show.

        Gene
 (Still with great effort, he turns some knobs)
Dave, nobody cares about our lives.

        Dave
I do. And that's what counts here. Remember make sure all the right things are turned on. I have this transistor.
  (Hands the transistor to him)

        Pat
You know you're ruining yourself and Gene. Can't you see that he's terribly sick?

        Dave
Tough.

        Pat
Don't you know that—

        Gene
 (Gaining his strength)
Pat, no more. I mean it. This is a situation you don't understand. So, please no more.

        Alice
Will you let us go after Gene says what you want him to say?

Dave
I don't know. I'll deal with that when I have to.

Burt
Can we at least call our families and tell them we're okay?

Dave
I said I'll deal with that later. Now be quiet. Gene needs quiet. The lights dim, the spotlight slowly comes up. Okay Geno, let's go, or we blow.

Gene
(Puts on the earphones and adjusts the microphone)
This is Gene Netti on WNAB and what you will be hearing for the next few minutes won't be very interesting. But I'm in a situation where I don't have much of a choice. We're under some pressure here... In fact, we're being held hostage by my stepson... We're all okay... So the friends and relatives of Pat O'Neil, Burt Johnson and Alice Jacoby don't worry, we're okay—

Dave
(In background)
Get on with it Geno.

Gene
Excuse me people.
(Turns some knobs and looks at Dave)
I can't and I won't. Dave I'm not going to embarrass your mother, myself and my friends. I'll be damned if I'm going to be forced on the air to say things which are nobody's business. I'm Gene Netti and no one tells me what to say. They tried that in Chicago and L. A., but I told them to all shove it. Sorry Dave I'm not doing it.
(Angrily takes off the earphones and slams them down)

Dave
Oh yes you are, Geno! Remember I was trained to kill and torture by your good guidance and with the help of the U. S. Army. Geno I have no problem doing the same thing to your friends if you don't get on with it.
(Motioning for Alice to come over)
Come here.
(She gets up and goes over to him)
Kneel in front of me.
(She hesitates.)
Kneel!
(She obeys.)
Good girl, very good. Nice girl.
(Gently he strokes her hair.)

Gene
Dave, why are you doing this? There's so much you could do.

Dave
I know Geno. Perhaps I can referee ping pong games or become an arm wrestler.
(Takes some matches out of his jacket.)

Gene
Look at the doctors, lawyers and teachers who are in wheelchairs. There is really so much—

Dave
I give a shit. I, me, this person right here
(Points to chest)
wants to be whole and normal. Normal, Geno! You hear! Not half a person sitting in a wheelchair the rest of his life! And not turning heads wherever he goes!... And there's no way that will ever be for me. And so I've made the decision not to be half a person. My decision, not yours, mom's, not the hospital's, not the nurses, doctors, mine!

Gene
But no one has the right to say it's time for him to die. You live life the best you can.

Dave
I will live life not this way. Self respect can't come very easily by peeing in your pants and not knowing it.

Gene
Whatever you say, it's still a sin—

Dave
Sin?! What the hell is sin Geno?! Especially when one's soul has been raped by the evil that lurks in mountains that crisscross like the breasts of large women. There Geno in a small village between two of those breasts, sin was sucked out of me when my sergeant shit and pissed on a baby-faced VC.
(Lights a match)
You have pretty blue eyes. I bet now you would like to shit and piss on my face.
(Brings the match close to her eyes)

Alice
(Screams)
Please don't!
(Crying)
Gene don't let him do it! Gene!

Gene
Jesus Dave, okay I do it! You're crazy!

(Dave takes the match and then gently reaches over and strokes her hair.)

Dave
That's basically the story, Geno. You catch on quick for someone who never finished high school.
(Looking directly at Gene)
You know I knew I had to go because of you. I mean I couldn't let down Gene Netti, The King of the Rock and Roll DJ's. God how proud I was of you then. All of those crazy stunts like in Buffalo when you stayed on a flagpole for two weeks. Everyone treated me like some kind of royalty because I was the son of a famous celebrity. And Geno couldn't be embarrassed by his stepson not going to kill people who slept twenty in a room. He was a fighter. You taught me since I was four about violence and how to fight those who get in your way.

Gene
How can you say that?

Dave
All I heard about since you came into my life was how you used to fight the hoods on the streets of Syracuse. You and your cousin Anthony taking on them and winning all the time. And how you were a mean son of a bitch when you played football. Tackle the guy and then sneak a hard elbow to the balls was the best way to show who was boss.

Gene
I just wanted to teach you that life is a fight. A real bitch, Dave. All living is fighting.

Dave
You just don't hear, like those letters I wrote to you from Nam. Crying out for some understanding. And all you could write was to "Hang in there, war is tough. Kill one of those son of a bitches for me." And one day I just about did that when I blew away, my legs, my balls, and they flew up to my neck... Okay Geno, enough reminiscing, let's get to work.

Gene
(Stares at the control panel)
We're not transmitting. No power is going out.

Dave
(Looks at Pat)
You better call them and tell them one more time they do that, we all go. Shit, do they think I'm stupid or something. Cops are such assholes. Go and call!

(Pat hurriedly gets up and dials the phone.)
Tell them if Geno can't transmit soon, I have no problem blowing us up
right now.
(Gently he rubs Alice's hair)

                              Pat
      (Talking into the receiver)
Brad, he says if Gene can't transmit, we're gonna die... No he means
it... He's already talked about his own suicide... I will...
      (Hangs the phone up)
They're gonna fix it. They said it won't be long. They did cut
some wires.

                              Dave
      (Shakes his head)
Asses. Okay sit down.
      (Pat obeys)
I got an idea for us while we're waiting. We're gonna to play a game
that a psychologist used to play with us in the hospital.
The object of the game was to get us to think about how important
life was and to forget about the suicide most of us were contemplating.
And believe me, atleast one and sometimes four or five a night would
get whole again by either OD'ing, drowning themselves in sinks,
pulling IV's out. One guy filled up his lungs with toilet paper and
choked himself to death. Screw it! Anyway here's how the game works.
You are four people on a sinking ship. And there is a lifeboat in the
water which has room for only one more. Now what the four of you have
to do is to take three or four minutes each to try to convince me
why you should be given the space on the boat. I'm the jury and will
make the decision on who lives and who dies. I am also free after
your presentations to ask questions of you. So why don't you take a
minite to think about what you want to say. I think I'm going to
like this.

                              Gene
Dave, please stop all of this.

                              Dave
Sorry Geno, I'm in control here, remember? I know that's hard to
accept. But that's how it is now, Geno. I, boss, you pissant.

      (Laughs)
Okay who's going first?
      (No one volunteers)
Okay you.
      (Touches Alice's head)
Start. And please stand. We may as well be a little formal about
this. You can't tell this may be the way I decide to save one of you.
But of course you Geno you have no chance for that. Your handicap
is death regardless how well you perform. See, isn't this fun, Geno?

Alice
(Slowly gets up)
I don't know if I can. Really this is not easy. I don't know what to say.

Dave
It's your life, think about that. And if you think it's important, then you'll try to save it.

Alice
Really I don't know what to say except that I am younger than the others here. And all I want really is to be someone other than Alice Jacoby from North Atlantic High. And I know I have the talent now to make it as a broadcaster because my journalism teacher has told me that and even Gene told me the same thing. Maybe, and I know it sounds corny, but maybe I could help wipe out some of the unfairness in this world. Stop people from hurting, you know what I mean? And just show them you really care about them. Be real to them, you know, and not be like some of the people around here who treat you like dirt because your mother is only a waitress and is divorced... I don't know, I guess... That's all.
(Crying a little)

Dave
Okay, thank you. Come back here next to me.
(She obeys and as she kneels beside him he gently pats her head.)
Okay, who's next.
(Slowly Pat gets up.)

Pat
Well, I just think if you gonna to save one of us, you should think of her last. I mean girls like her live in a dream world, and all they end up really doing is being a waitress or a clerk in a store. Then some boy gets them pregnant and they get married and have four or five more kids. And then what usually happens the husband runs out on them and they end up being a Saturday night girl and on welfare. Look at her mother.

Alice
(Angrily)
That's not true, you shithead and you know it! My mother works hard for everything she gets!

Dave
(Pats her on the head)
Okay okay, just let him go on. Remember, I'm the jury.

Pat

Anyway for Burt, my dear colored friend, he's gone as far as he could. Like it or not that's how it is in the south. Burt knows that too.
(Looks at Burt)
Don't you Burt? That's reality here. A white man is got a better chance of making it and helping his fellow man than a colored person today. Being a police officer, the power and law is on my side. Basically, it gets down to me having more skills that are needed by society than Alice or Burt. And yes, I also have a nice wife and two beautiful kids that need me and that's about it.

Dave

Okay, sit down please, Burt you're next.
(Pat Obeys.)

Burt

(Gets up)
Well I don't have much to say except that I have a lot of respect for what you're doing. I don't agree with how you're doing it, but I do respect your decision to die with self respect and dignity. I believe we have to do what we feel is right. I've always tried to live that way. And you know it's hard living by your principles, especially when you live amongst hypocrites like Pat. Pat sure loves his wife, especially when he's bowling at La Monicci's every Tuesday night. I know he and Debbie, the waitress over there talk about his wife and kids all through the night—

Pat

(Angrily jumps up and starts hitting Burt with his fists. Burt protects himself by covering his head.)
Shut up! Shut up! You dumb nigger! Shut up!

Dave

(Wheels over to them)
Sit down! Sit down! If you don't, we all die!
(Pat stops)
And now sit down! I'll take into consideration all the factors.
(Pat sits.)
Good. Okay, continue if you have anything more to say.

Burt

Well nothing too much, except to say that I think I'm changing the way people see blacks. I really work hard on speaking correctly and showing people that I'm no dumb nigger like he just said. I believe in my country and I want people less fortunate, black or white, to be given a chance to make it just like I had. That's if they're willing to do a lot of self sacrificing and hard work. But I also want to say this to you. Please let us all go, Dave, you seem to be really nice. And this is not going to do anyone any good. Follow the good, Dave, not that damn evil you met over there.

Dave

Thank you Father Burt for the advice, but my good will be followed! Now sit down!
    (Burt obeys.)
Okay Geno, your turn. But for you, of course, your audience will join us. Are we transmitting now? Go see.
    (Motions to Alice who gets up and looks at the control panel)

Alice

Yes.

Dave

Okay Geno, let's go. Time for the Truth Show.

Gene

    (Much of the fight has gone out of him as he speaks into the microphone.)
This is Gene Netti on WNAB. We're still doing okay. I don't know if you care about what I am about to say, but I have to say it to satisfy my stepson. It's about something that happened five years ago when he told me he was drafted. I didn't like the Viet Nam war any more than anyone else, but I felt if you're called you have to do your duty. It's as simple as that. We all must have the courage to fight for our country. And if you have the guts, you'll do it. This country offers a tremendous amount of opportunities for anyone who wants to get ahead, and we have to protect that right. Look at me, I started at seventeen and became one of the best DJ's in the country. What other coun—

Dave

    (Wheels closer and whispers)
Stop the bullshitting, Geno. They get enough of that every day from you.

Gene

Anyway we argued this night about him going in the Army. And after about four hours of arguing I convinced him that it was his duty to fight for his country. So he went in and came back without legs. Yes people, I feel guilty about that. But you parents out there know that you would do the same thing if you believe in this country and its principles. I mean would you tell him to run off to Canada? I couldn't. I have too much faith in this country. My parents—

Dave

    (Grabs the microphone away and speaks into it)
Bullshit and bullshit! Sorry people, he just can't tell the truth! Can you Geno?! The burning! The killing! The smell of dead bodies! I hated it! I loved it! I hated it! I loved it! The whole place was full of contradictions! So much beauty, almost dazzling but it was really a mask for a madman's soul! Sometimes you were fooled because it seemed like there was no war! For days, nothing would happen. Then it would start off like muffled caps going off in the

distance, just a ripple, and then it would build up to a roar until the deadly thunder began to rain pieces of flesh, blood, and white muscles...
(Chokes with emotion)
Old Geno said that night we must do things like fight in wars because that's why America is great. So people I couldn't let my famous stepfather down. And off I went to do my killings like a dutiful son I was...
(Starts to cry a little)
You know it's funny, those skinny little people never seemed to talk when we were around. All they did sometimes was whisper. But when they were being bombed or burned by us their screams and crying seemed to be coming from the lowest levels of hell... Then there are people in hospitals working on you and you can't talk. And you can't feel. But you think you can...

(Gene moves closer to him)
Keep away, or we go now!...
(Moves hand to button on wheelchair)

Gene

(Moves back)
Dave you're being so damn selfish now. And before too. If you would've only accepted your condition, a lot of things they tried to do for you would have worked. But we did think the hospital in Richmond was helping.

Dave

(Gaining his composure)
Sorry to disappoint you Geno. Remember I could never satisfy you anyway.
(The phone on the counter rings. He wheels over and answers it on the third ring.)
I'm serious... I don't know yet!
(Slams receiver down)

Burt

(Gets up)
Look Dave, really think about what you're doing. I don't care I'm not scared to admit it, but I don't want to die. Gene, tell him about you, at least for us. Tell him.

Gene

(Coldly)
It's none of his business. Forget it.

Pat

Burt is right Gene, he's gotta know. Maybe he'll come to his senses.

Gene

No!

                    Pat
Then I will. This has gone too far.

                    Gene
I said it's none of his damn business! Don't, Pat. Damn it!

                    Pat
I'm sorry Gene, but Dave your supposedly hateful stepfather is dying of cancer.

                    Dave
   (Unbelievingly)
You're kidding? You got to be kidding. Jesus, is that true Geno? Or is it another one of your lies?

                    Gene
One of my lies, I guess.

                    Alice
   (Looks up at Dave)
Dave, it's true. There're times when he leaves here that we almost have to carry him home because he's so tired. Look at him now. How many healthy people are that white?

                    Dave
Son of a bitch, I'll be damned! It is true, huh Geno?!

                    Alice
Tell him, Gene. Don't be so damn proud.

   (A long pause)

                    Gene
Okay, but I'm only telling you because of these people. Two years ago they found cancer in my colon. And they started treating me with chemotherapy. In fact, my doctors were in the same hospital that you were in in Richmond. But last year I gave up the chemotherapy because it made me too sick. Anyway every two months I have to come to Richmond to have it checked. Last time, they found some cancer in my neck. Then they found through surgery that I had a rare kind in there. I don't know but they said it's supposed to be caused by being near asbestos. I guess the early radio studios had a lot of it in them. You kinda choke to death when it gets bad. So you see coming to Richmond accomplished two purposes. And that's why sometimes your mother was there alone. I was in another part of the hospital being treated or examined. But I want to live more than ever, and a lot of that wanting to live is because of you. You understand? I know now that the most important things in life are not fame or material things, but it's you and your mother. That's why I was happy to hear last time we were there that things were going well for you.

Dave
I don't know I still don't believe you or your friends. Sure play on my sympathy and then I get my guard down. Nice try, people.

Alice
But it's true, really it is Dave.

Dave
Look, I don't care if it is or isn't now. It still doesn't change anything. The Gene Netti Truth Show must go on.

Alice
Can't you see Gene needs you, especially now?

Dave
He needs no one. Shit, even this, my finest hour, he's trying to control it with giving me a bunch of lies about having cancer. Damn you Geno!

Alice
(Gets up)
Gene, he won't kill us, will he? Not now? Why won't he believe us that you have cancer?! Why Gene?!

Gene
I don't know anymore. The doctors told us when he's depressed like this there's nothing you could do. Before he went to the hospital in Richmond he had tried to kill himself over the last four years with drugs, alcohol, not eating. I don't know, but now he seems more depressed than ever.

Dave
Depressed, I'm not.

Gene
You're not depressed?

Dave
No.

Gene
Then tell us what you think depression is, Dave.

Dave
Hard to say. I think it depends on the person. A person like me who thinks he is right but is constantly being shot down, then he's considered depressed. If however he is a famous disc jockey, then he would be considered as fighting the system. Depression is a word used for the no-counts of this world.

Gene
You just don't like anyone to tell you what to do.

Dave
Do you Geno? Tell me, do you?!

Gene
Sometimes if I think someone is right.

Dave
Another lie, because for the last four years you couldn't stand to see me make a decision about my life.

Gene
You're right because I believe you don't have the right to kill yourself.

Dave
Why not?

Gene
A lot of reasons, but especially because of your mother.

Dave
Don't give me that! You and I both know how much you care about her! It's all—
   (The phone on the counter rings. Dave puts the transistor up
   to his ear)
We're still on, great. All of this has been going out. Tremendous.
   (He motions for Alice to answer it.)

Alice
   (Picks up the receiver)
Hello... Yes.
   (Looks at Dave)
It's your mother.

Dave
Hell not now, damn it, okay.
   (She hands him the receiver.)
Hello Mom.

Mother
   (Worried voice)
Dave?

Dave
Yes.

Mother
You've been through enough Dave, please let them all go. Gene does have cancer, Dave. You know I wouldn't lie to you. Believe me.

Dave

I think Mom it's just a big ploy to get everyone to feel sorry for him because he's on the way out as a DJ. People do that Mom, I know I been with a lot of psychos over the years.

Mother

But it's true. If you only could see him some nights throwing up and screaming with pain.

Dave

I think you're lying too Mom. All of you are. Is that what the police told you to say?

Mother

No Dave—

Dave

Sorry Mom, I love you and understand why you're doing it. But also I know that you would lie to me to protect him. Bye.
(Hangs up and wheels toward the microphone)
Should I tell the people out there Geno about the time you thought my baseball bat was for hitting Mom and me and not baseballs? How about that people for a loving husband and father?

Gene

(Full of emotion, tries to get up but can't)
That's not true, not true! Sometimes I just didn't have much patience because all my energy was going out to record hops and the radio station's promos. Damn, I feel so helpless. It's not true!

Dave

He's lying again, people. Then there was the day when they told me at the station that he was in the record room. So I go in and there he is humping this girl on the floor. The girl didn't look any more than fifteen.

Gene

(Angrily turning some knobs)
It wasn't like that. I was lonely and things were not going right between your mother and me then.

Dave

Nice try Geno. More lies.
(Looking at Alice)
Are you the new one for humping?

Alice

Can't you understand he's dying? And he's a nice human being.

Dave

Bullshit!

                    Pat
    (Gets up)
Don't you have any compassion in your heart for Gene?

                    Dave
Look, all of you think I'm stupid or something. I know it's a plan
to save Geno's ass. Also you figure if you save him then you're all
saved. Sit down!
    (Pat obeys.)

                    Alice
I don't care what you believe. He does have cancer. And we do want
to help you.

                    Dave
Okay then get up and rub my neck. It's tightening up. That will
really help me.
    (Alice gets up and starts to gently rub his neck.)

That's good, ah that feels good. However, you others, I'm still in
control and my hand is on the button. God, that's great.

    (The lights dim over Alice and Dave and get brighter over Burt
    and Pat. Gene falls asleep in the chair.)

                    Pat
So?... So whataya think?

                    Burt
Nothing much.

                    Pat
I'm sorry Burt, about be—

                    Burt
Don't worry about it.

                    Pat
So here we are two outstanding leaders of the community and former
North Beach high school football stars, and now what?

                    Burt
I don't know. I keep saying to myself that I can use this situation
as something to learn from. I believe that everything we do we can
learn something from.

                    Pat
Yeah, right. You know Burt, at one time you and me had the world by
the balls. When we were playing football, everything seemed right
with the world. There was order. No problems. No worries. You go

out every afternoon and practice your ass off, then afterwards take a shower and it felt great. Your muscles ache, but it was a good feeling. Coach Bonley was a good coach too.

                        Burt
That's what I heard.

                        Pat
He was a mean son of a bitch but he like his football players. If you worked hard for him, he would do anything for you.

                        Burt
That's how Coach Jackson was at Brooker T. High. You worked your butt off for him because he was a great human being. He would say that what was important in football was that we are working toward a common goal. And that the feeling of closeness we would develop on the team we would never be able to find again. And you know, Coach Jackson was right.

                        Pat
I agree even though I still feel close to Tom Coleman our esteemed mayor and George Shriver who's my lawyer now. You know Burt both of them were great football players when we played. Hell remember the passes Shriver would throw?

                        Burt
Yeah, he was good.

                        Pat
I'll tell you Burt one time he threw the ball almost ninety yards.

                        Burt
I would say that's a good pass.

                        Pat
And he completed the son of a bitch.

                        Burt
Jesus, I thought our Jim Wynn was good.

                        Pat
Yeah, he was good too for your guys.

                        Burt
I heard a couple weeks ago they caught him hustling coke in Florida.

                        Pat
Well you know, that's the other thing. Once you lose contact on that closeness with a bunch of guys, something is lost. You don't have no common goal like you said. And you feel disoriented. That's why I joined the police. I tried selling cars, working on construction, and

a lot of stuff. But I just didn't like the people I worked with. But the North Beach guys on the force are good guys. You know, they're the kinda guys you can go out and get loaded with.

                    Burt
I wish I had that. In my business, I have to play boss because if I get too close to the guys in the gas station they'll take advantage of you. I've learned that by experience. But Pat, you're right there's nothing like the closeness on a football team. Something about everyone from the first string to the last string not being treated differently. Everyone, with Coach Jackson, had to do every exercise and every drill. That sweating and bitching about how hard it was with the guy next to you made you feel that you were all in the same boat. I think that's why we were undefeated for two years, Coach Robinson got us to be close during practice, and then it showed up during the games. We played like a well-oiled machine and that—

                    Dave
Both of you assholes make me sick!
        (The lights get brighter over him as Alice becomes startled
        and stops rubbing his neck.)
I've been listening here, and all that shit you're talking about reminds me of the crap they fed us day after day in basic training. Eventually they got me to believe that crap because Geno over the years had set the stage for them. Then before I knew what was happening I no longer had a love of life but was developing a passion for death. Soon I began to drift body and soul, like a leaf drifting in the wind currents. I began to drift without ever catching on to anything. All things since then have been against this life.

                    Alice
Is that why you're so morbid?

                    Dave
No, it's really because I can't go dancing.

                    Alice
I'm serious.

                    Dave
So am I. I used to love to dance before this happen. But what makes it even worse is everybody feeling guilty when they meet me, because I can't go dancing. That's a bitch.
        (She continues to rub his neck.)

                    Pat
Do you have any close friends?

                    Dave
I released all of them from feeling sorry for me.

Pat
How did they take it?

Dave
Wonderfully, I don't know. I just couldn't take all their compassion, all their sensitivity. I didn't like having them feel good about themselves because they were helping a poor cripple. I needed some self-respect at least.

Pat
I just think we need friends and family to help us get through.

Dave
I don't.
(Reaches up and brings Alice closer to him)
You know you have a lovely looking ass.

Alice
You're embarrassing me.

Dave
Well you do. You must know that it can excite any healthy male.

Alice
I don't know about that.

Dave
Even though I would love to have you, you don't have to worry.

Alice
Why?

Dave
Because I only have a dried-up prune in between my legs.

Alice
Don't say that.

Dave
Well I just want you to know that even though there's no feeling there I still have a tremendous amount of sexual desire when I see a lovely ass.

Alice
Would you like to have me, really?

Dave
Yes.

Alice
Well I wouldn't mind having you. I find you very attractive.

Dave
Well I'm sorry but I took the vow of chastity five years ago. However, maybe big Burt would like to act as my substitute. What about it, Burt? You can be honest with me.

   (A long pause)

Burt
Yes I would like to have her.

Alice
You would?

Burt
Yes. But I know if that ever happen I would be run out of town or burned to the stake if people found out.

Alice
But I still can't believe you want me.

Burt
I want you.

Alice
You know I find also many black men attractive.

Dave
Halleluyah! Truth is marching on!

Pat
This is crazy.

Burt
   (Winks)
Sure it is, but if you had a choice you do the same thing.

Pat
I don't touch young pussy.

Burt
   (Winks again)
I bet you would if you thought Alice wouldn't cry rape.

Pat
   (Smiles)
Okay, maybe I would.

Burt
You know I remember hearing you were the biggest stud of all the jocks in your school.

Pat
I was, I guess.

Alice
This could be interesting.

Dave
I love it.

Gene
(Opens his eyes)
Horny bastards!

Pat
You're just jealous because you're not getting any—

Alice
(Tries to signal behind Dave that she is only pretending)
Gene you know you can, if you want to.

Gene
(Confused)
I guess it makes no difference, anymore.

Alice
(Again she tries to signal to Gene that it's all a put-on.)
Maybe you and Dave can have a nice conversation while we go to the bathroom and start diagramming some football plays.
(Giggles as if she's embarrassed)

Dave
If I didn't have some sense of morality, I would watch.

Alice
That would be hard for me.

Burt
Well let's go. I waited for this a long time.

Pat
Burt I'll go up the left on thirty-two slant and you go up on the right on forty-six dive.

(They both laugh as they get up.)

Alice
Remember, no sneak plays.

Burt
No sir. Our strategy is to let you know what's coming and see if you can defend your position.

Pat
That's right. The harder we come at you, the harder you come at us.

(All three laugh as they walk into the "Employees Only" room.)

Gene
This is sick.

Dave
No sicker than you when you're in bed with her.

Gene
You know, the last five years has dulled me to your behavior. I don't care anymore.

Dave
Too bad.

Gene
And where do we go from here?

Dave
To die.

Gene
Do you really mean that without them around?

Dave
For me, my life is really over. I just don't want to live this way. And for you I won't be satisfied until I have my revenge. Do you understand?

Gene
No, you have so many good years left and you can do so many things. I mean with a little training and discipline you can do whatever you want.

Dave
Like what, Geno?

Gene
As I said before you can teach, be a doctor, a lawyer. Anything you put your mind to, you can be.

Dave
But I don't want to be a teacher, a doctor or lawyer.

Gene
What then do you want to do?

Dave
I want to be normal.

Gene
You can. They have artificial legs.

Dave
And yes as I stumble around with my aluminum crutches and plastic legs, people will look at me and wait for me to bring out the tin cup so they could pour their pity into it.

Gene
That's not true. And you can't tell in a few years they'll have legs which are computer operated. I saw something where scientists are now working on that.

Dave
Can't you see Geno, I don't want to wait around? I've made up my mind that this is what I want.

Gene
I still don't understand.

Dave
Geno, you never will.

Gene
You know I don't care if you believe them or me about having cancer. But I do want to say I made a lot of mistakes in raising you. And maybe by getting you to go to Vietnam was wrong, but I had to do what was right.

Dave
So do I.

Gene
It's funny that for twenty years we lived together and we still can't talk.

Dave
That's right Geno. We can't talk.

Gene
Does it matter that I'm leaving all my money to you and your mother?

Dave

No Geno, it doesn't matter.
(Laughing is heard coming from the "Employee's Only" Room.)

Gene

I just wanted to make sure.

Dave

(Sarcastically)
Okay, Geno. I'm glad you made sure.

Gene

Damn Dave, life is important! It's the only thing we have. I've come to see that after I found out I had cancer. Enjoyment is what I want now out of life. You know I always wanted to buy a yacht and live on it for the rest of my life. Just be free. Maybe now the three of us can go off to Greece and then Italy. We could drink wine, eat some good pasta and have stimulating dinner conversation with "alive" people of these countries. You know while I was breaking my hump to make, I lost out on too many pleasures. I want those pleasures now, Dave.

Dave

Of course a little screwing here and there with the native girls will help, right Geno?

Gene

(Smiles)
Why not? You can have all the ones I can't handle. Listen Dave, I put away close to three hundred thousand dollars. That should last as long as I'm around. Look after I get checked out in Richmond and if everything is okay, I'll come back here and we'll pack up and start taking some good bites of life.

Dave

How about my mother? And your need to fuck everything in sight?

Gene

She has always understood that need of mine.

Dave

That's right, she's always understood what a balling freak you are. That's true love.

(The laughing in the "Employees Only" room gets louder.)

Gene

(Gets up)
We should get in there and join the orgie.

                        Dave
I don't want to talk anymore.

                        Gene
    (Moves closer and stands so that Dave is facing him and
    downstage)
Listen Dave, all I'm saying is to live what time you have left. I
could see now that before I kept searching and searching for something
that would give me eternal happiness. But now I know that can never
be. You got to enjoy life now.

                        Dave
I can't believe Geno, how hard you're trying to talk. Are you
scared of dying, Geno?

                        Gene
Yes I am.

                        Dave
Good, that's what I like to hear Geno.

                        Gene
Aren't you scared?

                        Dave
No.

                        Gene
Sure you are. You're lying to yourself Dave. Your whole problem is
that you hate yourself for killing those fifteen VC's in that filthy
cave in Viet Nam. So what? That's war. And that's the real truth
why you're doing all of this.

                        Dave
Your truth, maybe, but not mine! Geno, you just don't listen or see
beyond only what you want to see.

                        Gene
Perhaps, but why don't you just admit it to yourself that you also
enjoyed killing those skinny little runts. Why do you keep lying to
yourself?

                        Dave
I don't! Geno, it's you who is the lying son of a bitch! That's
the real truth here! Sure I enjoyed it then, and I still feel bad
about shooting and shooting until they had no face except for raw-
burned flesh hanging down. And I still see those faces with only black
holes where their eyes were suppose to be. But old Geno, it's being
in this wheelchair for almost five years that has caused me more bad
nightmares. But you know what the real truth is is that you're a
damn coward. That's the real truth!

                    Gene
      (Sits down)
What do you mean?

                    Dave
I did a little checking and found out how you were drafted for the
Korean War, but you never went over there. You stayed right here in
the United States making training films. And all that shit you
gave me about being over there and fighting the Chinese was a big lie.

                    Gene
I wanted to go, but they said they—

                    Dave
Geno, you're a lying son of a bitch. And that is the real truth here!
You're a fucking coward! And fucking liar!

                    Gene
      (Gets up and goes after him. But Dave quickly tries to wheel
      away as Gene grabs hold of a wheel, and they begin to struggle
      for control of it.)
That's not true, you crippled bastard! I wanted to go! You don't
know anything!
      (Slaps him across the mouth and suddenly moves away)

                    Dave
There, Geno, don't you feel better?
      (Sings)
"Happy days are here again! Happy days are here again!"

                    Gene
Damn it Dave, I'm sorry. But you push and push—

                    Dave
Geno, that's the way it is my boy.

                    Gene
You keep goading and goading me like all the times before. Wanting to
take over and be the boss, just like your mother. How many fathers
would give up their authority? Parents need to be respected not
bossed around by their sons.

                    Dave
You're right Gene. You're always right. That's if I was your son.
But you know nobody can talk to you. You always have to twist things
around so you come out looking good.

      (Alice, Burt and Pat quietly and slowly come out and move up
      behind Dave. Pat attempts to grab Dave's arms, but Dave
      sees him and powerfully hits him across the face with the
      transistor. Pat moves back in pain. Burt and Alice go over
      to comfort him.)

Dave
Assholes! Now stand there and don't move! We've fooled around enough! Did you assholes forget that cripples are very sensitive to movement around them? Even though I'm half dead, I'm not stupid.
(He points to Alice.)
I'm surprised. And so it goes for my last sexual desire. Now listen. I want you to call them and tell them I'm opening the door and getting rid of you assholes. Of course, Geno stays. But if anyone tries rushing in, my hand presses this button. Now call my love, my Brutus.

Alice
(Picks up the receiver and looks at Pat)
Are they on or do I have to dial?
(Pat nods his head)
Oh, they are on.
(Putting the receiver up to her ear)
We're coming out but don't rush in because he says if you try he'll press the button on his chair... I'll see.
(Looks at Dave)
They want to know if that means Gene too.

Dave
No, I said he stays.

Alice
No, I guess he's keeping Gene...

Dave
Okay hang up.

(She obeys.)

Alice
I'm sorry, I really do like you.

Dave
Never mind the bullshit, get over to the door. But don't open it yet.

(Alice, Burt and Pat go over to the door.)

Alice
Please Dave give yourself up. Think of Gene. I know you have feelings for him.

Dave
Sorry, he stays.

Gene
(Completely exhausted)
Don't worry about me, Alice. We're both going in the same direction.

(She goes up to him and kisses him on the cheek and does the
same to Dave. He touches her, but quickly pulls his hand
away.)

Alice

I want to stay.

Dave

You won't stay. And now open the door.
(She hesitates.)
I said open the door! And you Geno come over here and stay right beside
me.
(With great effort, Gene comes over.)
Open the door!
(She finally opens the door. In the background, one hears
crowd noises and someone mumbling incoherently over a loud-
speaker along with sirens going off and on.)
Okay go.
(Alice is crying as she gives him another kiss on the lips.)
Please go. You two follow.
(Alice leaves as Burt and Pat follow. Then suddenly he
pushes Gene out the door and locks it. After a moment, he
wheels over to the microphone and speaks into it.)
Mom, I love you... And Gene, I guess I'm no good at killing important
people. Little yellow men are my specialty—
(A loudspeaker interrupts him.)

Mother

I love you too, Dave. Please come out, I promise no more hospitals.
We'll make things right again.

Gene

Dave, I need you. Both your mother and I need you. Let's start over
again. We'll get that show together like we used to talk about.

Dave

(Crying a little)
I shot this twelve-year old first in the arm and he screamed. Then
he held up the other arm and I shot him there and he screamed. He
wouldn't stop screaming until I shot him in the face. Then he
stop

Gene

Dave, it's over. It's all over. A senseless horror, I could see that
now, that should've never been. Please come out.

Dave

(Gaining his composure)
I'll see. Give me a couple minutes of quiet. Please just a few minutes...

                        Gene
We will.

                        Dave
Thanks.

        (After a long pause, he presses the button on the wheelchair.
        The lights dim and the stage becomes enveloped in red and
        yellow smoke.)

                        BLACK OUT

                        The End

THE BOILER ROOM SCHOOL

A SCREENPLAY

The Boiler Room School follows professor Vinnie Serrano as he attempts to teach children of Appalachia. He has a major drinking problem and has been showing up to class with alcohol on his breath. The chairman tells him to take over a special project in the hills of Appalachia or he's going to be fired. If he can make it go and can get sober, the university will consider keeping him on.

For several years, Vinnie has been bored by just talking about how to teach, but never really *teaching*. He's excited about implementing a humanistic education program he has developed and written extensively on for several years. But now that he has a chance to put it into action, he faces significant obstacles, including a rigid principal who is also a former marine. Vinnie does, however, get support from one other teacher who believes in him and his educational approach.

A major part of the program is having students learn subjects like math, science, and English by restoring an old car and preparing it for a NASCAR-type race. When the pressure of the race forces Vinnie to fall off the wagon, everybody has to come to terms with who they are and what they will do.

The Boiler Room School has been submitted to several film companies for consideration. Completed in fall 2012.

"The Boiler Room"

FADE IN:

EXT. SOUTHERN STATE UNIVERSITY IN WINTER

Camera moves in on Professor Vinnie Serrano, slightly built, about 40. He is partially clothed; no coat, hat or winter gear except for a long white scarf around his neck. He clutches a backpack and he stumbles through a driving sleet toward a university building, Smith Hall.

INT. SMITH HALL SCHOOL OF EDUCATION HALLWAY

The camera moves in on Vinnie's look. His black hair is streaked with gray along with dark, haunting eyes. He has a blank "out of it" look as he enters another teacher's classroom.

INT. CLASSROOM - Day

The camera shows the strained faces of a young professor and students as Vinnie pushes the professor away from the lectern and begins to lecture incoherently and obviously very drunk, and also full of anger.

> VINNIE
> We're all frauds my friends. We teach you about teaching and all we can do is lie to you. How many of you want to teach? Don't you see that this whole place is about lying? You don't, you young, poor, poor bastards!

He wanders away from the lectern, weaves out of classroom as the classroom teacher tries to help, he pushes him away. We see students with various stages of disbelief, anger, and amusement on their faces.

CUT TO:

INT. HALLWAY - DAY

As Vinnie staggers out into hall, he collapses. Students and professors surround him and try to help, as he drifts in and out of consciousness.

                    AD LIBS:
          "Call 911!" "Is he drunk?" "Is that
          Serrano?" "What the hell?"

Slowly he gets up and pushes people away as he staggers out
of the building.

          DISSOLVE TO: AERIAL VIEWS OF BOSTON, TRAFFIC LEADING INTO
                                                    CITY - MIDDAY

The camera moves in on a fairly new van approaching the
city. From the front view, we see Vinnie driving with his
wife, Karen, sitting in the passenger side. She is in her
mid-thirties with curling, sandy brown hair. Behind them sit
their two children, Joey and Pam. Joey, a ten year old, is a
miniature version of Vinnie, and likewise Pam, a seven year
old, is similar in looks to Karen. Joey is playing a
portable computer as Pam listens to an iPod. The camera
moves in on Vinnie's eyes as he seems to be lost in thought.

                                                    DISSOLVE TO:

INT. VINNIE'S CHAIRMAN'S OFFICE

We see Vinnie walking into the office. Glenn, Vinnie's
chairman, at the University. He is tall but overweight.
Everything about him is cold and unapproachable. Glenn
motions for Vinnie to sit in front of his desk.

                    VINNIE
          I'm sorry. Jesus, I don't know,
          Glenn. It won't happen again.

                    GLENN
          You bet your ass it won't. Hell, I
          had to deal with the president,
          parents, faculty over you being
          drunk in another professor's
          classroom. Jesus Christ, Vinnie. He
          shakes his head in disgust.

                    VINNIE
          God, I'm sorry.

                    GLENN
          Look, Vinnie, enough is enough.
          There are no more chances. You
          screwed up big time. I'm sick of
          these reports of you showing up to
          class drunk and unprepared. You're
          smart and have great ideas for
          teachers, but for some reason
          you're on a self-destructive path.

Vinnie is getting upset.

>VINNIE
>Perhaps I'm just tired of talking about policy number one hundred and fifty-four and what this committee found out, and what that committee found out, and how to fill out this form, and that form, and so on, and so on. Goddamn, Glenn, there's got to be something more that the shit we usually talk about. We're supposed to be dealing with how to teach kids.

>GLENN
>Sorry, that's how it is.

Vinnie angrily gets up.

>VINNIE
>Then why the hell am I here? Tell me, Glenn, for what?! To play nit-picking games... My God, Glenn, I'll tell you. It's getting so bad that at night I'm dreaming how to out-nit-pick the nit-pickers. I just want to teach!

Glenn is angry.

>GLENN
>Sit Down and listen, now!

VINNIE sits.

>GLENN
>Look, I've gotta go to another meeting. You've got tenure and I can't fire you, not yet, anyway. I decided because you haven't published anything in years to get you out of here and into a public school so maybe you could write about it. You were once professor of the year, now you're drunk of the year. Shit.

>VINNIE
>What school?

>GLENN
>Liberty Middle School. There's a special project being started this winter semester by Hannah McDowell. Her father is the President of the Board. He wishes that she would not do this, and would be more like his

GLENN
older daughter, Jennifer, who was
Miss West Virginia last year, and
now is making a lot more working
for a large pharmaceutical company.

VINNIE
I don't know...

GLENN
You better know, and make it work -
or you're out of here.

VINNIE
But what am I to do other than
write about it?

Glenn, getting up.

GLENN
Bring some of our older graduate
students to help you. Now, I gotta
go. The principal is John Masters.
I went to school with him and he
was a big jock. He thinks we at the
University are out of touch.
Anyway, I gotta go. Please don't
screw up or you're done.

Glenn leaves as Vinnie gets up slowly and follows.

DISSOLVE TO:

INT. VINNIE AND KAREN'S LIVING ROOM - NIGHT.

The camera shows her finding Vinnie passed out on the sofa
with blood dripping from his forehead. She gets a washcloth
and starts to wipe Vinnie's head. As she sits down next to
him, he slowly wakes up.

KAREN
Vinnie, you gotta stop. What's
going on?

VINNIE
I just tripped.

KAREN
No, I think you passed out, and you
were drunk again.

> VINNIE
> I don't know, no more drinking. I promise.

> KAREN
> Please, I've heard that for two years now. What's going on?

> VINNIE
> Nothing. Just let me go up to bed and get some sleep.

Karen is crying.

> KAREN
> I'm worried about you. I just want to make you happy.

> VINNIE
> Forget me. Don't try to live through me. I'm not worth it.

Karen is getting up.

> KAREN
> Damn it, Vinnie. You know my whole life has been set up so I could do what I'm doing now, and if I lose you or the kids, I don't know what I would do.

Vinnie sits up.

> VINNIE
> But you got to find other interests. You can't just depend on me and the kids for your satisfaction.

> KAREN
> Just promise me you'll get help.

> VINNIE
> Never mind me, what about you?

> KAREN
> You know you always do this. You twist it around and it becomes my fault. Then I feel guilty.

> VINNIE
> You just don't understand.

Karen throws down washcloth and begins to leave.

INT. PRINCIPAL JOHN MASTERS' OFFICE

We see VINNIE knocking on JOHN MASTERS' door and opening it. We see John Masters writing at his desk. He is big, balding, and looks in great shape, still very athletic. Masters is a man of the system. Doesn't like to deal with problems. These "Hollow kids" are problems. Sees Yankee professors as being out of touch with the real world, all theory, no practice He doesn't know, or care, about other ways of educating these kids. But he figures this attention from the University will reflect well upon him being a progressive educator in the eyes of the community.

     VINNIE
John Masters?

     MASTERS
Yeah.

     VINNIE
I'm Vinnie Serrano from State.

Masters gets up, goes over, and shakes his hand. He points to the chair in front of his desk. Vinnie sits as Masters sits.

     MASTERS
Look, to be honest, I think the program that Miss McDowell is working on will not work, but hell, her father is the President of the Board. What can I say?

     VINNIE
Right.

     MASTERS
Anyway, she is in Room 111 getting ready. The kids start tomorrow. I just don't want any trouble. Keep them under control and we'll get along.

     VINNIE
Okay.

     MASTERS
And don't bother with the parents/ They can care less as long as the kid isn't home. The less I see of you the better. Then I know the program is working. By the way, your graduate students are already

> MASTERS
> with Miss McDowell. You're late, my friend.

Vinnie leaves, and then we see him walking down the school's hallway in front of a classroom. We now see Vinnie opening the door to an industrial arts classroom. The teacher Hannah McDowell looks like she is in her late twenties and is talking to Vinnie's graduate students. She has short, blond hair with the body of a runner. She is small, but powerful. The graduate students are Jane Winston, in art, about 28. She is very competitive, strong on the use of art to teach kids math, science, reading with music, art and literature, respectively. Jack Rice, a Vietnam war veteran, about 50, working on his doctoral thesis. He has a small town background, and wants to be a principal or superintendent for more money, but his real love is science. Interested in seeing how and why things work. Bill Kingman, ex- Peace Corps, about 32, with an English specialization, he has a rural background, and is dedicated to "inspiring the third world" wherever he finds it. He believes it exists in rural America. Idealist, Ben Huffey, college basketball star, about 28. He was not quite good enough to stick with the pros. He wants his masters in physical education so he can coach and teach. He's rural, redneck. Jerry Spencer, math instructor from an upper middle class background, and can be disruptive himself. He has a bad attitude about family, team play, etc. More interested in Jane Winston than a bunch of hillbillies. All of them have Vinnie as a graduate instructor.

> VINNIE
> Hi, guys! And you must be Hannah.

Vinnie sticks out his hand, Hannah shakes it.

> HANNAH
> I'm glad to see you. I had you years ago in class. You're the reason I'm teaching.

> VINNIE
> That doesn't sound good. Sorry, don't remember you.

> HANNAH
> I'm serious. I told your students here it's your ideas I want to implement. I want these kids to be active, not passive, work on stuff that interests them, I want it to be an alternative to the same old education that doesn't work for these kids.

                    VINNIE
          Well, let's give it a shot. I don't
          have any other options left.

                                              CUT TO:

INT. INDUSTRIAL ARTS ROOM IN LIBERTY MIDDLE - STUDENTS COME
IN.

The camera shows Vinnie standing in between electrical saws
and equipment. He has 30 students in front of him. To one
side we see the graduate students, and on the other we see
Hannah. Even though there were chairs placed in a circle,
only one was occupied by a small, frightened boy. Most of
the students are anywhere from 14 through 15 years old. We
see some students lying upon saws and a worktable. Others
are punching each other, yelling at each other, and refusing
to pay attention to Vinnie. Some students are using tools in
the industrial art room as swords in their hands. In the
midst of the battlefield atmosphere, Vinnie and the other
teachers try to wrestle the tools out of their hands.

                    HANNAH
          Hey, can I have your attention? I
          want to introduce Doctor Serrano.
          He's from the University. He's
          gonna help me with a new program
          for you.

                    VINNIE
          We are going to be implementing a
          new program that I think you'll
          like.

A flat-faced, lanky, long haired student by the name of Pete
speaks. You sense he's a leader of sorts. He carries a big
attitude.

                    PETE
          I bet.

                    VINNIE
          Really. We want to be your friends
          and also your teachers.

Another student by the name of Gary speaks. He is small, red
haired, and troubled.

                    GARY
          How many paddles do you have?

                    VINNIE
Smiling
            None, we don't believe in paddling.
                    GARY
            You will.
                    PETE
            Hey Mister Doctorate, school ain't
            no way going to work for us. We're
            too stupid. My daddy says the only
            people stupider than us is blacks.
            Ask other teachers. They put us
            here to get rid of us. They want
            pretty rich kids. I bet if you stay
            around, you'll treat us like the
            other teachers. We don't need any
            dumb professor around.

Vinnie in desperation, getting angry.

                    VINNIE
            We want you to learn to be good
            with each other and love each
            other.

A heavy-set, pimple-faced girl student by the name of Sherry, answers in a demeaning tone,

                    SHERRY
            Go back to the University, asshole!

Students laugh mockingly

                                        DISSOLVE TO:

INT. CAR - DAY. Boston

We see a smile on Vinnie's face as the camera moves out to an aerial view and closes in on an apartment in the North End of Boston.

INT. SHOT. JIMMY'S BEDROOM

Jimmy's wife, Marjorie, sits in a chair in the bedroom, dressed in a white satin slip. She is in her early forties, with wrinkles breaking through a once smooth face. Jimmy, who is in his late forties, looks in perfect shape. His black hair looks dyed. Dressed in a jogger's suit, he sits on the edge of the bed putting on running shoes.

Marjorie slowly and seductively brushing her hair. Looking into a hand-held mirror, she tugs at the bottom of her eyes.

                    MARJORIE
          I hardly got any sleep last night.
          Who was up so early in the kitchen?

                    JIMMY
          Probably my mother.

                    MARJORIE
          But why so early? I looked at my
          watch and it was only about five.

                    JIMMY
          Italian mothers don't sleep. She
          stays up worrying.

                    MARJORIE
          About what?

                    JIMMY
          Everything.

                    MARJORIE
          It's her fiftieth anniversary party
          and she's doing all the planning.
          Why?

                    JIMMY
          I don't know, but my mom needs
          worries like normal people need
          sleep.

                    MARJORIE
          Do you think she and your father
          are excited about the party?

                    JIMMY
          Sure. Tough to tell with him.

                    MARJORIE
          Your dad doesn't seem to be the
          kind of monster you made him out to
          be.

                    JIMMY
          Wait. With you around and other
          strangers, you might not see the
          huge anger he carries in his heart.

MARJORIE
Did you talk to your father about
the investment and Vinnie's book,
"Boiler Room School"?

JIMMY
No. How could I? We just arrived
last night.

MARJORIE
I'm sorry, but you know I'm anxious
about the whole money thing we're
going through. It's still hard to
believe that most of my money is
gone.

Jimmy gets up, goes over to her, and massages her neck.

JIMMY
It's not gone. The money was put
into long term investments which
are draining us right now, but will
eventually pay off. Don't worry, if
we get the money for my father,
everything will be okay.

MARJORIE
I hope. But I still think, Jimmy,
the public is not ready to see me
as a serious actress. For eight
years, they saw me as naïve
sweetie-pie secretary sit-com star.
And they're just not ready to see
me as a sophisticated lawyer or
battered wife, or any of those
other roles you have gotten for me.
I think they want flighty Sallie
Peterson back. Really, Jimmy.

JIMMY
Look, don't worry, baby. Just have
patience. The public will come
around. Old Jimmy knows what he's
doing after twenty years in this
business. Another year or so and
the public will have completely
forgotten about Sallie Peterson.
You just gotta have patience, babe.

Marjorie, suddenly depressed.

> MARJORIE
> You know, maybe we are all living lives like Vinnie, and won't admit it.

> JIMMY
> What do you mean?

> MARJORIE
> Didn't you say he went a little crazy?

> JIMMY
> According to my sister, Toni, she said he did. But I'm not sure, I gotta find out from my parents what's exactly going on with Vinnie.

Marjorie, choking with emotion.

> MARJORIE
> You know, sometimes when I see us like this, I think, what's the use? I mean, I looked at you on the plane and you looked so worried and tired. Sometimes I get tired of it, and I say to myself, is it all worth it? I don't know.

DISSOLVE TO:

INT. LIBERTY MIDDLE SCHOOL GYM - EARLY MORNING

We see Vinnie walking through the gym. Kids are all over. On the floor, on the stage which functions as a theater when the gym is not in use. We see kids screaming and fighting, trying to play basketball, volleyball, or just milling around. Some kids who are lying on the floor grab onto Vinnie's legs. He drags them along as he walks to the boiler room, which is connected to the gym. The boiler room is also a small bathroom, and we can see water and urine leaking underneath the walls. Because it was cold outside, there were flies all around the boiler room, for it was the warmest place to be. Vinnie and his staff attempt to get everyone together.

INT. BOILER ROOM

Vinnie tries to speak, but no one seems to be listening.

> VINNIE
> Listen, everyone. This is where we
> have to be, because the industrial
> arts room didn't work out.

Vinnie moves closer to Pete.

> VINNIE
> Pete, I need your help if this
> going to work.

Pete walks away toward the door, giving him the finger as he walks out.

CUT TO:

INT. MARIO AND THERESA'S KITCHEN - DAY

We see Theresa cooking as Mario Serrano is looking out the window. He is small, like her, but intense and muscled. He is wearing a white barber coat. Theresa's face is wrinkled and thin, but has a figure and look that at one time you could tell she was good looking.

Theresa pleading, and placing plate on the table in the kitchen.

> THERESA
> Mario, come, eat, I'll watch. The
> ham is good in the sandwich. I just
> got fresh bread from Cato's, just
> like the kids like it.

Mario seems tired and depressed as he sits down.

> MARIO
> Yeah, the damn kids. I wish I never
> had them.

> THERESA
> Mario, stop talking crazy. How many
> did you have this morning.

Mario starts to eat his sandwich.

> MARIO
> Two. Five dollars for five hours
> work. It's nothing when I think
> about what I used to make.

> THERESA
> Maybe this afternoon will be better.
>
> MARIO
> The problem is that the damn people today go and make thirty dollars an hour for themselves, but still want to pay only twenty-five cents for a haircut.

Mario chews hard on his sandwich.

> THERESA
> Mario, please try to be nice today. The kids have gone through a lot of trouble to have this party for us tonight, especially Jimmy. Try to be happy.
>
> MARIO
> I'm always happy. It's you who gets depressed all the time now.
>
> THERESA
> Never mind, just be nice to them while they're here. It's the first time in years all the kids will be sleeping over night in the apartment. Don't spoil it.
>
> MARIO
> But I don't know why they have to have this party. We could eat here, and they could save all that money.
>
> THERESA
> Mario, that's what the kids want to do. Appreciate it. You're supposed to have something big on your fiftieth anniversary. Tonight is a big night for us.
>
> MARIO
> I do appreciate it, but I have to work tomorrow. Sat'day is my busiest day. You people could sleep all day.
>
> THERESA
> Mario, you're sixty eight years old. You don't have to work anymore. You could sleep all day too.

                    MARIO
          Not until my kids are settled.

                    THERESA
          I doubt they ever will be. Look at
          them now.

                    MARIO
          I know. You work and work, for
          what? To educate your kids so that
          they could get sick?

                    THERESA
          Everyone has problems, Mario.
          Anyway, it's just Vinnie who got a
          little sick. Toni, of course... You
          shouldn't let everything upset you.

Mario's mood changes as he comes over and affectionately
touches her.

                    MARIO
          Just think, if you didn't marry me,
          what kinda life you would have had
          with those brothers and sisters of
          yours. You would have been cleaning
          and cooking for them all the time.

Theresa embarrassed, but enjoying the attention. She kisses
him hard and passionate on the lips.

                    THERESA
          You forget how Joe Longo wanted to
          marry me. Look at all the money he
          makes now. I could have had
          anything I wanted he said, if I
          would marry him. I still remember
          that big Cadillac roadster he had.
          Remember?

Mario laughs.

                    MARIO
          Yes, but it was you who would come
          out and sweep the stoop every time
          I went to work. You and your family
          from Milan thinking you're better
          than all of us poor people from
          Naples.You son of a gun, you knew
          you had a good thing when you saw
          it, Longo or no Longo.

                    THERESA
          I don't know about that. I bet if I
          married him I would be living now
          in that big house in Cohasset I
          liked so much. Remember, Mario? All
          those big trees and how roomy it
          was.

JIMMY enters as he is zipping up his jogging suit.

                    MARIO
Jokingly
          Hey, I've been up since five
          working, and mister sunshine gets
          up at noon.

MARIO gets up and goes over to the kitchen window and looks out.

                    THERESA
          Mario, leave him alone. You forget
          that they didn't get in from
          California until after midnight.

MARIO goes over to him and, with exaggeration, pulls out a kitchen chair.

                    MARIO
          Oh, my poor, poor boy. Let me help
          you sit down.

MARIO gently sits him down. Jimmy forces a laugh.

                    JIMMY
          Yeah, some off the top. Leave the
          sideburns.

                    THERESA
          Your father is nuts. Jimmy, what do
          you want for breakfast?

MARIO goes back to the window and looks out.

                    JIMMY
          Nothing, just a glass of that
          carrot juice I brought with me.
          Have you tried it?

Theresa takes the carrot juice out of the refrigerator and pours him a glass.

                    THERESA
          I tried it this morning, but it
          gives me gas.

                    MARIO
          Listen to your mother talk.
          Everything gives her gas now, even
          water.

Mario smiles.

                    THERESA
          Shut up!

Theresa sets the glass of carrot juice in front of Jimmy.

                    THERESA
          Now don't spill it like you always
          do. Is Marjorie still sleeping?

                    JIMMY
          She's getting ready. What do you
          think of her?

                    THERESA
          She seems nice and friendly, she
          doesn't act like a big TV star. She
          acts just like one of us. I just
          wish you would stay with her. I
          miss my grandkids from your other
          wives, especially Judy.

                    JIMMY
          Hey, I see them and pay a lot of
          alimony to her. It's not about her.
          Dad, did you like Marjorie?

                    MARIO
          She speaks better Italian than you.

                    JIMMY
          I know. She took it in college.

                    MARIO
          Is she Italian?

                    JIMMY
          She's part Italian.

                    MARIO
          Well, at least she's better than
          some of those girls you've brought
          home since your last divorce. God,

MARIO
your mother and I will never forget
that girl you brought home last
year. Remember, Tree? It was
disgusting. Wearing all that cheap
make up and that tight silver suit.
I thought she was a TV antenna.

JIMMY
Mom, when is Vinnie coming home?

THERESA
Any time now.

JIMMY
Is he any better?

THERESA
Karen says he is. Supposedly he
doesn't drink anymore. Your father
and I flew down last month after he
got out of the rehab center. He
lost a lot of weight.

MARIO
I still say it was Karen's fault.
And those stupid hillbilly kids he
was working with.

THERESA
Sometimes, Mario, when you talk you
make no sense.

JIMMY
Was it a nervous breakdown over
some accident, Mom? You never
really said.

Theresa hesitates as Mario gets up and goes over to the
window.

THERESA
I don't know, but don't make it
sound so awful. Don't say anything
when he's here.

JIMMY
That's too bad. Well, hopefully the
party tonight will help him. Are
you set for it?

> THERESA
> You didn't have to spend all that money. Yes, I think it will be nice.

> JIMMY
> Mom, it's okay, I wanted to do it. You and Dad deserve it.

> MARIO
> I just don't know why you have to do all of this. Still, no one at the shop.

> JIMMY
> Dad, you need to retire. Enjoy yourself. Hey, when is Toni getting in?

> THERESA
> Late. Mario, forget the shop. Close it today. We have a big party to get ready for.

> JIMMY
> Well, I think it will be fun.

MARJORIE enters, dressed in her white terry cloth bathrobe.

> MARJORIE
> Buon giorno Signor Serrano. Che bella casa pulita che aveti tanto comida e intima.. Non posso credere che questo apartimento tiene tre camere di letto.
> (Good morning, Mr. Serrano. You really have a nice clean house. It's so cozy and comfortable. I can't believe you have three bedrooms in this apartment.

Mario turns on the charm and becomes "old world" and flirtatious.

> MARIO
> God, you speak good Italian, not like me. Mine is poor people's Italian. You speak the kinda Italian my wife's people speak. You understand her, Tree?

> THERESA
> No one in the North End has an apartment like this, thank you.

> MARIO
> There's a customer. I better go.
> MARIO yells out the window.

> MARIO
> Hey! I'll be right there.

Mario moves over to Jimmy.

> MARIO
> Come on Jimmy, after I finish this guy, I'll give you a trim. You look like a bum.

> JIMMY
> I just got a haircut. Thanks anyway, Dad.

Mario brushes up the hair on the back of his head.

> MARIO
> You should see the back of your head. It's all chopped up. At least let me fix it so you'll look halfway decent.

Jimmy gets up and starts to follow Mario out.

> JIMMY
> Okay, but please don't take to much off. I got an image to protect.

Mario now affectionately pushing him along.

> MARIO
> I give you an image. Come on.

EXT. MARIO AND THERESA'S APARTMENT - LATE DAY.

We see Vinnie's car pulling in front of the apartment. As they are getting out, Vinne's Uncle Louie, who is standing in front, comes over. He is the younger brother of Mario. Small, kind, cherub face, and well built. They embrace.

> LOUIE
> You've come home.

> VINNIE
> Yes, I'm home, I think.

> LOUIE
> Let me help you. I'm just doing nothing. LOUIE helps Vinnie, Karen, and the kids carry the luggage up to the apartment.

INT. MARIO'S BARERSHOP - MIDDAY

Mario is placing a barber's apron over Jimmy's jogging suit, and begins to cut his hair.

> MARIO
> Damn people. I can't believe I lost him because we were a minute late getting over here. My customers are spoiled.

> JIMMY
> You're right. Dad, did you see that piece on Marjorie in the "Star" last week?

> MARIO
> Yeah, and I didn't like it.

> JIMMY
> Why? It was great publicity for our production company.

> MARIO
> I just don't like it because they told the truth how you're after her money.

> JIMMY
> Hey, I was doing okay before I met her.

> MARIO
> Hell, what are you talking about? You didn't have a pot to piss in. You were selling goat's milk and seaweed when you met her.

> JIMMY

Getting angry
> That's not true! I was managing a health food store. And because of me it was making a lot of money!

MARIO stops cutting.

                MARIO
      But you still didn't have anything when you met her.

                JIMMY
      Well, I know I did but I'm not gonna fight with you on your anniversary. I don't care what you say.

Mario backs off.

                MARIO
      Don't be so sensitive or you'll end up like your brother.

                JIMMY
      I just don't like arguing.

                MARIO
      I'm not arguing, I'm just talking. A few years is okay to fool around, but it is more than twenty years and you still don't have a steady job.

                JIMMY
      You just don't understand.

                MARIO
      How long do you think her money will last? Get out of that business, Jimmy. It's a waste of time. You have such a good personality. You could have been selling computers for IBM, and you could be a millionaire by now. This country offers opportunities for people like you. Computer software is what to be in now. Think of how big Microsoft is.

                JIMMY
      I know.

MARIO takes the wallet out and forces some bills into Jimmy's hand.

                MARIO
      Take it.

JIMMY
No, I can't, Dad.

MARIO
Take it or I'll be mad. Show her you have your own money for the party tonight.

JIMMY
You'll get it back. I mean it, you will. In fact, Dad, how about making an investment in a movie project I have in mind. JIMMY puts the money in his pocket.

MARIO
Those types of things are for people who want to throw away their money. Ask your rich friends in Hollywod.

JIMMY
But I'm talking about making a movie out of a book Vinnie wrote. Before he went nuts, he sent me most of it written. It could be a big seller and a great movie. I mean it. The son-of-a-bitch has talent.

MARIO
Well, you talk to your brother, then I'll see. You're too free with my money. I still remember that time I gave you ten thousand dollars so you could start a record business, and then you ended up spending it on a party for the whole North End. You see what your brother says, then we'll talk. The things you kids did to me nobody will ever know.

JIMMY
But I've changed!

Mario laughs.

MARIO
The sun is green, too. We'll see. You talk to your brother like I said.

CUT TO:

INT. MARIO AND THERESA'S KITCHEN

THERESA opens the door with a plate of cookies in her hands as Vinnie and his family walk in. Marjorie is there. Louie is carrying the suitcases. They all hug and kiss.

                    THERESA
        You made good time.

Theresa placing cookies on the table.

                    VINNIE
    Yes.

                    THERESA
        And you, Louie? You're helping?

                    LOUIE
    Yes.

                    THERESA
        Let me introduce you to Jimmy's
        friend. Marjorie, this is my son
        Vinnie, his wife Karen, and their
        children Joey and Pam. And in back
        of them is my husband's brother,
        Louie.

ALL greet Marjorie by shaking her hand. Louie puts down the suitcases.

                    LOUIE
        I've enjoyed you on TV. You're
        good.

                    MARJORIE
        Thank you.

                    LOUIE
        Why they cut the program?

                    MARJORIE
        Not making enough money.

                    LOUIE
        That's America.

                    THERESA
        Louie, you eat?

Louie stares at Marjorie.

> LOUIE
> No, I can't. Concetta made some roasted peppers for me. Nice meeting you.

> MARJORIE
> Nice meeting you.

Louie leaves.

> LOUIE
> I'll see you tonight.

> THERESA
> Karen, sit down.

Karen obeys and Vinnie does the same.

> THERESA
> Vinnie, you want some lunch?

> VINNIE
> I'm not hungry, Mom.

> THERESA
> You kids want some cookies and milk?

> JOEY AND PAM
> Yes.

> THERESA
> Good.

THERESA heads for the refrigerator, gets the milk and hands some cookies to the kids.

> KAREN
> Are you ready for tonight?

Theresa pours the milk for the kids.

> THERESA
> I guess.

> JOEY
> Grandma, can we watch TV?

> THERESA
> Sure.

                    VINNIE
          Don't touch anything in there.

Children leave with cookies and glasses of milk and go into
the living room to watch TV.

                    THERESA
          Vinnie, how about some nice
          homemade soup?

                    VINNIE
          No, not now. Maybe later, Mom.

                    MARJORIE
          How's it feel to be home?

                    VINNIE
          Okay, I guess.

                    THERESA
          Please just have a little bowl. It
          will do you good. You look so pale.

THERESA moves to the stove and stirs the soup.

                    VINNIE
          Okay, I'll have a little. But just
          a little.

Theresa spoons some soup from a pot into a small bowl.

                    THERESA
          This is nice and hot.

THERESA brings the bowl and a spoon over to where Vinnie is
sitting.

                    THERESA
          You want a glass of milk?

VINNIE lights a cigarette.

                    VINNIE
          Okay, just a little glass.

MARJORIE gets up.

                    MARJORIE
          Well, I better get dressed. Jimmy
          and I still have some things to do
          for tonight.

                    THERESA
          I bet all of this planning for the
          party is too much for you.

Marjorie laughs.

                    MARJORIE
          No, I love it. My family was always
          having parties when I was younger.
          My mother would say having parties
          and going to wakes is what it means
          to be Italian. Really, the hotel is
          doing it all.

Theresa forces a laugh as she pours Vinnie a glass of milk.
Marjorie leaves.

                    KAREN
          She seems nice, real down to earth.

                    THERESA
          Yes, she is.

Theresa brings the glass of milk over to Vinnie along with
an ashtray.

                    THERESA
          You know you shouldn't smoke so
          much. It's just as bad as alcohol.

                    VINNIE
          I know.

                    THERESA
          Karen, you'll have some soup?

                    KAREN
          Thank you, it looks good. But I'm
          on a diet.

Karen hits her hips as she picks up a cookie from a plate on
the table. Theresa laughs nervously.

                    THERESA
          I should lose some too. Mario says
          I'm getting fat.

                    KAREN
          Stop it, I wish I'd look like you
          when I'm in my sixties.

                    THERESA
          You're not fat, just big-boned.

Theresa stirs the soup on the stove as she turns to Vinnie
                    THERESA
          Are you feeling better?

Vinnie gets up and starts walking toward the living room as
if in another world.
                    VINNIE
          Some days are better than others.

Theresa sits down and talks to his back.
          You watch tonight with everyone
          here, you'll forget all about your
          troubles. You think too much.

                                        DISSOLVE TO:

INT. BOILER ROOM - DAY

The camera moves in on a meeting Vinnie and Hannah are
having with Pete, Gary, Brandon, and Sherry. They are
sitting at school desks in a circle.
                    VINNIE
          Okay, what happened?

                    PETE
          He's stupid.

Brandon is crying.
          I just wanted to play with them. I
          love dodge ball.

                    VINNIE
          So, Pete, why couldn't he play?

                    PETE
          Because he doesn't know his ass
          from a hole in the ground.

                    HANNAH
          Please, Pete!

Pete and Sherry begin to laugh as they good-naturedly poke
each other. Vinnie angrily gets up.

VINNIE
Cool it!

Brandon is still crying.

BRANDON
All of you shit on me all the time.

Hannah taps him lovingly.
Bran, we'll work it out.

VINNIE
Okay, enough. Is there anything that you guys would be interested in? Anything? I'm lost.

PETE
Nothing.

VINNIE
Come on, there's got to be something you like doing.

HANNAH
Pete, I don't believe you're not interested in anything. You're always hanging around your Uncle Mike's garage.

PETE
I know, but it's not like school.

VINNIE
What do you mean?

PETE
It's fun with my Uncle.

GARY
We all like helping Mike get ready for the stock car races.

SHERRY
Yeah, I like it too. I feel free there, and grown up.

VINNIE
Okay, damn it; we'll get an old car.

GARY
My dad has an old '84 Chevy he'll give you.

                    HANNAH
          Tell him I'll be over with a tow
          truck to get it.

                    GARY
          It's really a piece of crap.

Hannah laughs.
          That's okay, I'm good at cleaning
          up crap.

They all laugh.

                              DISSOLVE TO

EXT. MARIO AND THERESA'S APARTMENT - EARLY AFTERNOON.

Toni, Vinnie's sister, who is in her mid thirties, small
bleached blonde and has angular features, runs into Vinnie
as he is walking across the street to his Dad's barbershop.
She is with her boyfriend, Neil. He is tall, dark, muscular,
and Jewish. Vinnie gives her a slight hug because she is so
fragile. Vinnie shakes hands with neil.

                    VINNIE
          Glad to meet you.

                    NEIL
          The same here.

                    TONI
          We're getting married next week.
          Neil's divorced and you know how
          old Mario feels about that.

                    VINNIE
Walking away.
          God, I don't know if I'll be able
          to handle all the joy that will be
          filling this house in the next few
          days.

                    TONI
          Where are you going?

                    VINNIE
          To see Ivan the Terrible.

                                    CUT TO

MARIO'S BARBERSHOP.

Mario is subdued, sitting in an empty barber chair. Vinnie comes in.

              VINNIE
     Hi, Dad.

Vinnie goes up to him and gives him a light kiss on the cheek. Mario seems upset and mad.

              MARIO
     Hi.

Mario gets up.

              MARIO
     I've only had one for almost the whole afternoon. You wanna haircut?

              VINNIE
     No, I just got one.

              MARIO
     You and your brother look like bums. Let me just touch up the back.

Vinnie gets into the barber chair.
     Okay.

Mario puts the barber apron around him.

              MARIO
     Are you working yet?

              VINNIE
     Not yet, maybe soon.

              MARIO
     You should have become a doctor, not a teacher.

              VINNIE
     I didn't want to. Where does money get you?

              MARIO
     Ahead, ahead of all those lazy son-of-a-bitches who know nothing about working for a living. Look at me, I worked until I became the best barber in the North End. When

MARIO
I first opened I would go from seven in the morning until twelve at night. I had better prices and I was good. Then almost everyone came to me. I would have had grocery stores, liquor stores, but because I can't do figures good this is what I had to do. When I think about how I had to live with my father leaving my mother in Italy with six kids, I don't know.

Chokes with emotion.
While he traveled all around in America so free his son had to beg for just a small cup of milk when I first came here. He came here and then would go back to Italy, get my mother pregnant, and leave again. Oh, God. You dream too much like him. And you're too good to everyone. You got to be a no-feeling bastard to make it in America or you'll end up in the gutter with all the other bums.

VINNIE
That's a good possibility.

MARIO
Not for you, I'm gonna get you all fixed up now that you're home. I'll get you straight.

VINNIE
I bet.

MARIO
I didn't have time before because I wanted to give you kids the best, the best clothes, the best education. But now I got time. I shoulda had a lot of the talks before when you were young.

VINNIE
You did.

MARIO
If I did, you never heard me.

                    VINNIE
          Yeah, right.

                                        DISSOLVE TO:

INT. MARIO AND THERESA'S LIVING ROOM - LATE AFTERNOON.

Vinnie walks in as Joey and Pam are fighting over the
remote. We can see Theresa working in the kitchen.

                    JOEY
          It's my turn.

                    PAM
          No, you had it last time.

The remote falls to the floor and it breaks.

                    JOEY
          Oh nuts! See what you made me do,
          pea-brain.

Vinnie looks over at the kids and then at Theresa.

                    VINNIE
          I really can't take him, mom. All I
          want is to be friends with him.

                    THERESA
          Let him be.

Fighting between Joey and Pam becomes louder and louder.
Vinnie sees the broken remote in Joey's hand. He goes over
and violently grabs it out of his hand. Joey begins to cry
loudly.

                    VINNIE
          Can't you kids do anything right?

                    THERESA

Yells.
          He lives in you too.

                    VINNIE
          I know.

Vinnie grabs Joey and hugs him tightly.

                                        CUT TO:

EXT. VINNIE ON COMMERCIAL WHARF IN THE NORTH END, BOSTON - NIGHT.

We see Vinnie standing at a railing overlooking the marina. He is in a trance-like state as he stares ahead. Coming into view, we see Jimmy jogging up to him. As Vinnie turns, Jimmy runs up to him and gives him a hug.

> JIMMY
> How are you doing? I'm glad you're home, buddie.

> VINNIE
> Thanks.

> JIMMY
> Are you feeling better?

> VINNIE
> I don't know.

> JIMMY
> I thought you Harvard types never got sick.

> VINNIE
> Right.

> JIMMY
> Hey, I read your Boiler Room School draft you sent me. I loved it.

> VINNIE
> Good. It's a rough draft. I still need to deal with the end because of the accident.

> JIMMY
> Well I think it will be a great movie regardless of the ending.

> VINNIE
> Emotionally, I just had to get it out.

> JIMMY
> Everyone loves seeing a story where someone is helping the poor kids. Ill work with you on the ending.

> VINNIE
> I don't need your help.

JIMMY
I might be full of shit, but I know what people want, especially seeing a teacher taking on a school system in Appalachia.

VINNIE
I don't know.

Jimmy angrily grabs Vinnie and shakes him.

JIMMY
Listen, I just want to show those assholes in Hollywood that a barber's son from the North End of Boston is just as good as them, and he's also got a Harvard education. He's no dummie.

Vinnie pulls away
We'll see.

Jimmy lets go. They walk together.

JIMMY
Every time I get home and he starts on me, it changes me.

VINNIE
Welcome to the Mario Fan Club.

They laugh.

JIMMY
Let's go over to Christy's and have a beer.

He hits his head with the palm of his hand.
Oh shit, I forgot.

VINNIE
Don't worry, I can handle one. I think.

DISSOLVE TO:

INT. BOILER ROOM - LATE AFTERNOON.

The kids (Pete, Gary, Brandon, Sherry, and about five other girls and boys from the Boiler Room) are working on an old Chevy in the back of the school. We see Vinnie, Hannah, Ben, and Jerry working with the kids. Vinnie is reading out of a large book.

> VINNIE
> Remove the parts cover and turn the flywheel in a counterclockwise direction until – Look, who knows what the flywheel is?

Pete is now pointing to something in the motor.

> PETE
> I do, here it is.

> VINNIE
> Great, now at position it says it should be "just" opening at fifteen thousandths of an inch. You're supposed to use that tool near Gary's hand.

Gary picks up a tool that looks like a small thin blade.

> VINNIE
> I guess that's it, Gary. Good. Now, do you know what fifteen thousandths of an inch is?

> GARY
> It has marks on each blade.

> VINNIE
> Yeah, good.

> BEN
> Okay, as the piston reaches the top of its travel on the compression stroke, an electric spark is featured at the spark plug. You all got it?

> VINNIE
> We're getting there, right guys?

> EVERYONE

Yells,
> Yeah!

Vinnie laughs.
> Now, let's see if you guys can get it started.

Pete gets in the car and tries to get it to start. After some false starts, it starts with huge puffs coming out from the exhaust pipe. Everyone is excited. They are all clapping.

                    VINNIE
          Great, now let me see what's
          happening in the boiler room.

Vinnie leaves, and Hannah follows.

                    HANNAH
          Damn it, I think you got their
          interest.

                    VINNIE
          Right.

                    HANNAH
          I hope we can sustain it now.

                    VINNIE
          We'll see. They will show us. We
          have to believe in them.

                    HANNAH
          Hey, let's get together at the
          Sunset Grill after school.

                    VINNIE
          Sounds good.

INT. BOILER ROOM - 10 MINUTES LATER

They now enter the Boiler Room. We see Jack and Jane working with the kids. The kids are at different learning stations around the room where different math, science, and language arts activities are using games of Monopoly, Password, Wheel of Fortune, cards, etc. Some students are standing around a snake in an aquarium. Another kid is listening to music on earphones and writing lyrics to the music. All the kids seem fully engaged with the learning stations. Still, we see Jack more interested in Jane than the kids as he stares at her.

A skinny red-headed student now comes running over to Vinnie and Hannah.
                    Mr. Serrano! Miss Nox said you
                    better come. Mister Masters is
                    paddling the hell out of Brandon.

Vinnie and Hannah run after the student as they head down the hall.

                                                  CUT TO:

INT. BOILER ROOM CLASSROOM

We see Jack Masters paddling the hell out of Brandon. Vinnie angrily runs over and grabs the paddle out of his hand, and then pushes him.

                    VINNIE
          What the hell are you doing?

                    JACK
          He deserved it. He was swearing. I
          had it with these kids swearing
          their asses off. Look, we're too
          soft on these kids. I would never
          have made it through Vietnam if I
          was undisciplined.

                    VINNIE
          Look, these kids are trying. That
          student you were paddling has been
          abused since he was two.

                    JACK
          I don't care. He's got to learn how
          to talk in this school.

                    VINNIE
          These kids need to be treated with
          respect and kindness, not paddling.

                    JACK
          That's a bunch of horse shit.

                    VINNIE
          Horse shit or not, next time we'll
          see who wins.

Jack begins to leave
          You better teach these kids how to
          talk or your program is done.

Vinnie is tightly hugging Brandon for a long moment.

                                        CUT TO:

INT. SUNSET INN - NIGHT

Vinnie, Hannah, Jane, Ben, and Jerry are sitting at a table in the Sunset Bar. The interior looks like the Cheers bar that ran on TV for so many years. They all have beers in front of them with a pitcher of beer in the center of the table. Sounds of sports games and rock music are in the background.

JANE
I can see why Masters did what he did.

VINNIE
Well, I can't.

JANE
I know, but sometimes these kids use language like fuck this, and that, and she's a bitch.... I mean I don't think you should talk like that in school.

VINNIE
I agree, but showing they got a rise out of you mean they'll only do it more. Ben I grew up like those kids, and that's how they talk.

JERRY
You just got to get them interested in something else. Hell, Jane, you have heard that language before.

JANE
Not where I grew up.

HANNAH
You mean in the suburbs you never heard the word fuck!

JANE
Yes, but...

VINNIE
Look, it's not about saying fuck or not fuck. Remember, many of these kids come out of homes where they heard that and lots more all the time. And lots of them are beaten up if they don't do what is asked of them. So remember if there are behavior problems that are disrupting the rights of others you either bring the problem to the group's attention and have them solve it, or confront the problem and identify the feelings the student has. And if you ever feel like letting a kid have it, leave the room until you gain your composure again, okay?

Everyone agrees as they pour more drinks.

INT. SUNSET BAR - LATER THAT NIGHT.

We see everyone getting up from the table as Vinnie motions he'll pay. Ben, Jerry, and Jane leave. Hannah stays.

>   HANNAH
>   You look like you're going to need
>   some help tonight.
>
>   VINNIE
>   I'll be fine. I sometimes drink a
>   little too much.
>
>   HANNAH
>   I heard.
>
>   VINNIE
>   So my reputation precedes me.
>
>   HANNAH
>   A little. My ex drinks a lot, but
>   unlike you, he got violent and
>   raped me.
>
>   VINNIE

Surprised,
>   What?
>
>   HANNAH
>   Three years ago.
>
>   VINNIE
>   How the heck could he rape you?
>
>   HANNAH
>   He did, but it's over, and what we
>   are doing with these kids is
>   helping me forget that asshole.
>
>   VINNIE
>   You know, sometimes I think I want
>   to get to know you better.
>
>   HANNAH
>   I know, I feel the same way. But
>   I'm still hurting from all the
>   stuff that went down with my ex.
>   And you're married. And from what
>   I've heard she's a good and kind
>   woman.

                    VINNIE
          She is, and I got two beautiful
          kids. I don't know, let's just see
          what happens.

                    HANNAH
          Yeah, it's probably best. But I
          want you to know if you want me to
          be your friend, I'll be your
          friend. If you want me to just hold
          your hand, I'll do that. But if you
          want me to be your lover, I can't.
          I need some clarity in my life now.
          You understand?

                    VINNIE
          Sure.

Hannah gets up and gives him a hug and a kiss on the cheek.
          You're a good man, Vinnie. Your
          wife is very lucky.

Vinnie laughs.

                    VINNIE
          Tell that to my father in Boston.

Hannah is confused.
          What?

                    VINNIE
          Never mind, just an inside joke.

                                              CUT TO:

EXT. OUTSIDE LIBERTY MIDDLE SCHOOL -NEXT MORNING.

We see the motor and its parts spread out on blue plastic.
Ben, Jerry, Hannah, and the motor pool gang are tagging the
parts with names. Vinnie walks over.

                    VINNIE
          God I hope you guys know what
          you're doing.

                    HANNAH
          We don't, but we're having fun,
          right guys?

They all agree.

                    HANNAH
          Sherry, pick up that piston and
          tell mister Serrano what it does on
          the exhaust stroke.

Sherry picks up the piston.
          Well, let's see, as this piston
          reaches the bottom of its strike,
          the exhaust valve opens. Now, as
          the piston moves up on the exhaust
          stroke, it forces the burned gasses
          out of the cylinder through
          something called the exhaust port.

                    BEN
          Wow! Jesus, you know your stuff,
          Sherry.

                    SHERRY
Giggles nervously.
          My brothers taught me

Sherry proudly goes on.
          Now, when the piston reaches the
          top of its travel, the exhaust
          valve closes and the intake valve
          opens. And the cycle repeats again
          with the intake stroke.

                    HANNAH
          Unreal. What to you think, Mister
          Serrano?

She gives Sherry a hug. Vinnie is a bit teary-eyed.

                    VINNIE
          God, I love you Sherry.

Vinnie also hugs her tightly.

                    PETE
          Hey, Mister Serrano, do you think
          if we get the car fixed we can race
          it? They have races at the dirt
          track every Sunday in Fairmont.

                    VINNIE
          Well, if you get the motor
          together. But none of you are old
          enough to drive. Who will race it?

                    PETE
          You will, man. We'll be your pit
          crew.

The kids and teachers root Pete on.

                    VINNIE
          Heck, I don't know anything about
          racing.

                    GARY
          We'll teach you. You'll be just
          like Jeff Gordon.

                    VINNIE
          Who?

                    GARY
          Jeff Gordon. He's one of the best
          NASCAR drivers today. My uncle
          Lloyd can help you, too. He
          sometimes races.

                    VINNIE
          Hannah, what do you think?

                    HANNAH
          I love it.

                    VINNIE
          Well, we'll see.

Everybody cheers.

                                                  CUT TO:

EXT: SCHOOL BUS COMING OUT OF LIBERTY TUNNEL PITTSBURGH - DAY.

Camera shows the kids looking out the bus windows as they move through the downtown area. The kids are in awe of the tall buildings and urban scene. We now see them getting off the bus in front of the Buhl Planetarium.

                                                  CUT TO:

INT. PLANETARIUM.

Camera shows Vinnie, Hannah, Ben, Jerry, and all the Boiler Room kids watching a film about the stars in a 360 degree theatre. We see Gary leaning over to Vinnie.

                GARY
You know, there's some small stars up there that you can't even see but they exist. You know a star is a sphere of gas held together by its own gravity. And you know the force of gravity is continually trying to cause the star to collapse but this is counteracted by the pressure of the gas...

                VINNIE
Interrupts.
Gary, how do you know that? What the heck?

                GARY
I've been watching a series on TV about stars and things.

                VINNIE
But everyone says you can't read.

                GARY
I can't, but I watch TV and learn.

                VINNIE
We will teach you how to read.

Hannah has been listening as Gary nods yes, whispering.

                HANNAH
They told me he was mentally retarded.

                VINNIE
I wonder how many others in today's schools have been misclassified. That's what they said about Einstein.

                                  DISSOLVE TO:

EXT. HEDGES IN FRONT OF VINNIE'S COLONIAL HOUSE IN WV -MIDDAY.

We see Vinnie in bathrobe and slippers following his father, Mario, as he trims the hedges.

              VINNIE
Dad, you didn't have to do that.

              MARIO
Be quiet. I don't sit around and do nothing all day like you.

              VINNIE
But you've come here to visit, not to work. I'll get to it once I get off these pills. I just can't get up the energy to do anything.

              MARIO
That's okay, you rest.

Mario clipping faster.
This place looks like a jungle. I just wonder what your neighbors think of you. At least now you can see some of your house. It will be respectable.

              VINNIE
I just haven't had the time the last few months, because of the Boiler Room, being sick, you know...

              MARIO
I understand. Why do you think I came to visit? Now you go in before you get sicker. How do you feel today?

              VINNIE
My headaches are not as bad in the mornings.

              MARIO
Did that hospital help you?

              VINNIE
I don't know. My doctor thinks it did, but what is he to say. He's on the staff there. He says I may need more that 20 days in rehab.

> MARIO
> Why did you have to work with those damn kids? The accident would never have happened.

> VINNIE
> It wasn't too much.

> MARIO
> You are both crazy, working with those kids. They don't appreciate it.

> VINNIE
> Dad, you don't understand.

> MARIO
> You're right, I don't understand. Almost killing yourself over some stupid kids. Just tell me why!

> VINNIE
> I believed in them.

> MARIO
> Believed in them?

> VINNIE
> I don't know, just believing in something is good.

Mario shows frustration.
> What the hell do you mean that you believe in something?

> VINNIE
> That I am worthwhile, and that those so-called stupid kids needed me more than anyone else did.

> MARIO
> Nuts to that! Your wife needs you, your kids need you, your mother needs you. And I need you to get well and stay well. So stop all that crap about feeling worthwhile and needed. You understand?

Vinnie forces a laugh.
> Let me do some.

Vinnie places his hands on the clippers.
> You look tired.

Mario moves the clippers away from Vinnie's hands.

                    MARIO
          No, you go in and rest I said.

                    VINNIE
          Please let me help. I need to turn
          my mind off for a while.

Vinnie takes the clippers away from Mario.

                    MARIO
          Okay, but do them even. You don't
          have to take too much off. Just a
          little of the new growth. Too much
          pruning, my grandmother used to
          say, will kill the plant, and
          that's not the way God wants it to
          grow. You understand?

Vinnie clipping at a fast pace.
          Yes, I do... yes, I do, Dad.

Mario points to a place on the hedge. Here, you missed here... Vinnie clips where Mario is pointing.

                    MARIO
          Good. Before I leave we'll have
          this piss-hole place fixed up and
          looking like a house again. Such a
          beautiful house and you had to let
          it go. It's sad.

Vinnie humors him
          Yes, it is sad.

                                  DISSOLVE TO:

INT. MARIO AND THERESA'S KITCHEN - NIGHT.

We see Toni taking a chair and motioning for Theresa to sit down. Toni is dressed in a very expensive dress. Toni begins to take curlers out of Theresa's hair.

                    TONI
          Mom, I really have to talk to Dad.

                  THERESA
          I was just saying, I just think he
          doesn't like how you have been
          living these last few years.

> TONI
> I know but it's because of him and his bitching is why I left.

> THERESA
> Try living with him every day and then listen to him bitch about this person, that person...

She is crying a little.

> TONI
> It's so depressing now to come home, Mom. I don't look forward to it at all anymore.

Theresa gains her composure.
> I don't know, maybe after Vinnie gets better he'll be happier. Toni, sometimes you forget and I forget how tough your father's life has been. Remember he came to this country when he was twelve with just five dollars in his pocket. His father was a lazy son of a bitch.

> TONI
> But Mom, you gotta start thinking of yourself. You can't live this way, always worrying about what you say so he won't blow up.

Theresa shrugs.
> We all have crosses to bear.

Toni gets angry and stands in front of Theresa.

> TONI
> You don't have to bear crosses for anyone, Mom! You should be only responsible for yourself! You understand?! Yourself!

> THERESA
> That's not true. He's my husband, and he's your father, and we must live with what God gives us. There's a lot of good in him. Look, things will get better when everything gets settled around here.

                    TONI
          Mom, I don't think it's going to be
          settled for a while. I'm getting
          married to Neil next week.

Theresa stands up with curlers half in and half out of her
hair.
          No, Toni, no. We got enough trouble
          with Vinnie now. My God, that's all
          your father needs to hear. It'll
          destroy him.

                    TONI
          I'm sorry, Mom.

                    THERESA
          You're not sorry! You're father's
          right! He's right! All you kids
          just think of yourselves! And he
          worries about you the most because
          you're not settled.

Theresa runs into the living room and sits on the sofa. Toni
follows.
          Mom, I don't want him or anyone to
          worry about me. I'm a big girl now.

                    THERESA
          Listen to her, she's a big girl
          now! You the Tinker Bell of toilet
          bowls? You who calls every time you
          have to go to the bathroom. You who
          calls when your left toe itches
          because you think it's some new
          disease. Oh God, I hate this
          arguing. Happy anniversary,
          Theresa!

                    TONI
          Mom, please don't make me feel
          guilty. I love Neil and he loves
          me.

Theresa works hard to control herself
          Whatever happened to that teacher
          you were going out with?

Toni sits on the coffee table across from Theresa.

                    TONI
          You mean Fagan?

> THERESA
> Yes, he seemed nice. What was wrong with him?

> TONI
> Everything. He had ulcers, colitis, high blood pressure, bad migraines. I know it's hard to believe, but he was more neurotic than me.

> THERESA
> What about the others? The doctor? And that Exxon salesman?

> TONI
> All bad.

> THERESA
> But isn't Neil divorced and Jewish? All he could give you is more troubles. Your kids would be Jewish.

Jimmy and Vinnie enter. They stagger a bit. You can sense they have been drinking.

> TONI
> Well, I told her about marrying Neil. One down, one to go.

> JIMMY
> I love the drama of it.

Vinnie sits down.
> Mom, it's her life. Let her live it the way she wants to.

Toni follows and sits across from Vinnie.

> THERESA
> Another one. One is worse than the other in this house. Well I'm not gonna think about it anymore. I'm gonna enjoy tonight if it kills me.

Vinnie pours himself a glass of wine from the bottle that is on the table and drinks some wine from his glass.

> JIMMY
> God, what a bunch of depressing people. I thought when I came home it would be your typical fun-loving Italian family. Kisses, pinching

JIMMY
cheeks, bear hugs, and all of that.
You know what I mean?

Jimmy goes over to Toni, and playfully hugs her.
Ah, my dear sister, what can I do
for you now before our dear father
comes dancing in. I'm perplexed.
Should I become your Friar Lawrence
or Tybalt, my dear sister?

TONI
Anything, just give me help. God,
my head feels like it's going to
explode.

VINNIE
Hold, daughter Toni: I do spy a
kind of hope, Which craves as
desperate an execution as that is
desperate which we would prevent.
If, rather than to marry Count Neil
Thou hast the strength of will to
stay thyself, Then it is likely
thou shalt undertake a think like
death to chide away. This shame,
That cop'st with death himself to
escape from it; And, if thou
dar'st, I'll give thee a remedy to
my dear sister.

Toni starts to laugh.
Will you stop, you're both crazy.

VINNIE
Call me what instrument you like,
dear sister, though you can fret
upon me, you cannot play upon me,
or upon my father.

Vinnie and jimmy laugh real hard. Toni becomes frightened.
Come on, Vinnie, please stop.

Vinnie, still laughing, holds up his glass.

VINNIE
And now to a happy prenuptial
affair and to the happiness your
parents will bestow on you.

CUT TO:

INT. ANNIVERSARY PARTY - NIGHT.

We see several people dancing to the "Tarantella" music. Jimmy is pulling on the hands of his mother and father. The party is held in a large ballroom of an opulent hotel in downtown Boston.

                  JIMMY
     Come on, Mom and Dad, dance! Mom,
     Dad, please, dance.

                  VINNIE
     Come on Mom, Dad, dance!

Couples now form a half circle around Mario and Theresa. Jimmy gentle pushes them into the center.

                  MARIO
     I doubt if an old man can do this
     anymore.

Theresa takes his hand.
     Do you remember this?

Theresa shows him a couple of steps as they begin to dance. The party group claps as they joyfully dance with energy. Jimmy and Marjorie join them. We see in the background Vinnie now forced by Karen to dance. Toni and Neil also join in. Jimmy motions everyone to be quiet, and stops the music.

                  JIMMY
     Mom and Dad, I know that all these
     years you both had a favorite song,
     and I also found out, Dad, that
     your mother sang this at your
     wedding fifty years ago.

The music begins and Marjorie sings the "Ave Maria." When she finishes, Mario and Theresa, with tears in their eyes, go up to her and kiss her. Mario then faces the party group.

                  MARIO
     I've been thinking what I could
     say. But after fifty years of
     marriage, all we could say is
     "thank you."

Theresa is crying as she goes around and kisses everyone. Everyone claps as the Tarantella music begins again. Vinnie mechanically claps as he watches Karen dancing with his Uncle Louie. Mario is dancing with Marjorie now. The music lowers as Jimmy leans over to Vinnie.

> JIMMY
> Look at my beautiful Marjorie over there. Wouldn't you like to have that beautiful lady next to you keeping you warm?

Vinnie shakes his head in disbelief.

> JIMMY
> I mean, wouldn't you like to fuck her? Wouldn't you?

> VINNIE
> Jesus, you're nuts.

> JIMMY
> So what? You're just like the Old Man and me. if there's a woman wanting and willing, you'll take care of her.

The dance stops and Marjorie comes over to them.

> JIMMY
> Well, brother, she's yours. Here she comes.

Looking at Marjorie
> Marjorie, take care of my poor lost brother, I want to see if the wine and food is holding out.

Jimmy joins the party. Marjorie approaches Vinnie and touches his arm, and gets close to him.

> MARJORIE
> Hi.

> VINNIE
> Hi.

> MARJORIE
> Jimmy gave me a couple of your plays and books of poetry to read, and you know, you're good.

> VINNIE
> I don't know about that.

> MARJORIE
> Well, you are. I would love to play the female lead in your book "Boiler Room School." Jimmy showed me the draft.

>   VINNIE
>   It's not done yet.
>
>   MARJORIE
>   I know, I wish we could find a
>   quieter place and talk more about
>   your thoughts on education. I
>   almost became a teacher before I
>   got into drama.
>
>   VINNIE
>   Sorry, I gotta find a bathroom. Too
>   much excitement, I guess.
>
>   MARJORIE
>   Just one more thing. You think...
>
>   VINNIE

Nervously,
>   Really, I must go. Do you know
>   where it is?

Marjorie is getting upset.
>   I think it's to the right and down
>   the hall.
>
>   VINNIE
>   Thanks.

                                                        CUT TO:

INT. ANNIVERSARY PARTY - LATER.

We see party goers still having a good time. Ties are loosened, jackets open, and dresses hang disheveled on bodies. The camera focuses on Mario and Louie, sitting and watching the dancers, especially Theresa, who is dancing with Jimmy.

>   LOUIE
>   You have good kids.
>
>   MARIO
>   I hardly know them anymore. It's
>   the mother who they're close to,
>   not me. I was always working.
>
>   LOUIE
>   You gave them a lot and look how
>   well they turned out.

Mario isn't listening, but is staring off into space.

                    MARIO
          Even the North End is a place I no
          longer know. All the Italians are
          moving out. Remember how it used to
          be the safest section in Boston?
          Now it's getting as bad as where
          the blacks live.

                    LOUIE
          I'd like to move to California.

                    MARIO
          Maybe that's where we should move.
          I'll find a little place near
          Jimmy. Then I'll get away from
          those big-mouth brothers of
          Theresa's.

                    LOUIE
          California is always sunny.

                    MARIO
          But the taxes and property are high
          there. Sometimes, Louie, I wish I
          went back to Italy. But some
          memories of sleeping on dirt
          floors, of working all the time,
          and of being poor...why should I go
          back?

                    LOUIE
          Mario, you don't know what you
          want. And then you complain about
          your kids being screwed up.

                    MARIO
          I know. I wonder how much they
          soaked Jimmy for this party.
          Everyone cheats you today.

                                        DISSOLVE TO:

EXT. LIBERTY MIDDLE SCHOOL PARKING LOT - LATE AFTERNOON.

We see Gary, Brandon, Pete, Sherry, along with Hannah and
the three teachers, pushing the car. Vinnie is inside,
steering. The car has been painted bright orange with a huge
#9 painted in black on its side.

                    VINNIE
          It's not starting.

> HANNAH
> Maybe we need someone who knows what's going on.

> VINNIE
> Maybe it's how we timed it.

> GARY
> My Uncle Lloyd can start anything.

> HANNAH
> Heck, call him. We need his help.

CUT TO:

EXT. PARKING LOT - LATER.

We see Gary's Uncle Lloyd with a huge body, good looking, and long blond hair approaching Vinnie and the others as they are looking at the motor. They all seem frustrated.

> LLOYD
> The motor is not going to start by looking at it.

They laugh as Lloyd begins to work on the motor, then looks up.

> Gary tells me you're going to race on Sunday.

> VINNIE
> I guess.

> LLOYD
> You know anything about racing?

> VINNIE
> Nope.

> LLOYD

Shakes his head in disbelief.
> Get in and try now.

Vinnie gets in and it starts. Everyone yells with excitement.

> LLOYD
> Look, professor, I'll be there Sunday if you want my help.

                    VINNIE
          I'll need it.

                    LLOYD
          Well, Gary tells me how much he
          likes you, so I guess I can give
          back a little.

He leaves as Vinnie high fives Hannah and the others.

                                                  CUT TO:

EXT. LIBERTY MIDDLE SCHOOL - LATE NIGHT.

We see Hannah sitting on a bench near the front door. She's
smoking a cigarette. Vinnie drives up, hurriedly gets out,
and goes over to her.

                    VINNIE
          I got your voicemail. You okay?

Hannah looks beaten with bruises with blood all over her
face.

                    HANNAH
          My ex came over and started to beat
          on me and my son.

Vinnie moves closer and moves her face into the light. It's
bruised and bloody.

                    VINNIE
          Jesus, let's go to the hospital.

                    HANNAH
          I'll be okay.

                    VINNIE
          At least call the police.

                    HANNAH
          He's a former cop.

Vinnie takes out his handkerchief and wipes the blood from
the bottom of her nose.

                    VINNIE
          Unreal.

                    HANNAH
          I dropped my son over at my Mom's
          and I just had to get away.

> VINNIE
> What are you going to do about him?
> How's your son?

> HANNAH
> Okay, he didn't touch him, just me.
> Sometimes I can't blame him because
> his father beat the hell out of him
> all the time.

> VINNIE
> But that doesn't make it right.

> HANNAH
> I know. I'm stuck. My teaching
> salary is not enough, and I need
> his child support to get by.

She cries and Vinnie brings her closer.

> VINNIE
> I'm here as a friend even though
> sometimes it can be more.

Vinnie brings her in close as he lightly kisses her lips. She pulls away.

> HANNAH
> But it's not worth the pain
> afterwards.

> VINNIE
> I agree.

He brings her in closely again as the camera pulls away.

> CUT TO:

INT. BOILER ROOM - MORNING.

We see Vinnie working with a group of students. He is showing them how to order from a catalog.

> VINNIE
> Now, once the order is done, you
> gotta add the items you have.
> Sherry, you help me add.

> SHERRY
> Okay, you got $5.69, $10.50, and
> let's see... $20.10, and that gives
> you... $36.29. Jesus, I can do it!

Vinnie high fives her.

> **VINNIE**
> Great! You sure can.

Mister Masters comes in, and asks to see Vinnie outside the Boiler Room. He's angry.

> **MASTERS**
> I hear you're going to race this Sunday with the kids.

> **VINNIE**
> Yeah.

> **MASTERS**
> You can't use the kids because it's not a school-sponsored activity.

> **VINNIE**
> You gotta be kidding.

> **MASTERS**
> No, it's school policy. If something would happen, we could be sued. It's not a school day. Do you have a sponsor?

> **VINNIE**
> I'll take responsibility. I'll also get some sponsors.

> **MASTERS**
> Shit. I'm already in a lot of trouble because of this program. Teachers are getting upset because you take the kids out of the building all of the time.

> **VINNIE**
> Well, maybe they should try it also.

> **MASTERS**
> Look, Vinnie, I'm telling you, you better not be involved Sunday. And that's it!

CUT TO:

EXT. I-79 RACEWAY - SUNDAY AFTERNOON.

From above, we see a small dirt racetrack with older cars racing around the track as they get ready for the race to begin. The atmosphere is festive and similar to a large tailgate party before a football game at the University. We now see the Boiler Room kids, Pete, Gary, Brandon, Sherry, Hannah, and Lloyd, working on their car. We see painted on the car "Lloyd's Garage" and "Smith's Funeral Home". Lloyd is tinkering with the motor as the kids and Hannah look on. Jane, Jack, Ben, and Jerry, are there also.

>   HANNAH
>   Look, I'm starting to get worried
>   about Vinnie. Did you guys tell him
>   it started at two?

>   GARY
>   Yes, he'll be here. I just hope
>   he's sober.

Lloyd raises his head.

>   LLOYD
>   What?

>   HANNAH
>   He drinks a little too much because
>   I think he hates his job at the
>   University, and there are some
>   other demons he's dealing with... I
>   don't know.

>   LLOYD
>   Too bad, I like him.

We now see Vinnie approaching. He is staggering a bit. He has sunglasses on, and his clothes look like he slept in them. He tries to straighten them.

>   HANNAH
>   You okay?

>   VINNIE
>   Yeah.

>   HANNAH
>   You sure?

>   VINNIE

Angrily
>   I'm fine.

Vinnie takes the racing helmet from Gary and then struggles to get into the car from the window.

                LLOYD
        Look, the clutch needs double
        clutching sometimes when you are
        shifting down. This baby should do
        100 or more with the new cam I put
        in.

                VINNIE
        I'm ready.

Vinnie revs the car.

                LLOYD
        Remember, it's 100 laps and after
        about forty laps come in and we'll
        check you out. These guys and girls
        are your pit crew.

Vinnie waves and he pulls up to where all the other cars are getting started. A black, sleek-looking car pulls up next to him. The racecar driver looks mean and dirty. He looks at him.

                RACECAR DRIVER
        Hey, asshole. Are you the one
        fooling around with my wife?

                VINNIE
        Screw you.

The flag comes down and they are off. Vinnie is way behind as he seems confused and still trying to shake off a major drunk from the night before. Hannah's ex bumps him and bumps and yells at him.

                HANNAH'S EX
        Go back to Boston, Yankee. This is
        a man's world here. You dumbass.

Vinnie seems to come to his senses as he now begins to race seriously and starts to pass some cars. After a while, we see his pit crew yelling for him to pull in, but he doesn't see them. Finally he does, and at the same time Hannah's ex sideswipes him as he comes toward the pit with a frantic look on his face. We see him trying the brakes but there are no brakes as he swirls into the pit. Everyone gets out of the way except Hannah, and we see her body bouncing off the front of the car.

                                            DISSOLVE TO:

INT. MARIO AND THERESA'S ANNIVERSARY PARTY - LATE.

Vinnie is drinking at the bar. He is alone as we see party guests saying goodbyes. He seems in a daze. Karen, his wife, approaches him.

          KAREN
I haven't seen you all night. Are you doing okay?

          VINNIE
Yes

          KAREN
You seem distant again.

          VINNIE
I'm sorry.

          KAREN
I wish you could turn that mind of yours off.

          VINNIE
So do I.

          KAREN
Please talk to me, Vinnie.

          VINNIE
I am.

          KAREN
I thought we had things all worked out.

          VINNIE
We did. Don't worry, I'm fine.

          KAREN
Vinnie, you're not slipping off into that world of yours again, are you? You've been so great to me and the kids these last few weeks, especially after the accident.

She kisses him on the cheek.

          VINNIE
Please don't worry, it's just that I feel so alone sometimes.

                    KAREN
            Just stay close, Vinnie.

                    VINNIE
            I'll try.

                                            CUT TO:

INT. MARIO AND THERESA'S LIVING ROOM - NEXT DAY.

We see Vinnie's Aunt Concetta entering. She is an overweight Sophia Loren. She is Theresa's sister, and Louie's wife. Vinnie is asleep on the soda. Pam and Joey are watching TV, and Theresa is in the kitchen cooking.

                    CONCETTA
            Hi, kids, what are you doing?

                    JOEY
            Looking at TV.

                    CONCETTA
            That's nice.

Concetta, looking at Vinnie.
            Your father is tired, huh?

Pam continues to watch TV
            Yeah.

Concetta goes into the kitchen, and gestures back at Vinnie on the sofa.
            Is that where Vinnie slept last
            night?

Theresa starts to set plates on the table.

                    THERESA
            I think so. He went out for a walk
            after we got home last night. Is
            Neil at your place still?

                    CONCETTA
            I think I heard him getting up just
            before I left to come over here.

                    THERESA
            You like him.

Concetta pours herself some coffee and sits down.
            He seems like a nice Jewish boy. A
            little quiet. How serious is Toni
            with him?

> THERESA
> Serious.

Mario enters the kitchen area from outside.

> THERESA
> Why are you home so early? It's only four.

> MARIO
> Why stay?

Mario sits down.

> CONCETTA
> Hello, Mario.

> MARIO
> Hello.

> THERESA
> Maybe it will be better next week.

> CONCETTA
> Well, Mario, you gonna quit now?

> MARIO
> Why?

> CONCETTA
> Because it's time for you and Tree to spend all the millions you saved. You could go visit your kids now.

Mario is sarcastic.
> Yeah, sure, millions. You go visit your kids.

> CONCETTA
> They all live here, remember? And they're sick of seeing me.

> MARIO
> I can't see why?

> THERESA
> Mario, that's not nice.

Concetta gets up.
> I better go.

> THERESA
> Why don't you stay? We're having an early supper.

> CONCETTA
> I can't. My supper is on too.

> THERESA
> You sure? At least have a little with us.

Mario gets up and goes to the kitchen window. Concetta starts to leave.
> I can't.

Concetta looks at Mario.
> Have a good supper, Mario.

Mario looks out of the kitchen window.
> Yeah, I think I hear Louie calling you.

> CONCETTA
> See you, Tree. I'll be by tomorrow.

> THERESA
> Why did you have to be so mean to her? God, you give me one night of being nice, and now I'll probably have to pay for it for the rest of my life. And why are you looking out the window? You're not going back to the shop, are you?

Mario rubs his eyes.

> MARIO
> I'm tired as hell, Tree. I just didn't feel like working today. That's really why I came home. I tried, but I can't keep looking for business.

> THERESA
> You can't go on like this, Mario. Why don't you go rest?

> MARIO
> I can't... you know John Rossi?

> THERESA
> Yes.

MARIO
He came in for a haircut today.
I've known him for at least thirty
years. But all the while he was
there, I couldn't think of his
name.

Mario is frightened.
Not even his first name. And, God,
I used to play bocci with him all
the time.

Mario is trembling, and Theresa comforts him by going over
and giving him a loving hug.

THERESA
Sometimes, we all forget. That's
nothing, don't worry about it. But
it's time to stop that job now. You
understand?

Mario chokes with emotion.
I'll miss the people and knowing
what's happening in the North End.
I don't care about cutting hair,
it's the people I need.

He regains his composure.
Where are my wonderful children?

THERESA
Well, you could see Vinnie is still
sleeping on the couch. Everyone
slept almost until now. Jimmy and
Marjorie went running after they
got up, and now they're changing
their clothes. Toni and Karen are
cleaning the bathroom. Someone left
hair all over the place.

MARIO
That's good for Karen. Maybe she'll
clean her house now. What a pigpen
she has.

THERESA
Stop it, she's got kids to take
care of. And her house is not
dirty.

DISSOLVE TO:

INT. MARIO AND THERESA'S KITCHEN - TWILIGHT.

The family is seated and they begin to pass around the spaghetti and meatballs. Neil and Toni sit next to each other. Jimmy sits next to Toni with Marjorie sitting across from him. Karen sits across from Vinnie. Pam and Joey sit at the end. Mario sits at the head with Theresa on his left. Everyone is talking at the same time and at times, loudly.

     MARIO
Mangia adesso, Marjorie.
 (Now eat, Marjorie)

     MARJORIE
Si, grazie, la mia dieta va al inferno per stasere.
 ((I will, thank you. The hell with my diet tonight.)

     MARIO
Right, forget the diet. This is good food, not the crap you people normally eat. And you know what, you're a pretty woman without a diet.

     MARJORIE
Thank you, you're a good-looking man yourself.

     JIMMY
Marjorie, remember that party in San Pedro last week? I wish Dad could have seen all that food, even though the hostess was a little weird. Here she is greeting us at the door with only rhinestone-framed glasses on, nothing else...totally nude.

Laughs uncontrollably

     MARIO
And this is your friend?

     JIMMY
No, just a person you got to mingle with so you can make deals. It's all deals out there, and who you know.

>   MARIO
> Have you talked to your brother
> about your plans for him?

>   JIMMY
> Sort of.

Mario looking at Vinnie.
> Whatya think?

No answer.

>   THERESA
> Vinnie, your father is talking to
> you.

>   VINNIE
> What?

>   MARIO
> I wanna know what you think of
> Jimmy's plan to make a movie out of
> that thing you did with the kids.

>   VINNIE
> I don't know.

>   MARIO
> Jimmy, did you tell him he could
> become rich like you, even though
> you want my money?

>   JIMMY
> That's not what I said, Dad, I
> said...

Theresa interrupts.
> Let's not start. Please eat,
> everyone. There's a lot here.
> Vinnie, have something to eat.

>   VINNIE
> I'm not hungry.

>   KAREN
> Are you okay?

>   VINNIE
> Yes, just a little tired.

>   KAREN
> What time did you get in?

VINNIE
I don't know.

NEIL
Vin, Toni told me about what you did with those kids in West Virginia. Would you like to do it again?

VINNIE
Perhaps...

NEIL
I bet they would love to get you back. I tell you there's just not a lot of good teachers around who care and can teach.

VINNIE
I'm thinking about it.

NEIL
When I think back at some of the teachers I had, I don't know how I got through.

TONI
I'm sorry, Neil, I can't wait any longer. Dad?

MARIO
Yeah?

TONI
I got some good news for you.

MARIO
Now what?

THERESA
Toni, I said wait. Not now.

TONI
Neil and I are getting married next week.

Neil gets up and faces Mario.
I love your daughter very much, Mister Serrano.

MARIO
What do you do?

                    NEIL
          I'm a lawyer.

                    MARIO
          Not a good profession to be in now.
          Too many lawyers.

                    NEIL
          I know, Mister Serrano, I want to
          be quite honest with you.

                    MARIO
          You like politics? I love politics.

                    NEIL
Nervously and scared.
          No, but I want to tell you I'm
          married, I mean divorced, and I
          have two kids.

                    MARIO
          I'm sorry to hear that, because she
          knows my feelings about divorced
          men. I won't allow it. Period.
          Jewish people getting divorced...
          you're Jewish, right?

Toni gets up as Neil sits down.
          I don't care what you say, Dad. I
          did want your approval, but if I
          can't get it, I'm sorry. This is
          the twentieth century, not the
          middle ages! I'm still getting
          married.

                    THERESA
          Maybe, Mario, I don't know, but
          maybe things will work out. Give
          her your approval.

Mario gets up, angry now.
          Work out, my ass!

                    VINNIE
          Dad, she'll be okay. Don't worry.

Depressed, Toni sits down.

                    MARIO
          That girl in the accident.... Is
          that a girlfriend of yours?

Smiles sarcastically.

                    THERESA
          Oh my God, you talk so stupid
          sometimes.

                    MARIO
          Yeah, we'll see, everything I say
          comes out true. You wait and see.
          And now we have Toni, who will be
          calling home because he took off
          with all the money I give her and
          she'll be left with his kids.

He looks back at Vinnie.

                    MARIO
          Why the hell are you drinking?

                    VINNIE
          I just needed a little to relax. I
          was tense.

                    MARIO
          Hell, I don't know what from.
          Professors don't work, all they do
          is talk. That isn't work. All of
          you kids just need a good kick in
          the ass. I should get the razor
          strap out.

Vinnie gives a toast.
          To razor straps, Dad! That's what
          we're all about!

                    MARIO
          You know I hate to admit it, but
          you're crazy. Why, God, why does my
          son have to talk crazy?

                    VINNIE
          Because it helps me forget.

                    MARIO
          Forget what?

                    VINNIE
          This world. Mario I can't talk to
          you anymore.

                    VINNIE
          We never have. It's you who talks,
          I just listen.

                    THERESA
          Mario, please for my sake try to
          get along tonight. Vinnie, you stop
          too.

Mario sits down.

                    MARIO
          Okay, let's see if we can talk with
          each other. I want the others to
          hear this. You know I always
          dreamed and hoped that someday
          maybe you would come back here to
          Boston and take over for me. I
          mean, I thought maybe one day you
          would see that writing and teaching
          will get you nowhere in this world.
          And with the money I have and your
          head we could own half the North
          End if you buy property and invest
          my money with smarts.

                    JIMMY
          I could do that for you, Dad.

                    MARIO
          Jimmy, I'm sorry, but you just
          don't have the business sense and
          head to make it. Your brother has
          it but won't use it. That's the
          problem. He would rather be
          depressed and a drunk instead of
          making money. If he didn't work
          with those hillbilly kids, that
          accident wouldn't have happened.
          Right, Vinnie?

Vinnie raises his glass.

                    VINNIE
          Right, Mario.

                    MARIO
          You don't see that if you had a lot
          of money you could do whatever you
          wanted.

                    VINNIE
          I guess not.

                    MARIO
          You mocking me?

> VINNIE
> No sir.

> MARIO
> God, I hate seeing my son like this. I can't understand it. Brains, a Harvard education... a drunk.

Vinnie angrily goes toward him. Mario is boiling over with anger as he stands up.
> Son, you're a crazy son of a bitch.

Theresa gets up, crying, and pushes Mario down in his seat.

> THERESA
> Mario, forget Vinnie. It's Toni we have to worry about now!

Mario looks at Neil and takes a long pause.

> MARIO
> I still don't like it, but if that's what my daughter wants and she loves you, you got my permission. Treat her good.

Neil shakes Mario's hand excitedly as Toni gets up and gives Mario a kiss.

> NEIL
> Thank you sir.

> THERESA
> You see how we are, Neil, in this house. We do this every day. One minute we're killing each other, the next we're throwing roses at each other. That's how it is.

> TONI
> It's crazy, but I love them. Thank you again, Dad.

Toni gives Mario another kiss as Vinnie begins to leave.

> THERESA
> Where are you going, Vinnie? You still haven't eaten anything.

> VINNIE
> I like sunsets.

                    THERESA
            Oh, I see.

Karen gets up.
            Do you want me to come?

                    VINNIE
            No, I just really like this time of
            day. Really, go ahead and eat and
            enjoy yourselves. I'm fine... Mom,
            why are you always cleaning?

Karen sits down.

                    THERESA
            Why do you ask that now?

                    VINNIE
            I just want to know. Please tell
            me, just tell me.

                    THERESA
            What else is there to do?

                    VINNIE
            I don't know, but there's got to be
            more to life than cleaning.

Mario gets up.

                    MARIO
            I haven't finished talking to you.

Vinnie abruptly turns around.

                    VINNIE
            I've finished talking to you.

                    MARIO
            It's a time to be happy. Your
            sister is getting married.

                    VINNIE
            I'm happy for her, but I'm sick of
            the lies that exist among us in
            this family. And being happy in
            this house is one of the biggest
            lies.

Mario sits down.

                    MARIO
          I don't care, go, go!... Tree, he's
          not my son anymore. You can have
          him. I thought when -

                    VINNIE
          Hi, ho, Mario! Hi, ho!

Vinnie gallops around the living room, as if he's on a
horse, and leaves.

                    VINNIE
          Hi ho, Mario!

Joey and Pam laugh.

                    KAREN
          Joey! Pam! Stop!

                                                    CUT TO:

EXT, COMMERCIAL WHARF - LATE NIGHT.

We see Vinnie sitting on the edge of the docks. He is
fishing. We also see his Uncle Louie approaching.

                    LOUIE
          I knew you would be here. Your
          mother called and told me what
          happened. Where did you get the
          pole?

Vinnie smiles.
          I bought it from a kid. Damn, Uncle
          Louie. I've missed this.

Looking up.
          Look at that moon tonight, Uncle
          Louie, pure as snow.

                    LOUIE
          Yes, it is beautiful. They say in
          Italian, "le raggi della luna
          passano nella tua vita e dolcemente
          toccaro la tua anima" which means
          in so many words that the moon
          beams go through your body and
          gently rub your soul.

                    VINNIE
          Beautiful. Hey, look at the line
          move. Maybe I have one, huh?

                    LOUIE
Touches Vinnie's shoulder.
          Yeah, maybe. They say there's sea
          bass here. What the hell is wrong?
          You look so pale.

                    VINNIE
          Nothing.

                    LOUIE
          It's not right, almost a sin. You
          are still young, you need to learn
          how to enjoy life. Too much is too
          much. Why don't you stay here a few
          weeks? Maybe you and maybe even
          your father will go fishing with
          us. Then you'll have a good rest.

Vinnie gets up.

                    VINNIE
          We'll see. But come with me to
          another dock. I want to walk.

Louie follows.

                    LOUIE
          I can't because your Aunt Concetta
          needs me to walk her home from a
          bingo game. It's only two or three
          houses down, but she thinks every
          man in the North End wants to rape
          her. But I'll come back if you want
          me to.

                    VINNIE
          No, I'm doing fine. I'll see you
          tomorrow.

                    LOUIE
          Are you sure?

                    VINNIE
          Yes, thanks.

                    LOUIE
          Take care, Vinnie, and remember to
          relax and be happy.

Louie starts to leave.

                    VINNIE
          I'll try. Uncle Louie, can I ask
          you just one favor before you go?

                    LOUIE
          Sure.

                    VINNIE
          Would you mind walking with me a
          little bit more and singing that
          aria from "Don Giovanni" that you
          always used to sing when you came
          fishing with us?

                    LOUIE
          My voice, Vin, is now an old man's
          voice.

                    VINNIE
          I don't care. I won't notice.

                    LOUIE
          Okay, for my favorite nephew, I'll
          try.

As they walk beside the docks, he sings a small aria from
Act I of Don Giovanni. At the same time, it gets darker as
the light from the moon shines on them.

                    LOUIE
          Oh che caro galantuomo! Voi star
          dentro colla bella, ed io far la
          sentinella, la sentinella, la
          sentinella. Voglio far il
          gentiluomo e von vogli piu servir,
          e no voglio piu servir, no, no, no,
          no, no, no, no, non voglio piu
          servir.
                    (Oh that dear gentleman! It's
                    for you to stay inside with
                    the pretty lady, and for me to
                    play the sentinel, the
                    sentinel, the sentinel! I want
                    to be a gentleman, and I don't
                    want to serve any longer, and
                    I don't want to serve any
                    longer, no, no, no, no, no, I
                    don't want to serve any
                    longer.)

                                                  CUT TO:

INT. JIMMY AND MARJORIE'S BEDROOM - LATE NIGHT.

We see Jimmy in bed as Marjorie sits on the edge of the bed. Jimmy is stroking her hair.

                    JIMMY
I'm sorry, I just can't. You saw my father tonight.

                    MARJORIE
But we don't have time. We have bank notes due next week, remember?

                    JIMMY
Maybe I could get more money on the residues yours getting from reruns. Also, Ashley at Fox owes me a couple favors. I'll see if he can help us.

                    MARJORIE
Jimmy, I can't depend on that. I trusted you with my money and all I know is that now we're on the brink of bankruptcy. I'm too fragile a person to start over again. That's why I called Gene tonight, I told him if this certain deal you were working on didn't go through, I would be in New York tomorrow to start rehearsals on that new sitcom.

                    JIMMY
Well at least let me see what Ashley will do for us? I want people to see you as a serious actress. Not one just delivering jokes.

                    MARJORIE
I don't care what you do with Ashley. But right now I'm going out to see if Vinnie is back.

                    JIMMY
I think you better forget it with him. Really, Marj, I don't think he could handle any more.

                    MARJORIE
You know, your brother and me have a lot more in common than you think.

                    JIMMY
          Why?

Marjorie turns around and shows him a long scar on her
wrist.

                    MARJORIE
          There was a time when I was just
          starting off as an actress and I
          just couldn't take all those
          rejections, and then on top of that
          living all alone in New York. It
          was just too much. So one night I
          tried with a razor blade.

                    JIMMY
          I thought that was a bike accident.

                    MARJORIE
          I lied.

                    JIMMY
          Damn you!

                    MARJORIE
          So you could see I've also known
          deep depression.

                    JIMMY
          Still, I don't want you to go out
          there. He's my brother, and I just
          can't stand to see him like this.
          My heart went out to him tonight,
          even though my fucking father
          favors him.

                    MARJORIE
          Well, should I tell Vinnie about
          your recent little problem?

                    JIMMY
          Come on, Marj, that's not fair.
          Everyone goes through that at my
          age.

                    MARJORIE
          But not Jimmy Serrano, the
          so-called perfect stud of
          Hollywood.

Jimmy yells as she leaves
          You whore!

                                             CUT TO:

INT. MARIO AND THERESA'S KITCHEN - LATE NIGHT.

We see Marjorie approaching as Vinnie sits at the kitchen table drinking wine.

          MARJORIE
You were out a while.

Vinnie seems to be in a trance.
I guess.

          MARJORIE
Your wife waited up, but got tired and went to bed. She's sweet. What does she think of your writing?

          VINNIE
She hasn't read any of it.

          MARJORIE
I don't believe it.

          VINNIE
She hasn't. She falls asleep as soon as she reads a page.

          MARJORIE
Wow, that's hard to believe... Vinnie, what are you thinking of now?

          VINNIE
Not much.

Marjorie sits across from him.

          MARJORIE
Tell me, I'm interested.

          VINNIE
That the more I try to get close to people, the more I know I can't. And perhaps the real truth is that I don't care anymore.

          MARJORIE
Why?

          VINNIE
Because there is very little depth to any of us in this world. We pretend there is, but there isn't. Our destiny in this world is only

                    VINNIE
          to adjust to the expectations of
          others, so that now I can only
          write words that are empty and
          meaningless.

                    MARJORIE
          You're a good writer, Vinnie, and
          you do expose some hard truths. I
          especially like your book, "A New
          Universe."

                    VINNIE
          You know, I forgot what I even
          wrote in that book.

Vinnie looks at the bottle of wine on the table.

                    MARJORIE
          I think your problem is that you're
          burned out. Jimmy said that you
          wrote seven books and articles in
          six years, and then just stopped.
          Is that why you worked with those
          poor kids in Appalachia?

                    VINNIE
          I don't know.

Vinnie pours himself another drink from the bottle, Marjorie moves her chair closer to him.

                    MARJORIE
          Vinnie, I know this is all wrong,
          but I felt something good inside
          when I first met you at the party.
          I know it's wrong because I do love
          Jimmy, but there's something in you
          that makes me want to touch you.
          Those eyes are so tragic and yet so
          soft.

Vinnie says nothing. Marjorie moves closer.

                    MARJORIE
          I want to touch you, Vinnie.

                    VINNIE
          You can.

She rubs his face, his hair, and his body. Then she leads him to the living room. They drop onto the sofa as she kisses Vinnie. After a long moment, he pushes off her and sits up. Marjorie reaches over to him as he covers his eyes with his hands. She strikes his arm.

>MARJORIE
>Can I help you?

Vinnie pushes her hand away.

>VINNIE
>Please go, please.

Marjorie puts her hand on his stomach.

>VINNIE
>Damn it, please go, go! I just can't!

DISSOLVE TO:

INT MARIO AND THERESA'S APARTMENT - EARLY MORNING.

We see Vinnie leaving with Joey and Pam with Karen following. They are carrying their suitcases toward their car.

>JOEY
>Can we go fishing tomorrow when we get back to West Virginia?

>VINNIE
>Sure. In fact, I already have a pole.

>JOEY
>You're not just saying that, like other times?

Vinnie grabs Joey and Pam and kisses them.

>VINNIE
>This time, you both will have my time.

Vinnie looks at Karen.
>You too, I love you.

>KAREN
>I love you, too.

                    VINNIE
          Let's go! One crazy has been freed
          from the asylum.

They hug, get in the car, and drive off. From above, we have
a shot as we see Vinnie's car moving with others along the
flow of traffic.

                                        DISSOLVE TO:

INT. HANNAH'S HOUSE -DAY

We see Vinnie entering with a bounce in his step. He's
smiling. Lloyd is there. Her head is bandaged and she has a
cast on an arm and a leg. Vinnie comes over to the side of
the sofa she is lying on.

                    VINNIE
          God, I'm sorry, so sorry.

                    HANNAH
          I'm gonna live.

                    VINNIE
          What can I do?

                    HANNAH
          Just get yourself clean from those
          demons in the bottle. I want you
          back with me and the kids. And
          don't worry, I'm not suing. Masters
          was fired because he paddled about
          sixty kids after you left. How was
          your trip to Boston?

                    VINNIE
          I'm better here than there. I need
          you and the kids. We got in
          yesterday and I went to a local AA
          meeting last night. No more
          drinking, I want to live and I need
          to stop blaming my family,
          especially my father. I need a
          fresh start with you and the kids.
          We know the program works, we just
          have to keep working with students
          who are looking to flip the
          education system. Kids and their
          parents come first now. You all are
          part of my recovery.

LLOYD
Great! Hannah conned me so that
I'll be teaching about cars. So I
am with you now. And I don't think
her ex will ever bother her again.

VINNIE
What happened?

LLOYD
His ass is in jail for what he did
to her the other night, and also we
have on tape how he ran into you.

VINNIE
Yeah, but if I was sober I could
have reacted faster.

LLOYD
Look, it's over, like Hannah said.

Hannah smiles

HANNAH
My friend, I look forward to
working with you.

CUT TO:

INT MARIO AND THERESA'S APARTMENT KITCHEN - DAY.

We see Toni, Neil, Jimmy, Louie, Concetta, Mario, and
Theresa sitting around the table eating. Theresa and Toni
are jumping up and down getting food from the stove.

JIMMY
I'm sorry Vinnie is not here. He
really would like this family thing
we're doing. I wish I could've seen
him before he left.

TONI
Well, I think he will be happier to
be in West Virginia.

Mario shakes his head.

MARIO
He could have so much here. You
educate your children and they
leave you.

              THERESA
Don't say that, he'll be back.

              LOUIE
Mario, just let him be.

              THERESA
Right. Now everyone eat. There's a lot of food. Jimmy, how's the sauce?

              JIMMY
Mom, you're the best.

              CONCETTA
Tree, you are a great cook.

Theresa gets up, goes to the stove, and comes back and gives everyone more food. As the credits roll, the *Tarantella* music plays in the background.

                                              FADE OUT...

THE COMEBACK
A SCREENPLAY

After losing his famed throwing arm from the elbow down, David, a cocky all-star high school quarterback, tries to return to the game he loves on his own terms and realizes what's most precious in life. His father wants him to succeed because, years ago, he was a great quarterback at the same high school. But David's mother doesn't care about football; she just wants him to be happy and forget about meeting the expectations of both his father and an insensitive high school coach. Throughout, her faith gives her strength to help him cope with all sorts of obstacles, especially a potentially lethal staph infection that attacks his throwing arm. Within the story, we see how his physical therapist— a young, kind Iraq vet—gives him hope to overcome his physical struggles and return to football.

Destiny Pictures producer, Mark Castaldo, is seeking investors for a film that can be made in or around West Virginia. Those interested can contact him at: destiny@destinypictures.biz.

FADE IN:

EXT. SISKIYOU COUNTY, CALIFORNIA - DAY

Snow blankets the expansive Sacramento Valley. An ice-capped Mount Shasta presides over the winter landscape.

In a meadow, a herd of CATTLE. Some chew on hay, exhale mist through their flaring nostrils.

Hibernating farmland as far as the eye can see. Icicles hang off an idle rusty tractor in an open field.

A homemade BANNER tied to the tractor reads...

Go Threshers! State Champs or bust! A crudely drawn FOOTBALL splits the uprights on the roadside sign.

On a nearby ranch, a GRAIN SILO bears a similar banner, spray painted onto the steel.

EXT. SMALL TOWN - MAIN STREET - DAY

For every thriving small business left, there's two that have gone under. An American flag flutters over the town's tiny post office.

Snow crowns the church's steeple. Most of the storefronts are full of Thresher fan banners.

A young man's voice guides us through the faded Americana...

                    DAVID (V.O.)
          Where I grew up, you were either a
          farmer or a football player.

EXT. VACANT LOT - DAY

Kids bundled up for winter run amok. They all chase ONE BOY that's holding a red DODGEBALL.

                    DAVID (V.O.)
         I had no interest in cows or corn,
         but my parents couldn't afford to
         buy me a football. So, I played a
         lot of Pick It Up, Mess Him Up. The
         rules are simple...

YOUNG DAVID (7), dressed in his Sunday best, clutches the rubber ball to his chest. He runs as fast as his little legs will carry him.

David's wool cap falls in his eyes as he sprints away from the ANGRY MOB of kids pursuing him.

                DAVID (V.O.)
        If you pick up the ball. Everyone
        else will try and mess you up.

They're gaining on him. A big BULLY with a COWLICK leaps and tackles David from behind. Face first into the frozen snow.

                BULLY
        Stay down, shrimp.

                DAVID (V.O.)
        It was as close to football as my
        grubby paws could get at the time.

The Bully strips the ball from David, then leaves. He holds the ball high. The mob chases the Bully next.

David rolls over, stares up at the blue sky and catches his breath. He's got a fresh welt over his right eye.

A blaring CAR HORN commands David's attention. He looks down at his Sunday best, curses his luck.

CONNIE (30s) steps out of the old sedan. She closes the creaky door, braces against a wind gust.

A tense look on her face, Connie yells...

                CONNIE
        David Anthony DelSanto, get your
        behind over here.

                YOUNG DAVID
        Yes, ma'am.

David makes the walk of shame across the lot. The Cowlick Bully and the mob laugh at him.

                CONNIE
        Hush up, you little heathens.

                DAVID (V.O.)
        One day that big bully that just
        laughed at me, will be tackling
        anything in sight to protect me.
        But right now, he thinks I suck.

Connie frets over little David.

She dabs his bruised cherub face with her spit-moistened handkerchief. Connie rubs his cheek as she talks...

                    CONNIE
          What happened to your face?

                    YOUNG DAVID
          They chased me and I fell.

                    CONNIE
          Why were they chasing you?

                    YOUNG DAVID
          Because I had the ball.

                    CONNIE
          Is it too much to ask that you mind
          me just one day a week?

                    YOUNG DAVID
          Sorry. Mom, you're making it worse.

David's right. His face is much redder now. Connie kisses his
crimson cheek, walks her son to the car.

                    CONNIE
          Come on, we'll be late for church.

                    YOUNG DAVID
          Mom, I don't think I'm fast enough
          to be a quarterback.

                    CONNIE
          Don't let your father hear you say
          that. He'll have a stroke.

INT. CHURCH - DAY

Barely awake, PAUL (30s) sinks in the pew. He's flanked by
his wife and son. David's welt has matured into a full blown
BLACK EYE. Much to the dismay of his mother.

The modest CHORUS wraps up singing a hymn.

                    DAVID (V.O.)
          My Dad preferred worshipping at the
          altar of football instead of the
          Almighty. His idea of a Hail Mary
          was a lot different than hers. But
          somehow they always made it work.

Paul falls asleep. Connie elbows him in the gut. He opens his
eyes wide, perks up.

                    PAUL
          Amen.

The PRIEST stands in his pulpit. He looks down at Paul, makes the Sign of the Cross, then closes the Bible.

     PRIEST
 Amen.

     CONNIE & YOUNG DAVID
 Amen.

INT. DAVID'S HOUSE - DAY

The rooms are small and the windows are frosted. An old cast iron radiator spits steam in the living room.

The furniture's second hand, maybe third, but Connie manages to give it a Woman's Touch.

In a corner, a CHRISTMAS TREE stands. Just a few presents nestled under the branches. The decorations are homemade, popcorn and cranberry garlands adorn the tree.

Football memorabilia fills the walls. Pictures of a YOUNG PAUL posing in football team photos. Sectional Champs 1988, Regional Champs 1989. Paul DelSanto #12. Regional MVP.

     DAVID (V.O.)
 Every Division One team on the west
 coast recruited my father. Until he
 tore three of the four ligaments in
 his left knee. Dad never got to win
 a state championship ring or be
 voted All-American. That mission
 was passed down to me, whether I
 wanted it or not.

Football trophies occupy most of the shelf space. They compete for real estate with Connie's collection of ceramic Dutch Boy knick-knacks.

An NFL game plays on the modest tube TV.

Paul and David sit close to the screen. They watch NFL legend LaDainian Tomlinson bust through the opponents' defense, then streak down the sideline for a...

     YOUNG DAVID & PAUL
 Touchdown!

David and Paul high five.

Connie watches them from the small kitchenette. She turns away from the celebration.

INT. DAVID'S HOUSE - KITCHENETTE - DAY

Connie wears an apron. She sits at the old dinner table, looks through a pile of mail and PAST DUE bills.

Something catches her eye...

It's a letter addressed to Paul from the Siskiyou County School District.

> CONNIE
> Paul, come in here.

> PAUL (O.S.)
> Can't it wait? LT just ran--

> CONNIE
> It's here.

Paul appears in the doorway. Connie offers the sealed envelope to her husband, but Paul doesn't take it.

> CONNIE
> Well, aren't you going to open it?

> PAUL
> You open it, sweetheart.

Connie takes a deep breath. She opens the envelope, starts to silently read the letter.

> PAUL
> What does it say?

Paul can't take the suspense. He's on pins and needles, until a big smile spreads across Connie's face...

> CONNIE
> The Siskiyou County School District is proud to welcome you to our staff for next semester. Your degree in Psychology will go a long way in helping guide our students towards a bright future.

> PAUL
> I got the job?

> CONNIE
> You got the job.

Connie and Paul kiss each other, then embrace. Tears of relief roll down their cheeks.

                    PAUL
          Which means Mommy doesn't have to
          work nights at the diner anymore.

                    YOUNG DAVID
          Yay.

That happy realization hits Connie. Paul cradles her smiling
face in his hands. They gaze into each other's eyes.

David watches his parents hug. The flickering glow of the NFL
game highlights his doe-eyed face.

                    DAVID (V.O.)
          Dad worked odd jobs for six years
          to put himself through night school
          to get that degree. It's the first
          time I ever saw my father cry, but
          it wasn't the last.

                    PAUL
          Let's celebrate, Connie.

                    CONNIE
          With what? We're broke.

LIVING ROOM

Paul's on his hands and knees. He looks through the pile of
presents under the Christmas tree. Connie hovers over Paul,
her arms akimbo.

                    PAUL
          Come on, just one?

                    YOUNG DAVID
          Please?

                    CONNIE
          Absolutely not. I forbid you to
          open a single present until the
          morning of Christ's birth. Do you
          hear me, Paul Ronald DelSanto?

                    PAUL
          Yes, ma'am. No opening presents.

Paul retrieves a FOOTBALL-SHAPED present from way underneath
the tree. As if it were hidden from a certain boy. Little
David sees the gift, his eyes light up.

                    YOUNG DAVID
          Is that for me?

EXT. DAVID'S HOUSE - DAY

The small yard's barren and fenceless.

David wears an oversized football jersey over his threadbare jacket. The uniform looks just like the one his father wears in the old photos. #12. Quarterback.

Paul throws the still GIFT-WRAPPED football to his son. David catches the ball, crumples the bow a bit.

Connie stands in a window. She glares outside at her two "boys" as they play a game of catch.

David and Paul talk as they toss the festive football...

          YOUNG DAVID
  You think I can be a quarterback,
  just like you, Dad?

          PAUL
  I know you can, Son.

          YOUNG DAVID
  How?

          PAUL
  Because it's your legacy.

EXT. EMPTY LOT - DAY

Young David grips the now unwrapped football. The dimpled pigskin glistens in the sunlight. He runs his small fingers over the pristine white laces.

          YOUNG DAVID (V.O.)
  What's a legacy?

          PAUL (V.O.)
  It's the best gift a father can
  ever give his son.

          YOUNG DAVID (V.O.)
  Even better than a football?

          PAUL (V.O.)
  The best.

          YOUNG DAVID (V.O.)
  When do I get one?

The Bully and the Mob see David. They run across the lot towards him. One boy stays behind, YOUNG MAX (7).

> PAUL (V.O.)
> You already have it. I gave it to you the day you were born.

> YOUNG DAVID (V.O.)
> What am I supposed to do with it?

> PAUL (V.O.)
> Make all your dreams come true. Be the legend I know you can be.

Max looks at David, waves his arms. He jumps up and down, thumping his little chest.

Young David stands his ground. He doesn't run from the approaching mob. David grips the football by the laces, his little knuckles white.

> YOUNG MAX
> Hey! Throw me the ball! I'm open!

The Cowlick Bully leads the charge, the mob not far behind.

David pulls his arm back, hurls the football as far as he can. The wobbly spiral soars high...

EXT. THRESHER FOOTBALL FIELD - NIGHT

The weak spiral _SUDDENLY_ flies straight and true... MAX, now 17, catches the football in the endzone during the biggest game of his young life.

The capacity crowd of Thresher fans scream. They rise up and cheer from the standing room only grandstand.

SUPER: TEN YEARS LATER.

DAVID, now 17, celebrates in the endzone with Max. The Thresher team rallies around the boys. Over the PA system...

> ANNOUNCER (V.O.)
> DelSanto connects with Max Robinson for their third score of the night. The Shasta Miners' defense has had no answer for this junior year duo in the second half!

The scoreboard reads: *Threshers 24. Miners 28.* There's about a minute left in the fourth quarter.

Connie and Paul, both 40s now, stand in the bleachers and root for their son.

ANNOUNCER (V.O.)
No quarterback has ever led the
Threshers to a state championship.
The only one to get close, was
David's father, thirty years ago.

Paul turns around. He regards the COLLEGE SCOUTS behind him holding their clipboards and taking notes.

PAUL
Yes sir, that's my David! That's
DelSanto with one "L", not two.
Remember that next year when you
come knocking on my door with a
jersey for my boy.

David, Max and the rest of the varsity football team trot to the sidelines. They wave to the crowd.

A blonde cheerleader, JENNA, runs up to David. He takes off his helmet, plants a big kiss on her eager lips.

JENNA
You were so hot on that drive.

DAVID
Yeah, but we're still down by four.

Another kid sits on the bench in a pristine uniform, ERIC. He glares at David and his blonde prize.

HEAD COACH BURNS (60s) claps his hands. No headset or tablets for this guy, he's old school.

COACH BURNS
Hustle! Special Teams, we need a
takeaway or the season's over!

The Thresher Special Teams unit takes the field, lines up and kicks the football. The pigskin sails high, end over end.

The Shasta receiver catches the ball, runs up field. He dodges Thresher defenders, until face to face with...

The Cowlick Bully! He's built like an NFL linebacker now. He tackles the receiver, strips and recovers the football!

CROWD
CRUNK!!!

ANNOUNCER (V.O.)
Craig "Crunk" Miller comes up with
the ball for the Threshers! It's
first and ten at midfield.

The team rallies around Crunk. David bear hugs him. Eric jumps up off the bench...

> ERIC
> Hey Coach. What about my trick play? Run the hook route with--

> DAVID
> You're the back-up quarterback.

> ERIC
> Come on, it's a great play.

> COACH BURNS
> This is DelSanto's team. He's a leader and you're not. Get it? He makes the play call, kid.

> ERIC
> He's making out with his girl.

> DAVID
> So what? Grab yourself a seat and watch the show. Because I'm about to make history, back-up.

David leans close, whispers to Eric...

> DAVID
> And keep your eyes off my girl.

> ANNOUNCER (V.O.)
> The Threshers have no timeouts and there's only thirty seconds left, DelSanto will have to work the sidelines to win the championship.

Max, David, Crunk and the rest of the Thresher's offense take the field and huddle up.

ASST. COACH WEATHERS (30s), Burns' "new school" assistant, puts a reassuring hand on Eric's slumped shoulder. He speaks in private to Coach Burns...

> ASST. COACH WEATHERS
> You didn't have to chew Eric out, all he wants to do is contribute.

> COACH BURNS
> Do you want to win the championship or not, Weathers? This team's for winners. Don't you forget it. Ever.

The Threshers break the huddle, line up at scrimmage. Taped fingers dig into the turf. Max goes into motion.

Crunk hikes the football. David drops back. He looks for his favorite target. Max runs along the sideline. David RIFLES the pigskin through the air.

Max turns, catches the ball between the numbers. He steps out of bounds. The Thresher fans cheer.

> ANNOUNCER (V.O.)
> Robinson picks up eighteen yards for a Thresher first down!

The teams square off at scrimmage. Crunk hikes the ball to David. He backs up, looks for a receiver...

Everyone's covered. The pocket collapses.

David runs towards the sideline, defenders in pursuit. Max's open on the other side of the field. David switches hands, throws the football across his body with his -- LEFT HAND!

Max dives for the wobbly pass. He makes the catch.

> ANNOUNCER (V.O.)
> Never have I ever! Unbelievable! Is there anything DelSanto can't do?!?

The clock keeps running: 0:09... 0:08... The players rush up to the line of scrimmage. David spikes the ball at the ten, stops the clock.

> ANNOUNCER (V.O.)
> Five seconds left!

Crunk hikes the ball to David. It's an all out blitz! A huge Shasta linebacker runs over Crunk. David looks downfield. Max slants across the endzone.

David stands tall. He throws the football. The linebacker's helmet SMASHES into David's FOREARM. Bones crunch. David grunts in sheer pain. Shasta players pile on top of him.

Max leaps, extends his body to the limit and catches the pass to win the state championship!

Coach Burns celebrates the win, fist pumps. Coach Weathers looks at David, concerned for his player.

Thresher fans scream and applaud. All but Connie and Paul.

> CONNIE
> David.

                    ANNOUNCER (V.O.)
          Threshers win state!!! But
          DelSanto's down. He took a wicked
          shot to his throwing arm.

David squirms on the ground, holding his lame arm. Max and
Crunk pull the Shasta players off their quarterback.

                    MAX
          Get off him!

                    CRUNK
          I'm sorry, man. I should've stopped
          that creep.

                    DAVID
          Hell yeah, you should have.

                    MAX
          Is it bad?

                    DAVID
          It's not good. Help me up.

Crunk and Max help David get up. He wobbles, keeps the broken
arm tight against his side. The crowd's quiet until...

David raises his LEFT FIST high into the air. The fans scream
and applaud their quarterback. Jenna runs up to David, kisses
him at midfield. Fans holler even more. Eric glares at David.

The Coaches run out onto the field. Burns congratulates his
players. Weathers runs straight to David. He checks the arm.

                    ASST. COACH WEATHERS
          Pretty sure it's broken.

EXT. MAIN STREET - NIGHT

An AMBULANCE speeds down the street. Not too far behind, Paul
follows in his car.

INT. AMBULANCE - NIGHT

David lays on a stretcher, his arm in a sling.

Connie sits next to him. She touches the GOLD CRUCIFIX around
her neck, blinks away tears.

                    DAVID
          Don't cry, Mom. I'll be fine. You
          don't have to pray. I got this.

David holds his mother's hand. Connie forces a smile.

INT. RECOVERY ROOM - NEXT DAY

David sits up in a hospital bed. He wears a CAST on his right arm, Skypes with someone on a LAPTOP.

On screen: The entire Thresher team...

     TEAM
  Go Threshers! Champions! We did it!
  Best quarterback ever!

David smiles at all his friends.

Players relay get well wishes. Some say they'll visit. The cheerleaders are there, including Jenna. Eric sits near her.

     MAX
  How does it feel to be the champ?

     DAVID
  Better when I get out of this cast
  in six weeks.

     CRUNK
  I still feel bad, man.

     DAVID
  You can spend all of next season
  making it up to me, big man.

     JENNA
  We all miss you, David.

Jenna blows a kiss to David. Much to Eric's dismay.

     DAVID
  Right back at you, princess. Did
  you miss me too, Eric?

     ERIC
  Yeah, sure.

     DAVID
  Good answer.

There's a KNOCK at the door. Paul peers through the narrow window, waves to David.

     DAVID
  I've gotta roll.

                    TEAM
          Goodbye. Get well. See you at the
          awards dinner. Go Threshers!

David closes the laptop. Paul enters the room. He can't help but stare at the cast.

                    DAVID
          It's not as bad as it looks.

                    PAUL
          Son, I've been right where you are,
          laying in bed wondering if I'd ever
          play football again.

                    DAVID
          I won't let you down.

                    PAUL
          I want you to have all the great
          opportunities that I didn't.

                    DAVID
          I know. I can handle this.

Paul hugs David.

                    PAUL
          That's my boy. That championship
          game. I've never seen anything like
          it. You were incredible. Next year
          will be even--

                    DAVID
          Where's Mom?

                    PAUL
          She's in the chapel. She wanted to
          say a few words for you.

                    DAVID
          They're called prayers, Dad.

                    PAUL
          I'm so proud of you. We're both so
          very proud of you. I love you, Son.

                    DAVID
          I love you, too.

                    PAUL
          The Doctor says you should heal up
          in plenty of time for training ca--

CONNIE (O.S.)
                Let the boy rest, Paul.

Connie stands in the doorway. She looks pale.

                    PAUL
                I'm almost done, sweetheart. Coach
                Weathers knows a rehab specialist
                that used to work in the NFL. We're
                gonna talk--

                    DAVID
                I don't need a specialist. Are you
                feeling OK, Mom?

David hugs his mother tight.

                    CONNIE
                I'm fine, just worried about you.
                When can you come home?

                    DAVID
                Day after tomorrow.

                    CONNIE
                Why so long?

                    DAVID
                My white blood cell count came back
                high. There's still some bacterial
                infection in the bone.

                    PAUL
                Don't worry about it, we'll get the
                best doctors to clear you for play,
                David. I won't let this affect your
                eligibility status for the All-
                American Bowl next y--

                    CONNIE
                Paul, can you get me a coffee?

                    PAUL
                Sure. I'll be right back.

Paul leaves. Connie and David share a knowing look.

                    CONNIE
                Your father only wants what's best
                for you.

                    DAVID
                And himself.

Connie kisses her Son's forehead.

NEXT DAY

Get Well cards and flower bouquets fill the room.

There's a KNOCK at the open door. Coach Burns and Coach Weathers enter the room. They both greet David, shake hands.

                COACH BURNS
        How's the arm, champ?

                DAVID
        A little stiff, Coach.

David mock-flexes his broken arm. Coach Burns laughs.

                COACH BURNS
        Sense a humor, I love it.

                ASST. COACH WEATHERS
        We brought you something.

Coach Weathers pulls a football out of his backpack.

                COACH BURNS
        It's the game ball. Weathers had
        the entire team sign it for you.

David holds the GAME BALL. He looks at the football for a while, reading every name. David chokes back some tears.

                DAVID
        This really means a lot to me.

                COACH BURNS
        You earned it, David. And that's
        only the beginning for you. There's
        a lot of game balls in your future.

                ASST. COACH WEATHERS
        We want you to work with a great
        physical therapist to help you
        rehab the arm in the off season.

                DAVID
        It's just a break. I'll be fine.

                COACH BURNS
        You're tough, DelSanto. I like
        that, but don't be stupid. That arm
        will get you all the way to the big
        show if you treat it right.

                    ASST. COACH WEATHERS
          Your father's on board. He'll drive
          you out to meet Joe next week. This
          guy knows his stuff. He's ex-NFL.
          Promise me you'll hear the man out.

David nods in agreement.

EXT. REHAB CENTER - PARKING LOT - DAY

Paul pulls up in his sedan. David, still wearing the cast, sits next to him.

An old man with a cane hobbles past the car.

                    DAVID
          You sure this is the right address?

                    PAUL
          I think so.

                    DAVID
          You think so? Give me the GPS.

                    PAUL
          This has got to be the place.

                    DAVID
          I thought you said this guy worked
          with the pros.

                    PAUL
          He does. Well, he did.

David spots a PRETTY NURSE in scrubs (early 20s) escorting an elderly woman using a walker. He hops out of the car.

                    PAUL
          Where you going?

                    DAVID
          To get some answers.

The Pretty Nurse watches David approach. Remember HAILEY'S sweet smile, you'll be seeing it again soon.

                    HAILEY
          Can I help you?

                    DAVID
          I sure hope so. I'm looking for the
          guy that works with injured
          football players.

                    HAILEY
          You mean, Joe?

David fishes out a piece of paper. He checks the name.

                    DAVID
          Yeah, that's the guy.

                    HAILEY
          Ask for Joe Hackett at the front
          desk. They'll page him for you.

Hailey starts to walk away with her patient. David pursues her, catches up. He walks alongside as they talk...

                    DAVID
          Can I ask you something?

                    HAILEY
          Sure.

                    DAVID
          Is this place a rehab center or a
          retirement home?

                    HAILEY
          Well, we help people of all ages,
          even some famous athletes.

                    DAVID
          Does Mister Hackett, you know...
          officially live here?

                    HAILEY
          You mean, is Joe a patient?

                    DAVID
          Yeah, is he some old Yoda-looking
          dude that talks to himself all day?

Hailey laughs.

                    DAVID
          What's so funny?

                    HAILEY
          Joe volunteers his time here. He
          helps rehab disabled vets.

David's five kinds of embarrassed. Their eyes meet. Hailey beams that warm smile again.

Paul watches the pair from the car. He BEEPS the horn.

DAVID
          I've gotta go. Let's keep that Yoda
          comment just between us, OK?

                    HAILEY
          OK. Your secret's safe with me.

Hailey watches David walk away.

EXT. REHAB CENTER - GARDEN - DAY

A tranquil flower-filled setting for residents.

JOE HACKETT (40s) sits on a bench. He keeps his salt-and-pepper hair cropped tight and his body finely tuned.

Seated next to Joe: CORPORAL LANE (20s) has the unmistakable physique of a soldier. Except for his entire left arm that's been replaced with a PROSTHETIC LIMB.

David exits the main building. He walks down a path, sees Joe and Corporal Lane. David stops. He fixates on the prosthetic limb, then looks down at his cast.

                    CORPORAL LANE
          I've been off the pain killers for
          two weeks and no spasms.

                    JOE
          That's great. Are you cleaning the
          gelatin sleeve after every swim?

Joe recognizes David, waves him over.

                    CORPORAL LANE
          Yes sir.

                    JOE
          Good man. David, I'm Joe Hackett,
          it's nice to meet you.

                    DAVID
          Likewise.

Joe stands up. He shakes David's good hand.

                    JOE
          Congratulations on winning state.
          So, how does it feel?

                    DAVID
          Well, with everything that's
          happened, the win hasn't really
          sunk in yet, but we've got an
          awards dinner coming u--

                    JOE
          I mean the arm, kid. The broken
          one. How does it feel?

                    DAVID
          Oh. It's OK. No problem.

                    JOE
          Really? I see. David, I'd like you
          to meet Corporal Tom Lane.

                    CORPORAL LANE
          I know who you are. My little
          brother plays for Shasta. That was
          a hell of a game. Get healthy.

                    DAVID
          Thanks, man. I promise, that won't
          be my last game.

Corporal Lane stands up. He instinctively offers his right
hand to shake, but David's wearing a cast.

David hesitates, stares at the prosthetic limb. He shakes
Corporal Lane's artificial hand with his left.

                    CORPORAL LANE
          See you next week, Joe.

                    JOE
          I'll be here.

Corporal Lane walks away. David watches him. Hailey exits the
main building, greets and KISSES Corporal Lane.

Much to David's dismay.

                    JOE
          He's one hell of a fighter.

                    DAVID
          What happened to him?

                    JOE
          Corporal Lane lost that arm saving
          a kid from a UXO in Yemen.

DAVID
What's UXO mean?

JOE
Unexploded ordinance.

DAVID
You mean like a land mine?

JOE
Yeah. Something like that.

Hailey ushers Corporal Lane inside. She looks back, catches David staring at her. He looks away.

JOE
Sit down, David. Let's talk.
Where's your father?

DAVID
He's in the bathroom.

JOE
Do you mind if we start without him? I'm on a tight schedule.

DAVID
Sure. No problem.

JOE
Your coaches are concerned about your rehabilitation. They want to get out in front of any potential muscular or neurogenic atrophy. So, we're going to take it very slow.

David laughs.

DAVID
Neuro what? You know I broke my arm, Doc, not my brain. Right?

JOE
I'm a physical therapist, David, not a Doctor. I've worked with hundred of athletes.

DAVID
Look, I appreciate that Coach Weathers is trying to hook you up, but my family can't afford to pay for any homeo-whatever st--

> JOE
> I volunteer my time here, kid. And no one's out to scam you. I strongly recommend no throwing for at least four months.

> DAVID
> Four months? I'd miss spring training. No way, That's crazy, the cast comes off in six weeks.

> JOE
> Well, seems like you've got all the answers already, so why're you here wasting my time?

> DAVID
> My Dad wanted me to hear you out. And now I've heard enough. I can see why the Seahawks dumped you.

> JOE
> I resigned, smart ass. You have to want to get better for therapy to work, David. You can't heal, unless you want to. See yourself out, kid.

> DAVID
> Whatever.

David storms off back the way he came. Just as Paul steps out of the main building, David walks past him.

> PAUL
> What happened?

> DAVID
> I'm out of here.

> PAUL
> But we just got here.

> DAVID
> And now we're leaving.

EXT. VFW - PARKING LOT - NIGHT

The parking lot's filled to capacity. More cars park on the street. Along the side of the old brick building...

Max, Crunk and David, all wearing suits, drink BEER. Crunk's suit is too small for his linebacker build.

                    DAVID
          He said I didn't want to heal.

                    CRUNK
          What? That guy sounds whack.

                    MAX
          Forget him. We've got a state title
          to defend next year.

                    CRUNK
          Together.

                    DAVID
          Hell yeah.

The trio of boys fist bump.

David cracks open another brew, takes a big swig. Max and
Crunk notice he's sweating, looks a little pale.

                    CRUNK
          Maybe you should slow down.

                    MAX
          David, are you OK?

David finishes the beer fast. He crushes the can, spikes it
on the ground.

                    DAVID
          Never better.

Jenna arrives with a bunch of cheerleaders. Eric's tagging
along with her group. Crunk and Max see him.

                    MAX
          Not again.

                    CRUNK
          Will that boy never learn?

                    DAVID
          What? Oh hell, no. Hey! Back-up!

David glares at Eric. He jogs over, gets in Eric's face.

                    DAVID
          I told you before to keep your
          hands off my girl.

                    ERIC
          At least I got two of them.

JENNA
David, leave him alone.

David pushes Eric. A shoving match escalates. Until David PUNCHES Eric square on the jaw with his left.

Eric falls on his ass. He rises fast, fists clenched.

DAVID
Go ahead. Take your best shot! Come on. What you waiting for?!?

JENNA
Stop it!

Max restrains Eric from behind, pulls him back. Crunk bear-hugs David, holds on tight.

DAVID
Get off me, man!

CRUNK
Calm down and I will.

David resists. Jenna steps in between the boys. David yells at a bloody Eric over her shoulder...

DAVID
You'll always be a back-up while I'm around! That's who you are!

JENNA
David, please. Nothing happened, Eric just needed a ride.

DAVID
I bet he did.

Sweat beads up on David's forehead. Jenna holds his hand, concern on her face...

JENNA
Your hand, it's warm. Are you feeling alright?

David pulls his hand away from Jenna. Before he can answer her, Coach Burns exits the building. He sees his team divided over the conflict.

COACH BURNS
DelSanto? Break it up! What the hell's going on out here?

INT. VFW - BANQUET HALL - NIGHT

Everyone's decked out in formal attire, from star players to proud parents. They're all seated at large round tables.

The walls are decorated with Thresher memorabilia and blown-up photos of the championship season.

Coach Weathers stands at a podium on STAGE. He looks at David as he clears his throat and speaks into the MICROPHONE...

     ASST. COACH WEATHERS
  Teamwork. There is no championship
  season without it. No one athlete
  carries the burden alone. As a
  team, we either succeed or fail.

Connie and Paul flank David. They notice him rub his right arm. Crunk, Max and their parents also sit at the table.

     ASST. COACH WEATHERS
  The lessons we learned this season
  will help us to grow as a team and
  as individuals.

David looks away. On the wall, he sees a big POSTER PRINT of himself. In the photo, he's poised to throw a football. David stares at his larger-than-life throwing arm.

Applause all around. On stage, Coach Burns approaches the podium. He shakes hands with Coach Weathers, then speaks into the microphone...

     COACH BURNS
  David DelSanto, #12 come on up
  here. Give your future All-American
  Bowl candidate a warm welcome!

Everyone claps, but Eric. A bright SPOTLIGHT shines on a sweaty David. He shields his eyes, stands before the crowd.

     CONNIE
  Are you alright, David?

     DAVID
  Never better.

David smiles at his mother. He walks up on stage.

     DAVID
  You see this?

David raises his cast as high as he can. He looks into the bright light... The room starts to SPIN.

The POSTER PRINTS on the wall TWIST and DISTORT.

      DAVID
  I want you all to know, that this
  isn't going to stop me! Not ever.
  #12 has got this! I'll do anything
  to win! And anyone that gets in my
  way is going down!

      COACH BURNS
  David, we've got something special
  for you. It's the prototype for our
  championship ring. Coach Weathers
  and I want you to have it.

Everyone stands and claps for David. He looks down at his proud parents, tears in Paul's eyes.

      DAVID
  Dad, this is for you. Come on up
  here and get your legacy.

Connie encourages Paul. He steps up on stage. The crowd claps even louder. David gives Paul the ring. Father and son hug.

      DAVID
  I love you, Dad.

David breaks the embrace, staggers. He PASSES OUT, collapses on the stage. The crowd gasps. Connie and Jenna scream.

      PAUL
  David!

Paul opens up David's shirt, listens to his chest. David's right arm is swollen and red.

INT. INTENSIVE CARE UNIT - DAY

David sleeps, an oxygen mask over his face. The EKG keeps a steady beat. There's a thick IV stuck into his arm.

Connie prays over David. Her eyes closed and hands clasped tight around ROSARY BEADS.

In the hallway, Paul listens to a SURGEON...

      SURGEON
  David's suffering from a very
  severe bacterial bone infection.

      PAUL
  But he took every pill.

> SURGEON
> Antibiotic-resistant bacteria is becoming more and more common.

> PAUL
> Well, give him something stronger.

> SURGEON
> I wish it were that simple. The bacteria has compromised both the radius and ulna. I'm very sorry.

> PAUL
> What're you saying, Doc?

Connie stands in the doorway.

> CONNIE
> He's saying that David will never play football again.

> PAUL
> No. There's got be something you can do for him, Doctor. Please.

> SURGEON
> There are other antibiotics we could try. But if they don't work, your Son could die. If we amputate right now, David should have a long and healthy life ahead of him.

> PAUL
> But football is his life.

> CONNIE
> Doesn't David have a say in this?

> SURGEON
> In his weakened condition, inducing consciousness would only make matters worse. I'm sorry, but this is a decision you're going to have to make for your Son.

Paul and Connie have no words. Until they do.

> PAUL
> It'd kill David if you amputate.

> CONNIE
> No, it'll kill him if they don't.

INT. CHAPEL - DAY

Connie sits in a pew. She looks up to the statue of Christ presiding over the modest church.

Paul paces in the aisle.

          PAUL
No parent should ever have to make this decision.

          CONNIE
We're the only ones that can.

          PAUL
I won't let them do it. David's got his whole career ahead of him. I won't let them take that away.

          CONNIE
Sweetheart, you reversed your fortune after football. David can do the same.

          PAUL
No. I don't want him to end up like me. He deserves better!

          CONNIE
David can still have a life without football, can you?

Paul sits next to Connie, cries on her shoulder.

          PAUL
What're we going to do?

          CONNIE
Be there for him and hope he can forgive us. Who knows, maybe in time we'll even forgive ourselves.

INT. RECOVERY ROOM - DAY

Paul and Connie sit at David's bedside, watch him sleep. She holds David's left hand and prays. His right forearm's been AMPUTATED up to the elbow, the rest cocooned in bandages.

The signed GAME BALL sits at the foot of the bed.

Paul holds his wife's free hand, joins her in prayer. Mother and Father bow their heads. Tears fall from their weary eyes.

They mouth silent prayers for their son. Until David grips Connie's hand.

                CONNIE
     David?

                PAUL
     Son? Can you hear me?

Connie squeezes David's hand. He starts to wake, GROANS in pain. As David opens his eyes...

Paul and Connie sit up, trying to block David's view of his amputated arm. Connie wipes away tears.

                CONNIE
     Our prayers have been answered.

                DAVID
     Mom? Dad? What happened?

Paul and Connie look at each other... *Where do we start?*

                CONNIE
     What's the last thing you remember?

David blinks away confusion. He looks at the CHAMPIONSHIP RING on his father's finger.

                DAVID
     The ring. Giving Dad the ring. What
     happened after that?

                PAUL
     You passed out. Your broken arm was
     infected, Son. Infected real bad.

                DAVID
     My shoulder's numb. Why can't I
     feel my arm?

                PAUL
     We love you so much.

                CONNIE
     We're just so happy you've been
     delivered back to us, David. Thank
     God you're alright.

David pushes back his parents back. He looks at what's left of his throwing arm. David can't process this.

                DAVID
     Alright? You call this, alright?!?

He kicks the GAME BALL off the bed. The autographed pigskin tumbles end over end onto the floor.

                DAVID
        Nothing is alright! Nothing will
        ever be alright again!!!

David panics. He pulls out his IV, peels off electrodes as multiple ALARMS sound off.

                DAVID
        What have you done to me?!?

Connie trembles and cries. Paul tries to put a reassuring hand on his son's shoulder.

                PAUL
        David, please understand.

                DAVID
        Don't touch me!

                CONNIE
        It was the only way we could save
        you, David.

                DAVID
        Save me? You both killed me!

The accusation sends Connie into a sobbing fit. Paul tries to comfort her in vain.

David throws the IV POLE across the room. A trio of ORDERLIES rush in, try to restrain David. BLOOD seeps through bandages.

Paul and Connie watch in horror. A NURSE enters. She preps a SYRINGE full of liquid, regards Paul and Connie.

                NURSE
        I need you to leave now. Please go,
        we'll take good care of him.

Paul pulls Connie away from the bed. She reaches out to David, ROSARY BEADS wrapped around her frail fingers.

INT. HOSPITAL - HALLWAY - DAY

Paul holds his crying wife. Another ORDERLY rushes past the couple into the recovery room. David's horrific screams echo into the corridor.

Connie breaks down in her husband's arms. Paul tries to comfort her. He kisses Connie's forehead.

                    PAUL
          We did the right thing. You hear
          me, sweetheart?

She doesn't acknowledge him, keeps crying.

INT. HOSPITAL - WAITING ROOM - DAY

It's been a few days.

Paul looks ragged. He stares blankly at whatever reality show plays on a FLATSCREEN.

Crunk, Max, Jenna, Coach Burns and Coach Weathers enter. Paul doesn't see them at first, eventually snaps back to reality.

                    MAX
          Hey, Mister D.

Max hugs Paul.

                    CRUNK
          We brought David's laptop.

                    PAUL
          Hello, boys. Jenna, you look nice.

                    JENNA
          Thanks, Mister DelSanto.

                    COACH BURNS
          Paul, good to see you.

                    ASST. COACH WEATHERS
          How's David doing?

                    PAUL
          They tell us he's stable. David
          won't talk to me, or his mother. We
          even tried leaving voicemail.

                    JENNA
          I tried too, his mailbox is off.

                    COACH BURNS
          I can't imagine what you must be
          going through, Paul.

                    ASST. COACH WEATHERS
          If there's anything we can do to
          help, please let us know.

PAUL
          There is one thing.

                    ASST. COACH WEATHERS
          Whatever it is, consider it done.

                    PAUL
          David doesn't want this anymore.

With regret, Paul reaches into a bag. He pulls out the GAME
BALL, offers it to Coach Weathers.

                    CRUNK
          What? No way.

                    PAUL
          I thought the team should have it,
          for the school trophy case.

Paul manages a half-smile. Coach Weathers accepts the ball.

INT. DAVID'S BEDROOM - NIGHT

The room hasn't been cleaned in weeks. David sits huddled in
a dark corner on the bed. The glow of a LAPTOP SCREEN lights
his zoned-out face.

He watches a YouTube video of the championship game...

On screen: The crowd cheers for a Thresher touchdown. David
and Max HIGH FIVE in the endzone. The ANNOUNCER decrees that
David will be the best quarterback in state history.

The video ends. David opens a PRESCRIPTION BOTTLE of pain
killers. He chews on two tablets, like they're Tic-Tacs.

On screen: Max calls David on Skype. The familiar jingle
chimes again and again. Until David logs out.

David lays back. He clicks the REPLAY icon. The state champ
video starts up again. The crowd chants...

                    CROWD (V.O.)
          Threshers! Threshers!

There's a KNOCK at the closed door.

                    CONNIE (V.O.)
          David, time for dinner.

David ignores his mother.

INT. DAVID'S HOUSE - HALLWAY - NIGHT

Connie stands in the corridor, worry on her face. She listens through the door, hears the video. Another knock.

>   CONNIE
>   I made your favorite.

Still no answer.

>   CONNIE
>   David, you have to eat somet--

>   DAVID (V.O.)
>   (through the door)
>   Leave me alone.

>   CONNIE
>   David, please.

>   DAVID (V.O.)
>   Go away!

A dejected Connie touches the closed door, then slowly retreats down the dark corridor.

INT. DAVID'S BEDROOM - DAY

A lethargic David lays flat on his back, stares up at the ceiling. He hasn't shaved in weeks.

Traditional bandages around his stump have been replaced with thick layers of Flex Wrap. There's a KNOCK at the door...

>   PAUL (V.O.)
>   (through the door)
>   Max and Crunk are here to see you.

David ignores his father. More knocks.

>   PAUL (V.O.)
>   David, I'm not sending them away
>   again. You hear me? David?

Paul knocks harder. David just stares into space, his eyes unblinking. The knocks give way to pounding. Again and again.

Until Paul barges into the room. David bolts upright, points his stump at his father.

>   DAVID
>   Get out of my room.

                    PAUL
          David, please talk to me. I know
          what it's like to be where you are.

                    DAVID
          No, you don't. You got to keep your
          leg. I'm a freak.

David waves the stump in Paul's face. He grabs David's upper
arm. Father and son struggle as they talk...

                    PAUL
          Don't say that.

                    DAVID
          Why not? That's what I am. Come on,
          say it. Say, "My Son's a freak."

                    PAUL
          Shut up.

                    DAVID
          My Son's a freak! My Son's a freak!

In the heat of the moment, Paul shoves David back against the
wall. Regret on his face, Paul tries to hug his son.

David swats away his father with the stump. He grabs his
FOOTBALL HELMET off a shelf. David slams the helmet into a
framed team photo on the wall. The glass shatters.

                    PAUL
          What're you doing?

                    DAVID
          Something I should've done a long
          time ago.

He smashes trophy after trophy on top of his bureau.

                    PAUL
          Stop it!

Paul tries to wrench the helmet out of David's good hand.

Max and Crunk stand in the open doorway. They watch father
and son grapple.

                    DAVID
          Get your hands off me! I hate you!

Max and Crunk rush in, restrain David. They push him against
the wall. He kicks and struggles, like a beast.

> CRUNK
> Relax, man. We're your friends.

> MAX
> You OK, Mister D?

David finally stops resisting. A shocked Paul stares at his wild-eyed son. Connie stands in the doorway, weeps.

NEXT DAY

All of the football memorabilia has been removed. No more trophies, pennants or pictures to be found here.

David sits on the bed. He re-wraps his STUMP, starting with the pale mound of excess flesh. There's a KNOCK at the door.

> DAVID
> Go away, whoever you are.

> JENNA (V.O.)
> (through the door)
> David, let me in. Please? I need to see you.

David wasn't expecting her. He looks at himself in a MIRROR, stares at his face, like he hasn't seen it in weeks.

LATER

David sits on the bed with Jenna. They look through a HIGH SCHOOL YEARBOOK together.

Jenna settles on a picture of her and David, arm in arm. The caption under the image reads... *Future Prom King & Queen.*

> DAVID
> Good times.

David reaches for Jenna's hand. She pulls away.

> JENNA
> David, there's something important I need to tell you.

> DAVID
> I'm listening.

This is hard for Jenna too...

JENNA
We haven't gone out since you came home and we barely text. I want my senior year to be special, it only happens once in a lifetime and--

DAVID
And you want to spend it with a football player, not a cripple.

JENNA
It sounds so awful when you say it like that.

DAVID
There's no other way to say it. That's all I am to you now.

JENNA
Fine, keep feeling sorry for yourself. Good luck with that.

Jenna starts to leave.

DAVID
Jenna, wait. I get it. You want someone who can hold you in their arms and protect you. And I can't do that anymore.

JENNA
I feel like such a monster.

DAVID
You're a beautiful princess. And don't let me hold you back. I couldn't even if I wanted to.

David holds up his stump, smiles at his bad joke. Jenna shakes her head, tries not to smile.

DAVID
What? Too soon?

JENNA
Promise me one thing. Don't shut out Max and Crunk. They miss you.

DAVID
I'm not a quarterback anymore.

JENNA
They don't need a quarterback, they need their best friend back.

ANOTHER DAY

David's clean shaven now. He downs a couple PAIN KILLERS, opens the door, greets Max and Crunk. The trio hug it out.

>DAVID
>Sorry about before, guys.

>MAX
>We miss you, man.

>CRUNK
>Remember, sunshine is your friend.

>DAVID
>I hear you, big man.

LATER

David, Max and Crunk enjoy ESPN Classic. It's the very same game Young David watched live with his father...

On screen: NFL legend LaDainian Tomlinson busts through the defense, sprints down the sideline for a--

>DAVID, MAX & CRUNK
>Touchdown!!!

Paul stands in the open doorway, watches the boys with a nostalgic smile on his face.

A stone-faced David notices his father. A dejected Paul walks away. David swallows two pain killers, then pops a third. The opiate kicks in fast. David's feeling real good.

>CRUNK
>Take it easy on those, man.

>DAVID
>Why? You want one?

>MAX
>Coach says that Eric will be the
>starting quarterback next season.

>CRUNK
>It won't be the same without you.

>DAVID
>I'm done with all that.

>MAX
>Maybe you could come back someday.

DAVID
As what? A water boy? No thanks. My
throwing days are over.

CRUNK
You could get a bionic arm and win
back-to-back championships.

MAX
The Bionic Quarterback.

DAVID
Hell yeah, that takes performance
enhancement to a whole other level.

David moves his stump, like a robot would. He makes gear-grinding noises, winds up and throws an imaginary football to Max. His friend catches it right in the chest.

DAVID
(robotic voice)
Perfect spiral.

The boys have a big laugh.

Crunk Googles "bionic arm" on his LAPTOP. He scans the search results, stops at: *BIONIC MODEL*. Crunk clicks the link.

On screen: A brunette poses against a neutral background for the camera in a studio. Her right stump's fitted with a sleek black PROSTHETIC BIONIC ARM with hyper-articulated fingers.

CRUNK
Guys, check out this website.

DAVID
She's hot.

MAX
And bionic.

DAVID
There's a link to the company.

Crunk clicks the link. David and Max look at the screen over his big shoulders as he reads...

CRUNK
Touch Bionics revolutionized
prosthetic myoelectric hands with
the Quantum i-Limb. The same one
worn by super-model Rebekah Maine
in Time magazine.

On screen: A close-up of a man using the Quantum i-Limb to focus the lens of a camera. The articulation's perfect. David stares at the state-of-the-art limb...

David dares to hope for the first time since he came home.

A KNOCK at the door brings David back to reality.

    DAVID
 Come in.

Connie enters with snacks. She's all smiles, until she sees the website and the sci-fi looking robot hand.

    DAVID
 Mom, look at this.

    MAX
 Isn't it awesome, Misses D?

    CRUNK
 What do you think?

EXT. FOOTBALL FIELD - DAY

The stands are empty, the field barren and brown. Connie and David walk across the sod towards the bleachers.

    DAVID
 Why did you bring me here?

    CONNIE
 I want to show you something.

David follows his mother up into the grandstand. Connie counts to herself as she climbs the old wooden steps...

    CONNIE
 One... two... three... four...
 five... six... and seven.

She pivots, sits down on the bench. Connie pats the spot next to her. David sits beside his mother.

They look at the empty field marked with faded chalk.

    DAVID
 Looks like the same old sod to me.

CONNIE
I always sat in the aisle seat next to my parents, so I could rush the field after the game and hug your father. This seat, right here. Every season. Every game.

Connie touches the weathered wood and chipped paint. She smiles at a hand-carved inscription: *Connie loves Paul*.

DAVID
I didn't know that.

CONNIE
And after your grandfather died, I sat here with your father and watched you play your heart out on this field. Every season. Every game. Win or lose.

DAVID
You're always there for me, Mom.

CONNIE
David, I need to tell you something very important.

DAVID
What's wrong? Are you sick?

CONNIE
No. I'm fine, sweetheart.

DAVID
Well, then what is it, Mom?

Connie hesitates, then reveals her big secret...

CONNIE
I hate football. But I sat here because the two most important people in my life loved to play. And I loved seeing that passion.

DAVID
Sometimes, I think Dad can't stand to look at me anymore.

CONNIE
It's not your fault. For years, he tried to rehab his knee and it nearly killed him.

> DAVID
> What happened?

> CONNIE
> He almost wound up in a wheelchair. But your Father eventually accepted that for new dreams to begin, sometimes the old ones have to be taken away from you.

> DAVID
> I don't understand.

> CONNIE
> Stop chasing your father's dreams, and start chasing your own.

> DAVID
> I still love the game, Mom.

> CONNIE
> I think you love your Father more. You stayed on your feet long enough to give him that ring. And then you just went limp, like an old dog dying in his owner's arms.

Connie cries. She reaches into her purse, pulls out a tissue and dabs her cheeks. David wipes away tears of his own.

> DAVID
> I'm so sorry that you had to see that. I didn't know I was sick, but I should have.

> CONNIE
> You have to stop hurting yourself to please others, David. No child can redeem their parent. If you want to play football again, you play for yourself. You hear me?

David nods his head yes, blinks away tears.

> DAVID
> Yes, ma'am.

> CONNIE
> And no more overdosing on your pain meds. Promise me.

> DAVID
> I promise, Mom.

> CONNIE
> That's my boy.

> DAVID
> I do want to play football, with all my heart and soul.

> CONNIE
> OK, but I'm not sold on this robot arm thing. Is there someone you can talk to that has one?

David thinks for a moment. He does know someone.

EXT. REHAB CENTER - PARKING LOT - DAY

Max pulls his pick-up truck into an open spot. David sits in the passenger seat, Crunk between them in the back.

David adjusts his spandex STUMP SLEEVE, looks nervous.

> MAX
> You want us to come with you?

> DAVID
> I got to do this part on my own.

> CRUNK
> Good luck.

INT. DAVID'S BEDROOM - DAY

Connie puts away clean laundry in David's bureau. Heavy footsteps pound down the corridor.

Paul stands in the doorway, glares at his wife.

> PAUL
> I knew I'd find you in here. You had to encourage this bionic crap, just to spite me, didn't you?

> CONNIE
> I encouraged David to make his own choice, which is more than you ever did for him.

> PAUL
> He'll make a fool out of himself in front of the entire school.

CONNIE
Better a fool than a bitter man that lives in the past.

PAUL
It's our job to protect David from making terrible mistakes.

CONNIE
I am protecting our Son. From you.

Paul storms off.

INT. DAVID'S HOUSE - HALLWAY - CONTINUOUS

Anger in his eyes and CELL PHONE in hand, Paul walks down the creaky narrow corridor.

He scrolls through his contacts, stops at -- COACH BURNS.

EXT. REHAB CENTER - GARDEN - DAY

The same scenic area and BENCH where David met Joe. But this time, Corporal Lane is sitting with Hailey.

David watches them talk and laugh from afar.

Hailey and Corporal Lane share a sandwich. They look happy together, in sync. Something David wishes he had.

Corporal Lane notices a skulking David, waves him over to the bench. Hailey turns around, recognizes David.

CORPORAL LANE
Sorry to hear about the arm.

DAVID
Thanks, man. I didn't mean to crash your personal time. I can wait.

CORPORAL LANE
No worries. I told Hailey all about your plan.

HAILEY
I was thinking, maybe I can help.

DAVID
Yeah?

> HAILEY
> Absolutely. And your secret's still
> safe with me, Yoda.

She still remembers their first meeting. Hailey's sweet smile looks even better in this sunny garden.

> CORPORAL LANE
> Have you two met before?

> DAVID
> We have. So, how long have you two
> been a thing?

Corporal Lane and Hailey have a laugh at David's expense.

> DAVID
> What?

> CORPORAL LANE
> Hailey's my baby sister.

David's five kinds of embarrassed in front of Hailey, again.

> HAILEY
> I'm only two years younger than
> you. And I'm not a baby.

> CORPORAL LANE
> Yes, you are. And your break ended
> two minutes ago, young lady.

David and Hailey stare at each other. Corporal Lane notices the chemistry, much to his dismay.

> HAILEY
> Nice seeing you again, David. Good
> luck with Joe.

> DAVID
> Thanks. I'll see you around.

Hailey leaves. David watches her walk away. She looks back.

> CORPORAL LANE
> (clears his throat)
> So, what's the sit rep?

David turns away from Hailey, sits down.

> DAVID
> The what?

                    CORPORAL LANE
               The situation report, Thresher.

                    DAVID
               I need some intel from you.

                    CORPORAL LANE
               What kind of intel is that?

LATER

David leans forward, stares at Corporal Lane who's silently pondering something...

                    CORPORAL LANE
               Bionic quarterback, nice. Do you
               think that qualifies as a
               performance enhancement?

                    DAVID
               Maybe. No one's ever tried
               something like this before.

                    CORPORAL LANE
               You need Joe to pull this off. So,
               why are you talking to me?

                    DAVID
               I bombed our first meeting, big
               time. Could you talk to Joe for me?

                    CORPORAL LANE
               I don't know, man.

                    DAVID
               Having Joe's support would help me
               make my case to Coach Burns.

Corporal Lane ponders the request.

                    CORPORAL LANE
               I'll talk to Joe and put a good
               word in for you with Coach Burns.
               But on one condition, Thresher.

                    DAVID
               Name it.

                    CORPORAL LANE
               You can't date my sister.

                    DAVID
               What? You're kidding, right?

> CORPORAL LANE
> Don't even bother denying it, I saw that "Luke and Leia are brother and sister" look in your Han Solo eyes.

David's guilty as charged. He sighs in defeat.

> DAVID
> You drive a hard bargain, Corporal.

> CORPORAL LANE
> Damn right, Thresher. She's my only sister. So, do we have a deal?

David nods yes, fist bumps with Corporal Lane. David's CELL PHONE chimes... It's a text from -- COACH BURNS.

INT. COACH BURNS' OFFICE - DAY

Coach Burns sits at his modest desk. All the walls and shelves are stocked with decades of Thresher memorabilia, including Paul and David.

There's a KNOCK at the door.

> COACH BURNS
> Come in.

David enters the office, shakes hands with Coach Burns. The coach can't help but stare at the stump.

> DAVID
> You wanted to see me, Coach?

> COACH BURNS
> Take a seat, David.

David sits down. He notices the pictures of him and his young father near the GAME BALL David returned.

> DAVID
> I'm sorry about the game ball. I didn't mean any disrespect.

> COACH BURNS
> I know. You wanted a clean break from football, I get that.

> DAVID
> Yeah. I thought I did at the time.

> COACH BURNS
> So, your father told me about the prosthetic arm.

> DAVID
> He did? What do you think?

> COACH BURNS
> It's not a good idea, David.

> DAVID
> Why not, Coach?

Coach Burns hates to be the one to say it, but...

> COACH BURNS
> David, you're not a football player and you never will be ever again. It's a damn shame, but there it is.

The words are like a dagger in David's heart.

> DAVID
> But Coach, the bionic arm is great, you can control it with Bluetoo--

> COACH BURNS
> We're defending our championship next season with a second string quarterback. There's no room for any distractions.

> DAVID
> A distraction? That's all I am to you now? Coach, give me a chance.

> COACH BURNS
> You don't want to drag the team down, do you?

> DAVID
> No, Coach.

> COACH BURNS
> I'm sorry. The answer's no, David.

> DAVID
> You think I'm a freak, don't you?

> COACH BURNS
> I think you're a kid in pain. And the sooner you accept that football is no longer an option, the better.

                    DAVID
          Please, Coach. I could paint the
          bionic arm up in our team colors,
          so no one would stare.

                    COACH BURNS
          They're always going to stare, Son.

David absorbs that horrible sentiment. He looks down at his
stump, then the floor. David chokes back tears.

                    COACH BURNS
          I won't let you humiliate yourself
          or tarnish the Thresher legacy with
          this robot arm crap. The Principal
          and your Father are in agreement
          with me. This nonsense ends now.

David storms out of the office, brushes past a surprised
Coach Weathers in the hallway.

INT. PAUL'S OFFICE - DAY

Paul sits at his desk. A long WINDOW affords a view of the
MAIN OFFICE. The brass name plate reads: *Paul DelSanto, Head
Guidance Counselor.*

Thresher collectibles and photos surround Paul's framed
degree in Psychology, some of them taken from David's room.

Max sits across from Paul. They don't see David standing in
the MAIN OFFICE watching them through the window...

                    PAUL
          You've already got a dozen Division
          One scouts lining up to meet you.
          And when they come visit your home,
          and believe me they will, I'll be
          there to help. I know exactly what
          those scouts like to hear, Max.

                    MAX
          Thanks, Mister D. You've been
          really great. You're the closest
          thing I have to a father.

David watches Paul and Max hug. He barges into the office,
upstages the embrace.

                    DAVID
          Does Max know what you told Coach?

                    MAX
          What're you talking about?

                    PAUL
          Max, you should leave.

                    DAVID
          No, I want him to stay. I want him
          to see the real you, Dad.

                    PAUL
          David, watch your mouth. This is
          not the time or pla--

                    DAVID
          Why did you throw me under the bus
          with Coach Burns!?!

                    PAUL
          I did that to protect you from
          yourself, Son.

                    DAVID
          You did that to protect yourself
          and your precious legacy.

                    PAUL
          I don't want you to embarrass
          yourself or the school.

                    DAVID
          All you care about are these dumb
          trophies that I won! For you! You
          used me up and now you're trying to
          do the same to my best friend!

Paul SLAPS David across the face. Max looks at his disgraced
father figure.

                    MAX
          Mister D?

Shocked CO-WORKERS watch the argument. Paul notices his
colleagues looking at him, regains his composure.

                    PAUL
          David, I was only trying to help.

                    DAVID
          I don't want your help ever again.

David and Max walk out on Paul. He stands in the doorway
alone. His disapproving colleagues stare at him. Paul
retreats to his office, closes the door.

INT. DINER - DAY

David and Joe sit at a BOOTH. *On David's laptop screen*: The Quantum i-Limb website. A skeptical Joe ponders the web page, then closes the laptop.

>   DAVID
>   I can even pre-program dozens of
>   hand grips for ball management.
>
>   JOE
>   How does that work?
>
>   DAVID
>   Through my phone, I can use my
>   muscles to select which one.
>
>   JOE
>   So, it's kinda like having a
>   playbook for your hand?
>
>   DAVID
>   Yeah! Exactly.
>
>   JOE
>   You already had one near fatal bone
>   infection, David. Why risk another?
>
>   DAVID
>   Because if I can make this work,
>   I'll be the first quarterback in
>   the history of football with a
>   prosthetic throwing arm.

Joe ponders the gravity of that lofty goal.

>   DAVID
>   But I need a hard ass physical
>   therapist I can trust to keep me
>   honest. Do you know where I could
>   find one?
>
>   JOE
>   That's one hell of a pitch, kid.
>
>   DAVID
>   Thanks, my friends helped me.

David points out the window into the parking lot...

Max and Crunk sit in Max's old pick-up truck. The two boys smile and wave hello to Joe.

Joe smiles, waves back to Max and Crunk.

EXT. INTERSTATE 5 - DAY

JOE'S SUV approaches the city limits of SEATTLE. David sits next to him, looks at the SPACE NEEDLE.

INT. TOUCH BIONICS - LOBBY - DAY

Joe ushers David into the upscale office space.

Behind the FRONT DESK on a wall-mounted FLATSCREEN: An animated i-Limb demonstrates common grips... Like shaking hands, holding a steering wheel and catching a round ball.

David likes what he sees on screen.

Joe regards the RECEPTIONIST.

     JOE
  Hi, David DelSanto's here to see
  Doctor Vang.

A Chinese woman wearing a lab coat, DOCTOR VANG, steps out of an elevator. Her long black hair's tied in a tight bun.

     DOCTOR VANG
  Joe Hackett, it's been too long.

     JOE
  It has been. I had no idea you were
  working here now.

Joe and Doctor Vang hug.

     DOCTOR VANG
  I needed a fresh start after the
  divorce. I should have reached out
  to you after Bobby passed away. I
  meant to, but I g--

     JOE
  Of course, I forgive you. The
  flowers you sent were beautiful.

David wonders silently... *Who's Bobby?*

Doctor Vang realizes she's touched a raw nerve. She smiles, then switches proverbial gears...

     DOCTOR VANG
  You've got a fine rehab man here,
  Mister DelSanto. Joe saved my ex-
  husband's football career. Come on,
  let's get you fitted for an i-Limb.

INT. TOUCH BIONICS - EXAM ROOM - DAY

David sits on an EXAM TABLE. Joe helps him put his T-shirt back on over his head.

MRI FILM in hand, Doctor Vang enters. She secures the film to a wall-mounted LIGHT BOX, turns it on.

On the MRI, David notices an oval-shaped WHITE SPOT on the bone at the base of his stump.

          DOCTOR VANG
  We've got your MRI results back.

          JOE
  What's that white area?

          DOCTOR VANG
  That's bone marrow. And it's been compromised by the infection much more than we were led to bel--

          DAVID
  But the hospital said I was fine.

          DOCTOR VANG
  X-rays can't detect the micro-softening of the bone marrow.

          DAVID
  Am I going to lose more of my arm?

          DOCTOR VANG
  No, but it does mean you're no longer an i-Limb candidate.

          DAVID
  I did all of this for nothing?

          DOCTOR VANG
  I'm truly sorry, David, but I can't help you play football again.

The weight of it all crushes David, his throat tightens. He opens the door, runs out of the room.

          JOE
  David, wait.

INT. TOUCH BIONICS - CORRIDOR - DAY

David bursts through swinging double doors. He sprints past a LEGLESS PATIENT in a wheelchair.

INT. TOUCH BIONICS - WAITING ROOM - DAY

Patients and loved ones sit in the reception area. A sweaty and out of breath David approaches. Everyone looks at him. A closed exam room door opens...

A young GIRL (5) with TWO PROSTHETIC ARMS exits. She sees her DADDY. He gets up, smiles at his pride and joy.

                PROSTHETIC GIRL
     All done. Pick me up, Daddy.

David watches the Girl reach up with her bionic hands. The mechanical digits touch her father's real fingers. Daddy scoops her up, sets the Girl down on his broad shoulders.

                DADDY
     You're the wind, baby girl, and I'm
     the feather.

The Girl holds out her arms, like she's flying. David watches her hug her father with both hands. Something David can never do again. He looks at his stump. The Girl waves to David.

David waves hello back. He tries to smile.

EXT. TOUCH BIONICS - ROOFTOP - DAY

David stands close to the edge. He stares at the SEATTLE skyline, contemplates the tiny people far below.

The wind makes the tears in David's eyes sting. Behind him, the ROOF ACCESS DOOR opens. Joe steps out into the open air.

                JOE
     David, turn around and look at me.

                DAVID
     It looks so easy from up here.

                JOE
     What does?

                DAVID
     Living.

                JOE
     Come here and we can talk about it.

                DAVID
     I don't want to talk anymore, Joe.

> JOE
> You know when we first met, I was glad that you walked out on me.

> DAVID
> Because I acted like a jerk.

> JOE
> Because you remind me of my son. Bobby never listened to me either.

> DAVID
> What happened to him?

> JOE
> After losing his left leg in a car accident, Bobby took his own life.

> DAVID
> I'm sorry.

> JOE
> He couldn't accept that his surfing career was over. And I couldn't see past my training to help my son, but that's my cross to bear alone.

> DAVID
> You know, someone I respect once told me that before you can heal, you have to want to heal.

> JOE
> That's some pretty good advice. And so is, don't jump. By the way.

Joe offers David his hand. David surprises Joe with a big hug. Eventually, Joe embraces David.

> JOE
> It's gonna be alright. Come on, let's get you home.

EXT. DAVID'S HOUSE - NEXT DAY

Paul sits atop a RIDING MOWER that's custom-painted in the Thresher colors. He cuts the grass in the front yard.

Across the street, Joe's SUV slows to a stop.

> JOE
> You want me to come in with you?

                    DAVID
          Thanks, but I got this, Joe. I
          appreciate everything you've done
          for me. I owe you.

                    JOE
          You owe me nothing. What're you
          going to do now?

                    DAVID
          I don't know. Get a job. Find a
          girl. Forget about football.

                    JOE
          You don't always have to be so
          damned tough, you know.

                    DAVID
          I know. Thank you for believing in
          me, Joe.

                    JOE
          I still do, son.

David shakes hands with Joe, then exits the SUV and closes the passenger door. He waves goodbye to Joe.

Joe waves back, watches David cross the street. He starts up his SUV, then PUNCHES the dashboard.

FRONT YARD

David trots up the walkway towards the front door. Paul sees his son and no prosthetic arm. He turns off the mower.

Behind father and son, Joe's SUV drives away.

                    PAUL
          Where's the bionic arm?

                    DAVID
          I'm not a suitable candidate.

                    PAUL
          Says who?

                    DAVID
          My bone marrow, it's too soft. I
          can never use a prosthetic. Ever.

                    PAUL
          David, I'm so sorry.

                    DAVID
          Really? Because I thought you'd be
          relieved that I can't play anymore.

                    PAUL
          That's not true.

                    DAVID
          I wish I could believe you.

Father and son stare at each other. Until Connie opens the
front door, concern on her face...

                    CONNIE
          David, what happened? Come inside.

David walks into the house. Connie closes the door behind
him, leaving Paul alone with his Thresher lawn mower. He
hears his wife and son talk inside, starts up the engine.

INT. JOE'S SUV - DAY

Joe turns off the radio, drives in silence. Until he gets an
IDEA. Joe pulls over, grabs his SMARTPHONE. He scrolls
through his contacts until he finds: ASST. COACH WEATHERS.

INT. SPORTS BAR - KITCHEN - DAY

It's dinner time. The WAITSTAFF bustles to and fro. David's
got a few weeks of stubble on his sweaty face. He wears a
greasy apron, flips burgers on a GRILL.

Meat sizzles, hot oil droplets BURN David's hand. He's got
some nasty blisters on his knuckles.

The COOK rounds the corner, tucking his CELL PHONE into his
pants pocket. He takes the steel spatula from David.

                    COOK
          The test came back negative, my mom
          can come home tomorrow.

                    DAVID
          That's great, man.

                    COOK
          Thanks for covering for me.

The MANAGER sees David chatting up the Cook.

                    MANAGER
          DelSanto, get back to your station.

LATER

David loads dozens of dirty plates into a rack. He pushes the full rack into the steaming industrial DISH WASHER. David sighs, wipes the sweat from his brow. More dishes pile up.

EXT. SPORTS BAR - PARKING LOT - DAY

David shoulders an overstuffed TRASH BAG.

Behind him, Joe stands by his SUV. David opens the dumpster, strains to lift the bag. The plastic splits, trash spills all over David. He recoils from the stench, kicks the garbage.

>   JOE
> You'd have an easier time lifting
> that if you listened to me. How's
> the new job?

>   DAVID
> Lousy and the pay's worse, but it
> beats sitting around the house
> feeling sorry for myself all day.

>   JOE
> You got a minute to talk?

INT. SPORTS BAR - BOOTH - NIGHT

Joe watches David approach. He balances two cheeseburger dinners on a tray with his left hand.

David sets the tray down on the table, flexes his left arm.

>   DAVID
> See? Being a dish dog isn't all
> bad. I'm getting stronger.

>   JOE
> That's what I wanted to talk to you
> about. Your arm.

>   DAVID
> OK. After you try my cooking.

Joe bites into the burger. He enjoys the meal, notices the fresh blisters on David's hand.

>   JOE
> Not bad. How did you know I like my
> burgers medium well?

DAVID
Lucky guess. What's on your mind?

JOE
Well, what would you say if I told you there's a way that you could play football again?

DAVID
I'd say that you're probably drunk.

JOE
I believe you can be a quarterback again, David, with just one arm.

DAVID
I take it back, you're crazy.

JOE
Hear me out, D--

DAVID
A one-armed quarterback? That's even crazier than a bionic one.

JOE
I think they're equally nuts.

DAVID
So, how many one-armed quarterbacks have ever played in high school?

JOE
Not a single one.

DAVID
I spent my life being a right-handed quarterback, Joe. I can't just change arms my senior year.

JOE
David, if anyone can reprogram ten years of muscle memory in six months, it's you. You have more guts and talent than any young man I've ever known.

DAVID
I'm not a charity case that you can use to feel better about yourself.

                    JOE
          You're not a charity case, David,
          you're a champion. And you'll
          always be one.

That fact almost punches through the fear on David's face,
but he pushes away the plate of food.

                    DAVID
          I'm moving on with my life. And if
          your son was anything like me, he'd
          want you to do the same, Joe.

                    JOE
          This isn't about the past. It's
          about your future.

                    DAVID
          How would I even hand off the ball?

Joe stands up, demonstrates with a football as he talks...

                    JOE
          Take the snap with your left, tuck
          your knuckles against your spine
          and the running back does the rest.

                    DAVID
          You look like you're trying to wipe
          your butt.

                    JOE
          Just take the football and try it.

Joe offers him the football. David stares at the white laces.

                    DAVID
          It'll never work, Joe. I'd need at
          least a hundred thousand reps.

                    JOE
          I was thinking more like a hundred
          and fifty thousand.

                    DAVID
          The ball spin from a lefty is
          completely different than a right-
          handed quarterback.

                    JOE
          I saw the tape. You threw a left-
          hander to win the championship.

> DAVID
> I floated a wobbly pass to Max. He has great hands, but all the other wide receivers would have to adapt.

> JOE
> I'm glad you brought that up.

Joe WHISTLES, waves someone over to the table.

David turns around, sees Crunk and Max! They walk over to the table, it's hugs and fist bumps all around.

> JOE
> I'm going to need your help to convince him, boys.

> MAX
> Don't worry, Crunk's got you covered at center. And I'll work with you now, then drill the other receivers in the fall.

> DAVID
> Coach Burns won't let you bail on spring training to help me.

> CRUNK
> We don't have to. Coach Weathers will let us leave early most days.

> DAVID
> Why would he do that?

> JOE
> Because he believes in you, like the rest of us do. Even if Coach Burns doesn--

> DAVID
> That's not me anymore! I'm not a football player!

David gets up, walks towards the nearest exit.

> CRUNK
> David, come back.

> JOE
> Let him go.

EXT. SPORTS BAR - PARKING LOT - NIGHT

David looks up at the star-filled night sky for answers to silent questions. He notices the overflowing DUMPSTER, kicks the trash. Joe rounds the corner, confronts David.

SOMEONE sitting in a dark unfamiliar car WATCHES them.

     JOE
  David, listen t--

     DAVID
  Don't you get it? I had my shot.

     JOE
  Then take another one.

     DAVID
  It doesn't work like that.

     JOE
  It does if you want it bad enough.
  You lost your arm, not your heart.

     DAVID
  I saw it in his eyes, Joe. Coach
  Burns was ashamed of me.

     JOE
  Then shame on him!

That someone steps out of the car...

     ASST. COACH WEATHERS
  Sorry, I'm late Joe. You worry
  about your arm, David. And I'll
  take care of Coach Burns.

     DAVID
  What if he won't give me a chance?

     ASST. COACH WEATHERS
  Then I'll resign. I won't coach a
  team that's ashamed of its players.

     DAVID
  You'd do that for me?

     CRUNK (O.S.)
  We would too.

Max and Crunk join the group.

                    ASST. COACH WEATHERS
               You given us all so much of
               yourself, David, it's time to let
               us give back to you.

That sentiment brings tears to David's eyes. His best friends
and supporters stand before him, united.

                    JOE
               If we all do our part and you work
               harder than you ever have before,
               you will be ready for opening day.

David ponders this life-altering decision. All eyes on him,
until he finally nods his head -- YES.

                    DAVID
               OK. Let's do this.

Crunk and Max whoop and cheer approval. David shakes hands
with Coach Weathers, then hugs Joe.

                    CRUNK
               With all this extra work, I'm
               really gonna have to bulk up.

Everyone looks at the gargantuan Crunk.

                    DAVID
               How about a couple of cheeseburgers
               before I turn in my apron?

                    CRUNK
               Yeah! With extra bacon.

INT. REHAB CENTER - TRAINING ROOM - DAY

WHISTLE around his neck, Joe watches Crunk hunker down,
poised to hike the football to David a few feet behind him.

Joe blows the whistle. Crunk hikes the ball. David reaches
forward with his left, drops the football. He strains to
maintain his balance, his stump flails.

                    JOE
               Stop trying to use an arm you don't
               have anymore, David! You hear me?

That remark stings David. Hailey empathizes.

                    JOE
               Lean forward more, flex your wrist
               to control the ball. Again.

Joe blows the whistle. Crunk hikes. David flexes his wrist, gooses the football with his fingertips, almost got it.

        JOE
    Better. Again.

Hike after hike after hike, Joe blows that whistle. Sometimes he waits longer, forcing David to hold his low stance.

        JOE
    Again!

INT. REHAB CENTER - WEIGHTS ROOM - DAY

David holds up a football in his left hand. He bends his arm as tight as he can. Hailey wraps a thick latex strap around his wrist and upper arm. She knots the rubber tight.

He strains his left bicep through a crude throwing motion.

        HAILEY
    Slow, sustain the burn. You're
    imprinting new muscle memories.
    Good. Now do a thousand more.

        DAVID
    And then what?

        HAILEY
    Thirty minutes of free weights,
    then a quick lunch with me?

        DAVID
    Deal. Count me down.

        HAILEY
    One-thousand, nine-hundred and
    ninety-nine...

David completes rep after rep. Never taking his eyes off Hailey. Much to the dismay of CORPORAL LANE, who's watching them in secret.

EXT. REHAB CENTER - RUNNING TRACK - DAY

Several patients use the facility. But none of them have a football DUCT-TAPED to their left hand.

Joe wraps sticky tape over David's knuckles, securing the fingers over the laces.

JOE
          This will hyper-stretch the
          lumbrical and interosseous muscle
          groups to simulate years of
          handling a football. Now, I'll turn
          you over to your running partner.

                    DAVID
          Running partner?

                    CORPORAL LANE (O.S.)
          You ready, Thresher?

                    DAVID
          Oh, hell no.

David knows that voice. He turns around, sees a grinning
Corporal Lane wearing a U.S. ARMY shirt and shorts. David
sighs, notices the WHISTLE around Lane's neck.

                    JOE
          Every time Corporal Lane says...

                    CORPORAL LANE
          Hut!

                    JOE
          You raise your arm and grip that
          ball as tight as you c--

                    DAVID
          Yeah, yeah. I got--

                    CORPORAL LANE
          Hut!

David doesn't raise his arm in time. Corporal Lane blows a
whistle right in his face.

                    JOE
          Every time you fail to execute,
          Corporal Lane will blow his whistle
          in your face. You got that?

                    DAVID
          Yes, Coach. Very loud and clear.

                    JOE
          Good. Now run six laps without
          missing a single Hut.

                    DAVID
          Six laps? But that's three miles.

>   CORPORAL LANE
>   Correct. Hit the track, Thresher!

Joe salutes Corporal Lane. The soldier salutes him back. Side by side, David and Corporal Lane run the oval as Joe watches.

>   CORPORAL LANE
>   Hut!

Every time Lane gives that command, David raises his left arm mid-stride, works those muscle groups. Until he misses one, then Corporal Lane blows that whistle near David's skull.

>   CORPORAL LANE
>   Start over. Hike!

David raises his left arm, even though he wasn't given the proper command. Corporal Lane chirps the whistle.

>   DAVID
>   You tricked me.

>   CORPORAL LANE
>   My track, my rules. Hut!

David pumps his left arm. Each white knuckle clamps down tight on the football's ivory laces.

LATER

Joe sees David laying on the grass, huffing and puffing. The sweaty football still taped to his blistered hand.

>   JOE
>   How many laps did you complete?

>   DAVID
>   One.

INT. REHAB CENTER - TRAINING ROOM - DAY

Joe double-chirps the whistle in his mouth. Crunk hikes the football. David cradles the ball in his left palm.

>   JOE
>   Come on! Fast--

>   DAVID
>   Faster! I know!

With each blow of the whistle, Crunk and David become more and more in sync, just like they used to be.

EXT. CHURCH - COURTYARD - DAY

Behind the brick building, there's a manicured garden filled with religious statues. Connie and David walk together...

>   CONNIE
>   Did I ever show you this place?
>
>   DAVID
>   You used to spank me here when I
>   talked in church.
>
>   CONNIE
>   Oh yeah, but this is also the spot
>   where I married your father.

The mention of him sours David's mood.

>   CONNIE
>   You haven't spoken more than ten
>   words to him since you started
>   training, David.
>
>   DAVID
>   I don't know what to say to him.
>
>   CONNIE
>   Don't talk, just listen.

Paul stands next to a MARBLE STATUE of a hopeful angel. He looks at his son, tries to smile. David starts to leave.

>   PAUL
>   David, wait. Please. I'm sorry that
>   I let you down, Son.

That admission stops David in his tracks.

>   DAVID
>   Why did you never want to be my
>   guidance counselor, Dad?
>
>   PAUL
>   I thought an outside opinion w--
>
>   DAVID
>   Why would I need an outside opinion
>   when my father's the best guidance
>   counselor in Siskiyou County? How
>   could you help Max build a future
>   while you were tearing mine down?!?
>   Because you're ashamed of me!

> PAUL
> No, because I'm ashamed of myself.
> I was always there for you when you
> were a champion. But I was a no
> show when you needed me most. Don't
> make the same mistake I did. Don't
> hang on to an impossible dream.

It's too much for David. He runs off. Connie starts after him, then falters. She looks disoriented. Paul steadies her.

> PAUL
> Are you alright?

> CONNIE
> Yes, I'm just upset.

INT. REHAB CENTER - WEIGHTS ROOM - DAY

David stretches the latex wrapped around his left arm much easier now. Hailey nods approval at his progress.

Stump and arm crossed over his chest, David lays on the floor, then sits up. Hailey holds down his feet. She tries to not stare at his sweaty torso. She fails. He notices.

EXT. REHAB CENTER - RUNNING TRACK - DAY

Corporal Lane's in hot pursuit of his trainee. David sprints around the half-mile oval.

> CORPORAL LANE
> Hut!

Football taped in hand, David's arm bends in a blink of an eye, poised to launch the ball. Corporal Lane hounds him...

> CORPORAL LANE
> Hut! Are you dating my sister? Hut!

> DAVID
> No sir! Just lunch.

INT. REHAB CENTER - TRAINING ROOM - DAY

Joe slides a BLACK SLEEVE over David's stump as he talks...

> JOE
> It's made from the same micro-
> fibers used in training gloves for
> wide receivers. Very slippery.

David wears a thick glove on his left hand. Joe moves David's limbs to demonstrate as he talks...

                JOE
    When you get a bad snap, use your C-
    TACK glove. Tuck your right arm in
    and roll the ball over the sleeve
    until you see the laces.

Joe underhand-throws a football to David. He catches it, looks at the sleeve, shifts the ball and grips the laces.

                JOE
    Take your eyes off the coverage to
    play catch with yourself and you'll
    get sacked all day long. Again!

ANOTHER DAY

Crunk's poised to hike the ball to David, but there's one big difference. They're lined up in a SHOTGUN FORMATION.

Wearing a helmet, David's set up about fifteen feet behind Crunk. Joe blows his whistle. Crunk hikes the ball. The pigskin hits David square in the chest, falls to the ground.

                JOE
    Elbow facing out! Use your stump's
    inner bicep to control the ball!

ANOTHER DAY

Six numbered TRASH BARRELS are stacked like a pyramid on top of a long folding table. ONE is the top barrel. TWO and THREE make up the middle row. FOUR, FIVE and SIX are on the bottom.

Max and Crunk flank David, there's a big pile of footballs at their feet. Joe blows his whistle.

                JOE
    Accuracy is everything! Four!

Max tosses a football. David catches it, lines up the laces with the sleeve. He throws the ball at the lower left barrel, comes up way short. Joe blows the whistle.

WEIGHTS ROOM

Hailey stands behind a seated David. She MASSAGES his sweaty left bicep, while admiring his six pack.

                    HAILEY
          Is it OK if I massage your right?

                    DAVID
          Yeah, I'd like that.

David pulls off the sleeve, holds out his stump. Hailey faces
him, then works her magic. They smile at each other.

EXT. DAVID'S HOUSE - DAY

Green buds sprout from naked tree branches.

Football in hand, David stands in the FRONT YARD on a cloudy
SPRING day. He looks at someone, throws a weak spiral.

Connie wraps her hands around the pigskin, laughs.

                    DAVID
          Good grab, Mom.

Through a window, Paul watches his wife and son play catch
together. Connie throws a shaky spiral through the air...

EXT. REHAB CENTER - OPEN FIELD - DAY

The weak spiral _SUDDENLY_ flies straight and true... The
cloudy day gives way to blue skies and lush trees of SUMMER.

Max plucks the laser-guided pass out of the air! Hike after
hike from Crunk leads to a completed pass. Joe loves what he
sees, fist pumps.

                    JOE
          Yes!

Hailey and Crunk clap. From hiding, a concerned Paul watches
the training. He calls COACH BURNS on his SMARTPHONE.

Crunk flops on the ground. David offers him a water bottle.

                    DAVID
          Here ya go. How do you feel?

                    CRUNK
          Awful, I think I'm losing weight.

Hailey approaches, offers her water to David. He takes the
bottle. Their hands touch. They linger, smile at each other.

                    CORPORAL LANE
          Hailey, can I talk to you?

EXT. REHAB CENTER - GARDEN - DAY

Brother and sister walk and talk in private. They're flanked by the summer flowers in bloom.

> CORPORAL LANE
> Look, David's an athlete. And once he's back in the saddle, don't expect him to stick around. OK?

> HAILEY
> Why would you say that to me? Because he's a Thresher?

> CORPORAL LANE
> Because all David cares about is football. I don't want to see you get hurt by some cocky jerk that's using you to inflate his own ego.

Hailey slaps her brother hard across the jaw. Corporal Lane sighs, rubs his face. Hailey storms off...

> HAILEY
> It takes one to know one, brother.

EXT. THRESHER FOOTBALL FIELD - DAY

Eric, last year's bench-warming back up that old David loved to torment, now runs the Thresher offense.

He throws a tight spiral. Max leaps, catches the pass.

Something on the sideline catches everyone's attention. They all stare at David and Joe. Jenna sees her ex-boyfriend.

The team gathers, greets David. Some hang back. Some stare at the stump. Eric removes his helmet, looks over his old rival.

> DAVID
> You've bulked up.

> ERIC
> You've lost a little weight.

Eric flexes his right arm, plays to the crowd. Several team members laugh. Jenna joins the group, at Eric's side.

> DAVID
> You're looking good, Jenna.

> ERIC
> What do you want, cripple?

David clenches his fist, right in Eric's face. The team circles the pair, many eager for a fight.

                    JOE
          Easy, David.

                    DAVID
          You're gonna have to do a lot
          better than that, if you want to
          bait me into a fight, back-up.

Eric and David stare each other down. Until a long shrill WHISTLE BLAST cuts through the silence.

                    COACH BURNS (O.S.)
          DelSanto! In my office, now!

From the locker room doorway, Coach Burns glares at David and his divided team. Eric grins.

Joe steps between the boys. He pulls David away from Eric.

INT. COACH BURNS' OFFICE - DAY

David, Joe and Coach Weathers look at Coach Burns. He watches a SIZZLE REEL of David's training on a laptop. The triumphant video ends with David throwing a long bomb to Max. Touchdown!

Coach Burns looks at his assistant...

                    COACH BURNS
          This was your idea, Weathers?

                    JOE
          It was mine, Coach. With all due
          respect, David deserves another
          chance to play football.

                    COACH BURNS
          With all due respect, if you were
          my assistant, I'd fire you.

                    ASST. COACH WEATHERS
          David worked hard all s--

                    COACH BURNS
          You don't have to tell me how tough
          the best quarterback I ever coached
          is, boy! One more word out of you
          and you're fired.

                    DAVID
          I want to be a Thresher again, sir.

COACH BURNS
I know you do, you remember what a
thresher machine does, David?

DAVID
Separates the chaff from the wheat.

COACH BURNS
That's right. And as head coach of
this team, that's my job too.

Tears well up in David's eyes. Joe glares at Coach Burns.

DAVID
Please give me one chance, Coach, I
won't let you down.

COACH BURNS
I wish it were that simple, but you
weren't even back two minutes
before a fight broke out.

JOE
That your player star--

COACH BURNS
My starting quarterback is the
uncontested leader of this team. I
can't have David's presence on the
field undermine that.

DAVID
Did my father put you up to this?

COACH BURNS
This morning, your father tried to
convince me to take you back. He
asked me not to tell you that, but
I thought you should know.

That eye-opening fact shocks David into silence.

COACH BURNS
I'm sorry, David, but there's no
room for you on my football field.

ASST. COACH WEATHERS
Then what about the sideline?

COACH BURNS
What? Don't play games with m--

                    ASST. COACH WEATHERS
               I'm serious. No one's volunteered
               yet, I still need an assistant.

                    COACH BURNS
               You mean, a water boy.

                    ASST. COACH WEATHERS
               My assistant is also responsible
               for maintaining the playbooks.
               David knows those books better than
               anyone on the practice squad.

                    COACH BURNS
               Is this what you really want, son?

David looks up at the Thresher memorabilia on the walls. All
those past teams led to glory, some by Young Paul and David.

                    DAVID
               I'll do whatever it takes to get
               back on this team, Coach.

                    COACH BURNS
               All right, we'll give this a try.
               You can assist Weathers, but if
               there's even a whiff of trouble
               between you and Eric, you're off
               the team for good.

David nods in agreement. He shakes hands with Coach Burns.

INT. DAVID'S HOUSE - KITCHEN - DAY

The unseen front door closes. An excited David trots into
view. He looks around.

                    DAVID
               Mom? You home? Guess what?

David's all smiles...

                    DAVID
               I made the team! Sort of. I'm the--

Until he sees Connie face down on the floor. David struggles
to roll her over with his one good arm. She's unconscious. He
shakes her shoulders. No response from Connie.

                    DAVID
               Mom! Wake up!

INT. HOSPITAL - INTENSIVE CARE UNIT - DAY

Paul stands in a corridor. He watches David pray at Connie's bedside. A bearded NEUROLOGIST in scrubs approaches Paul.

> PAUL
> Is she going to be alright?

> NEUROLOGIST
> Your wife had a severe saccular brain aneurysm, which caused a subarachnoid hemorrhage. We stopped the bleeding, but the damage was already done. I'm so sorry.

> PAUL
> What can we do for her?

> NEUROLOGIST
> Give the brain time to heal, keep her comfortable. She may regain some of her motor functions, we'll know in a few days.

INT. CHURCH - DAY

David lights a VOTIVE. He sets the candle amongst all the others burning for loved ones. David makes the Sign of the Cross with his left hand.

In the back row: Paul watches David pray, then looks at the statue of Jesus Christ presiding over his son. Paul leaves.

INT. INTENSIVE CARE UNIT - CONNIE'S ROOM - DAYS LATER

David's been up for days. He prays at Connie's bedside, his hand clasped over hers. David's fingers touch his sleeping mother's ROSARY BEADS. Paul enters, closes the door.

> PAUL
> We have to talk. It's time.

> DAVID
> Pray with me, Dad. Just one time. She prayed for me. Please?

Paul nods yes, sits next to David. Father and son hold each others' hands. They bow their heads, pray in silence. Lips moving, tears falling...

Until Connie wakes up. She looks around, disoriented. Paul hugs and kisses his wife, but it brings her no comfort.

>   PAUL
>   Sweetheart?
>
>   CONNIE
>   We're late for David's game.
>
>   DAVID
>   Mom, it's OK. Relax.
>
>   CONNIE
>   Paul, we have to go now or someone
>   will take my seat.
>
>   PAUL
>   Connie, please lis--
>
>   CONNIE
>   Where's my seat?!? I can't find it.
>
>   DAVID
>   It's OK, Mom. It's right here, just
>   follow me up the steps.

Mother and son hold hands. They count the rows together...

>   DAVID AND CONNIE
>   One... two... three... four...
>   five... six... and seven.

Connie relaxes, she's at peace. David smiles at his dying mother. Connie closes her eyes for the last time.

Father and son weep.

EXT. HILLSIDE - DAY

It's a secluded spot that provides a clear view of the distant Thresher football field. The team practices.

Paul, SILVER URN in hand, crests the hill. David, wearing a BACKPACK, trails his father.

They take in the scenic view. David stares at the football field, watches his team practice without him. Paul opens a LETTER. He reads in silence...

>   CONNIE (V.O.)
>   The only thing I hate more than the
>   sport of football is the thought of
>   being buried in the cold ground.

Paul smiles as he reads...

CONNIE (V.O.)
Spread my ashes somewhere I can
always watch my two favorite people
do what they love most. And I'll
keep cheering until we meet again.
I love you both so very much.

Paul puts away the letter, dries his tears.

PAUL
I think this is the spot.

David opens his BACKPACK. He pulls out two HAND SHOVELS, gives one to Paul. Father and son dig holes. They plant FLOWER SEEDS as they talk...

PAUL
I never knew my wife hated football
so much. How could I miss that?

DAVID
Because all we ever saw was that
face of love in the grandstands
rooting for us.

Father and son finish planting the seeds. They open the URN, take turns spreading Connie's ASHES. The fine mist dissipates in the blue sky.

On the distant field, someone blows a WHISTLE. The tiny players stop practicing. David watches his team leave the field, stares at the GRANDSTAND where he and Connie sat...

DAVID
I hope Mom can see me play at least
one more time.

PAUL
Did I ever tell you the story about
your first baby steps?

DAVID
No.

PAUL
Your mother wanted to record your
second birthday, but we couldn't
afford a video camera or even a
casette recorder. I set up my old
reel-to-reel and played records.
You sang all night long, when you
weren't too busy chewing on that
poor old microphone.

                    DAVID
          I kind of remember that.

                    PAUL
          Shirley Bassey was your favorite,
          but what you don't remember is I
          had nasty gas that night. The
          worst. It was so loud, you could
          hear the farts on the playback.

Paul and David share a laugh.

                    DAVID
          I definitely don't remember that.

                    PAUL
          After five or six of those: You
          stood up, gave me the stinkeye and
          walked out of the room as fast your
          little legs would go. And you never
          stumbled or looked back, not even
          once. I thought it was a blind
          luck, but your mother knew better.

                    DAVID
          What do you mean?

                    PAUL
          Connie figured you must've been
          practicing alone for months. Even
          back then, she knew you were a
          perfectionist that would succeed in
          whatever you set your mind to.

David nods yes. Father and son embrace.

                    PAUL
          I love you, Son.

                    DAVID
          I love you too, Dad.

INT. COACH BURNS' OFFICE - DAY

Coach Burns sits at his desk, reviews paperwork. There's a KNOCK at the closed door.

                    COACH BURNS
          Come in.

David enters, closes the door behind him.

                    COACH BURNS
          Sit down, David. I'm sorry for your
          loss. Your mother was a kind human
          being and a hell of a booster.

                    DAVID
          Thank you, Coach.

                    COACH BURNS
          Given everything that you've been
          through, everyone would understand
          if you decided to quit the team.

                    DAVID
          Since Mom died, I've given it a lot
          of thought.

                    COACH BURNS
          Of course you have. There's no
          shame in walking away, Dav--

                    DAVID
          And I want to stay on the team. I
          want to be a Thresher.

Not what Coach Burns wanted to hear, but he smiles and shakes
David's left hand anyway.

INT. THRESHER LOCKER ROOM - DAY

Coach Burns escorts David into the empty room.

The floor's covered with sweaty practice gear. Jockstraps,
shoulder pads, helmets and filthy jerseys aplenty.

                    DAVID
          So when do I start, Coach?

                    COACH BURNS
          Now. Lock up when you're done.

Coach Burns hands David a KEY RING, then leaves. David looks
at the huge mess, then sighs.

EXT. THRESHER FOOTBALL FIELD - ANOTHER DAY

The team practices offensive plays, mostly passes.

David pushes a CART down the sideline, there's a bright
orange Gatorade container on top. David watches the team.

Coach Burns blows his WHISTLE, Crunk hikes the ball. Eric throws a tight spiral. Max catches the pass.

                COACH BURNS
    That's what I like to see.

Eric notices David watching him. David turns away, pushes the cart towards the bench. Eric throws the football, hits David in the back of the head.

Most of the players laugh. Crunk and Max glare at Eric.

                ERIC
    Hey water boy, that ball's a little
    deflated. Grab me a new one.

All eyes on David. He stares at Eric, absorbs his anger. The prank backfires. David grabs a fresh ball, throws a tight blistering spiral.

Eric barely manages to corral the speedy pass. The team marvels at David's skills.

                DAVID
    That one better?

David and Eric glare at each other.

                ERIC
    Yeah, thanks water boy.

                CRUNK
    Get a life, Eric.

                ERIC
    Shut up and hike the ball, fat ass.

Both coaches take note of the strife.

LATER

The team practices tackling.

David wears a numberless jersey, just like the rest of the PRACTICE SQUAD. He holds a TACKLE DUMMY, braces for impact.

A big linebacker smashes into the dummy, drives David to the ground. The team winces. Eric laughs. David gets to his feet.

              ASST. COACH WEATHERS
    Are you alright, David?

                    DAVID
          Never better. Nice one! Who's next?

                    ERIC
          Me.

                    DAVID
          Alright. Bring it, QB.

Eric lines up, runs into David as hard as he can. David backs up, digs in with his heels and repels Eric with the dummy.

                    DAVID
          Nice one. For a back-up QB. Come
          on! Hit me like you mean it!

David slaps the pad with his one good fist. Eric takes a running bash into the dummy, knocks down David hard. Eric whispers in David's ear...

                    ERIC
          Stay down, cripple.

Max pulls Eric off of David. The team takes sides. Some fist bump Eric, the rest glare at him. Coach Burns doesn't like what he sees, neither does Coach Weathers.

EXT. THRESHER FOOTBALL FIELD - NIGHT

It's the season-opening kick-off. The pigskin sails high.

                    ANNOUNCER (V.O.)
          And the Thresher's quest to defend
          their championship begins!

From the sideline in street clothes, David watches Eric lead the Threshers down the field. A dropped pass ends the drive.

                    COACH BURNS
          Come on! Eyes on the ball!

The team trots off the field. David offers towels to the dejected players. Eric rips one out of David's grip.

INT. THRESHER LOCKER ROOM - NIGHT

Coach Burns addresses his somber team. David stands alone.

                    COACH BURNS
          38-7. Worst season opener in
          Thresher team history!

He throws the PLAYBOOK on the floor.

>   COACH BURNS
> Unless you start acting like a
> team, this season's over!

>   THRESHER TEAM
> Yes, Coach.

>   ASST. COACH WEATHERS
> Alright. Hit the showers.

The players undress. David picks up the crumpled playbook.

EXT. THRESHER FOOTBALL FIELD - NIGHT

Another night, David stands on the field alone next to some kind of waist-high portable machine. He doesn't see COACH BURNS high up in the dark grandstands watching him.

At midfield, David sets a football down on the metal cradle of the CENTER SNAP SIMULATOR.

David pulls a lever. The machine clicks faster and faster, until the cradle flips the ball to David.

In one quick motion: David catches the ball with his stump and hand, rotates it, grips the laces and throws a laser-guided spiral all the way into the ENDZONE.

Where it lands near TWO DOZEN other footballs.

ANOTHER NIGHT

Another football flies, this time during a Thresher game.

Max sees the pass, it's high and off the mark. He adjusts his running route, times his leap. The ball grazes his extended fingertips, sails out of bounds. Game over.

>   ANNOUNCER (V.O.)
> That dropped pass dooms the
> Threshers to their first oh-and-
> three start in twenty years.

In the grandstand, Hailey sighs in defeat. Paul does too.

INT. REHAB CENTER - TRAINING ROOM - DAY

David wears his practice gear, ready to train. He sees Hailey sitting alone in a corner, concern on her face.

                    DAVID
          What's wrong? Where's Joe?

                    HAILEY
          Joe turned in his resignation this
          morning. He left this for you.

Hailey hands David a SEALED ENVELOPE. He tears it open, scans
the letter. It's not good news. David shakes his head no.

                    HAILEY
          What does it say?

                    DAVID
          I've gotta go.

She reaches out to him. He pulls back his hand.

                    HAILEY
          David? Talk to me.

                    DAVID
          I'm sorry, I can't be here.

David runs back the way he came. Hailey sits alone, just like
her brother said she would.

INT. JOE'S GARAGE - DAY

In the CLOSED GARAGE, Joe waxes a pristine SURFBOARD that's
laid out on a long table. Someone knocks on the unseen front
door. Joe ignores them, hangs the waxed board on the wall.

                    DAVID (O.S.)
          Joe, you home?

More knocks annoy Joe. He stares at pictures of a SURFER
that's David's age. Father and son smiling. They hold a big
trophy together. A promising career that was cut short.

The knocks finally stop. Joe stares at the memorial to his
son in silence. Until David pulls open the garage door,
exposes a nostalgic Joe to bright sunlight.

                    JOE
          You make a habit of breaking into
          people's homes?

                    DAVID
          Only when they walk out on me. I
          don't get you, man. Why'd you quit?
          What did I do wrong?

JOE
Nothing. Nothing at all. Dav--

DAVID
So that's it, you're just done? I can't do this all by myself.

JOE
Yes, you can. Use the automatic ball snapper twice a week to keep your arm in shape.

DAVID
Joe. I'll do whatever you say, I'll run however many laps you want. Just please don't stop coaching me.

JOE
I have nothing left to teach you. Besides, I g--

DAVID
Half the team hates me! And the other half can't stand looking at me on the sidelines. I can't take it! Eric rides my ass every day!

JOE
Of course he does. Who do you think he looks up to? Tom Brady? His father? No! He looks up to you! Help Eric step out of your shadow.

DAVID
I don't know how to do that.

JOE
Respect your quarterback. Rise above your pride and be a better man than I ever was.

Tears well up in David's eyes as he laughs...

DAVID
What? Pride? What pride?!? I'm the water boy, Joe!!!

JOE
David, wait I--

David turns away from Joe. He leaves, slams the garage door down behind him. Joe sighs, frustrated.

EXT. THRESHER FOOTBALL FIELD - DAY

The team lines up for a scrimmage game. The PRACTICE SQUAD plays defense against the varsity starters.

On the sideline, David organizes the PLAYBOOKS. A winded Max joins him, gulps down some Gatorade.

>   MAX
>   I don't get it. Eric hasn't been
>   the same since you came back.

Someone on the practice squad comes up lame. Coach Burns blows his whistle, yells across the field...

>   COACH BURNS
>   DelSanto! Take his place!

>   DAVID
>   Maybe I can shake Eric up a little.

Max and David fist bump. They don helmets, take the field on opposite sides. Eric breaks the huddle, lines up his offense.

>   ERIC
>   Blue twenty-three. Hut!

Crunk hikes the ball. David sprints through a hole in the offensive line. Crunk hesitates to tackle him. David breaks the line, lunges through the air.

Eric's ready for the blitz. He rises up, flips David end over end in midair! David pinwheels, then hits the turf hard.

>   ERIC
>   You like that, has been?

David lays on the ground, catches his breath. He holds up his open palm, gesturing for a hand up. But all Eric does is spit on the ground. Coach Weathers blows his WHISTLE...

>   ASST. COACH WEATHERS
>   Eric! That was uncalled--

>   COACH BURNS
>   Break the huddle, line up!

>   ERIC
>   The next loser that lets the water
>   boy through can ride the bench for
>   the rest of the season!

Play after play: Eric lines up. Crunk hikes the ball. David lands flat on his back every time.

                    COACH BURNS
                Last snap, boys. Make it count.

Crunk shovels the ball to Eric. David finds a seam, spins
away from a tackle and pounds Eric to the turf! The two
grapple and smash helmets, like dueling mountain goats.

                    ERIC
                Get off me, cripple.

                    DAVID
                  (whispers)
                Ten o'clock, tonight. Midfield.
                Come alone, unless you're afraid.

Eric nods and shoves David off him. Max offers David a hand,
helps him to his feet. The coaches take note of the strife.

                    MAX
                What's going on?

                    DAVID
                I need your help tonight. Meet me
                here at nine. Bring Crunk.

THAT NIGHT

Crickets chirp. The field's slick with fresh rain. Not so
distant thunder rumbles. David stands alone on the dark turf.

Until Eric appears out of the shadows.

                    ERIC
                You're never going to play QB
                again. Not while I'm a Thresher.
                And keep your eyes off Jenna!

                    DAVID
                She's your girl now. I get that.
                But If you want to lead this team--

Eric charges David, knocks him to the wet muddy turf. The
boys wrestle. David cracks Eric across the jaw with his
stump. The boys scramble to their feet, square off.

                    ERIC
                I am the leader!

                    DAVID
                No, you're not! Not until you stop
                second guessing yourself out there.
                You've got all the talent you need
                to lead us to the playoffs.

>   ERIC
>   You really think I do?
>
>   DAVID
>   Yes, I believe in you. But no one
>   else will follow you. Until you
>   show them that you're worth
>   following. 'Bout time you guys...

Crunk and Max step onto the field...

>   CRUNK
>   Sorry we're late. When I first met
>   David, I flattened his worthless
>   butt into the snow. And now, there
>   is nothing I wouldn't do for him.
>
>   MAX
>   Because we know there isn't
>   anything he wouldn't do for us. On
>   or off the field, David has got our
>   backs. We respect each other.
>
>   DAVID
>   I wouldn't be here without their
>   help, now let us help you be the
>   leader I know you can be.

Eric ponders the offer, then nods. David and Eric shake hands. Max and Crunk fist bump with the boys.

High up in the shadowy grandstand, Coach Burns watches his star players bond.

NEXT DAY

David and Eric play a game of catch together. They start close together, whipping short fast passes at each other.

Max and Crunk toss them ball after ball.

As Eric and David step back from each other, the throws become longer and longer, neither one dropping a ball. The boys complete pass after pass. Athletes in perfect sync.

From a hidden spot, Coach Burns watches his two missile-throwing quarterbacks with pride.

ANOTHER NIGHT

Another game. The Threshers are driving deep into their opponent's territory. Eric throws a TOUCHDOWN to Max!

David stands on the sidelines, clutching the PLAYBOOK. He
jumps up and down, cheers for his team.

>   ANNOUNCER (V.O.)
>   Touchdown Threshers! What a
>   turnaround! The defending champs
>   have won six in a row. One more
>   victory sends them to the playoffs!

ANOTHER NIGHT

Threshers in command on the SCOREBOARD, 41-10. Eric catches
the hike from Crunk, takes a knee and runs out the clock.

>   ANNOUNCER (V.O.)
>   A record-breaking night for the
>   junior quarterback! The Threshers
>   are going to defend their Title in
>   a rematch with the Shasta Miners!

The crowd cheers. The victors rally around Eric, then trot to
the sideline. David greets the team with towels and high
fives. No one shies away from his stump anymore.

David collects the PLAYBOOKS from the coaches. He's a cog in
a machine much bigger than himself now. Jenna hugs Eric. She
waves to David with a smile. He smiles back at her.

EXT. SPORTS BAR - PARKING LOT - NIGHT

David holds the door open for Hailey. They walk hand in hand
towards her car...

>   HAILEY
>   That's the first time someone
>   brought me to a restaurant and then
>   made me dinner.

>   DAVID
>   I'm tight with the cook.

In the corner of his eye, David spots the old dumpster. It's
still overstuffed with garbage. He turns away from his past,
towards a hopeful future with Hailey...

>   HAILEY
>   You nervous about the game?

>   DAVID
>   A little, but my team will do their
>   best. I'd like you to be there.

                    HAILEY
          I will be there.

                    DAVID
          Good.

Hailey flashes that familiar smile that's only grown sweeter
the longer she's known David...

                    HAILEY
          Rooting for my little brother to
          kick your Thresher asses.

                    DAVID
          What? Oh hell no. That ain't right.

David shakes his head no. Hailey laughs, then shrugs. Before
she can unlock her car, David steps in front of the door. He
stares into Hailey's unblinking eyes. They're face to face.

                    DAVID
          And what if I was playing
          quarterback this weekend?

                    HAILEY
          Then I'd settle for a tie. You two
          can share the trophy.

                    DAVID
          But I don't like to share what I
          want. What do I get if we win?

                    HAILEY
          A kiss. At midfield.

                    DAVID
          In front of everyone? Corporal Lane
          isn't going to like that one bit.

                    HAILEY
          No, I suspect he won't.

They stare at each other. Until Hailey TICKLES David. He
recoils and giggles. She unlocks the car, slides inside.

                    DAVID
          That's cold-hearted, girl. Tickling
          a one-armed man.

Hailey sticks her tongue out at David. He grins at her.

EXT. JOE'S HOUSE - DAY

Paul pulls up to the yard in his sedan. He's very surprised to see a MOVING VAN parked in the driveway.

Joe steps out of the house, coffee mug in hand. Paul steps out of the car, looks at the furniture in the van.

> PAUL
> Mister Hackett, we never formal--

> JOE
> I know who you are, Mister DelSanto. Coffee?

> PAUL
> No, thanks. Are you moving?

> JOE
> Yes, back to Seattle.

> PAUL
> Does David know about this?

> JOE
> No, he doesn't. What can I do for you, Mister DelSanto?

> PAUL
> I came to give you a ticket. The championship game's this weekend.

Paul offers Joe a TICKET to the big game.

> JOE
> Keep it. I won't be there.

> PAUL
> But it will probably be the last game of David's career. He needs your support.

> JOE
> David needs his father, not me.

> PAUL
> But you believed in him when I didn't. Just think about it. Please? Take the ticket, in case you change your mind.

Joe stares at the ticket.

EXT. DAVID'S HOUSE - DAY

Bare trees flank the home. A stark contrast to the colors of summer last seen here.

Parked across the street: Joe's MOVING VAN. In the FRONT YARD, Joe plays a game of catch with David as they talk...

                DAVID
I'm sorry I broke into your house and yelled at you. So, you hooked up with Doctor Vang? Nice.

                JOE
No, she hooked me up with a job.

                DAVID
Doing what?

                JOE
Working with kids, like you. I'm sorry I couldn't get you back on the field.

                DAVID
You did something far better for me. You got me back on the team.

                JOE
I wish I could've seen you play, just one time.

                DAVID
It could happen. You should come to the game and see for yourself.

                JOE
David, I don't want to watch you warm a bench all night. I can't do that. It's time for me to move on.

Joe offers the TICKET to David. He declines.

                DAVID
Keep it. As a souvenir.

                JOE
Thank you. For everything.

David hugs his mentor tight. Joe looks over David's shoulder, down the long stretch of road that lay ahead of him.

Joe climbs into the truck. David stands by the side of the road. He watches Joe pull away, waves goodbye.

INT. THRESHER LOCKER ROOM - NIGHT

David sets the team helmets in front of the lockers, then hangs the pristine jerseys next to them.

He stares at the team colors, longing in his eyes. David looks down at his street clothes, then sighs.

LATER

The players prep for the biggest game of their lives. David sits with Eric. They review the PLAYBOOK together, until David stops. He realizes something.

>   ERIC
>   What's up?

>   DAVID
>   I don't want you to play for the
>   wrong reasons, like I did.

>   ERIC
>   I got you. Loud and clear.

David nods in satisfaction. The two quarterbacks fist bump. A shrill WHISTLE upstages the boys.

Coach Burns and Coach Weathers step into view. The team huddles around them. The coaches address the boys...

>   COACH BURNS
>   To get back here and how we got
>   back here, means a lot to me. You
>   boys are already champions. And
>   tonight on this field you're going
>   to make sure those Shasta Miners
>   never forget it!

Cheers all around from the team.

>   ASST. COACH WEATHERS
>   You boys found your way to come
>   together as a team. Whether you're
>   catching the winning touchdown...

All the players love that idea, some of them high five.

>   MAX
>   Don't be shy Coach, we all know
>   you're talking about me.

Max smirks at his teammates. Some boo. Others throw dirty towels at their star receiver, including David.

                    COACH BURNS
          Button it, Max.

                    ASST. COACH WEATHERS
          So, whether you score a touchdown.
          Or you're supporting the team from
          the sidelines, I know deep down in
          the bottom of my heart, that all
          you boys contribute to this team
          the absolute best way you can.

Coach Weathers looks at David. The team follows suit. David
smiles at all of his teammates and the coaches. He fights
back tears, his jaw tight.

                    DAVID
          Huddle up!

All the players huddle around David. He puts his one good
hand in the center. All the other players place their hands
on top of his.

                    DAVID
          Go Threshers on three. One...
          Two... Three!

                    EVERYONE
          Go Threshers!

EXT. THRESHER FOOTBALL FIELD - NIGHT

The Thresher team bursts through a paper barrier, rush onto
the field. The Thresher fans scream and cheer, give their
team a standing ovation.

In the opposing grandstand, the Miners fans BOO.

Including Corporal Lane. Hailey sits next to him, her mouth
shut. Until her older brother glares at her. Then Hailey
belts out a few half-hearted BOOS.

In the Thresher grandstand seven rows back, Paul sits in the
same spot where David talked with his mother. Next to Paul:
There's an open aisle seat where Connie used to sit.

Paul stands. He watches David, wearing street clothes, walk
to the sidelines with the PLAYBOOKS in hand. Paul sighs.

David looks up into the grandstand, sees his father. Paul
waves to his son, cheers his brains out. David smiles.

Paul keeps cheering, until the Miners take the field. Leading
the charge for the team: Two huge Polynesian linebackers!

The entire Thresher team marvels at their size. Crunk shakes his big head in amazement.

                    COACH BURNS
          Jesus, Mary and Joseph. In what lab
          did they engineer those boys?

                    ASST. COACH WEATHERS
          Hawaii, I think.

                    MAX
          They're even bigger in person.

                    CRUNK
          They're gonna cook me and eat me.

                    DAVID
          Protect Eric with everything you
          got tonight, big man. You hear me?

David punches Crunk's helmet. He nods yes at David.

                    ANNOUNCER (V.O.)
          Since the Kekoa brothers joined the
          Shasta Miners, they're undefeated.
          Expect this gargantuan Polynesian
          duo to be making Division One
          quarterbacks miserable next year!

The teams line up for the KICKOFF. The REFEREE blows his whistle. The Threshers kick the football to the Miners.

The Shasta receiver catches the ball. He lines up behind the Kekoa Brothers, runs up field. The big duo repel all Thresher defenders in their path. Finally, someone makes a tackle.

                    ANNOUNCER (V.O.)
          Shasta takes possession on the
          Thresher forty yard line. That's
          exactly the kick start the Miners
          we're looking for.

Coach Weathers shakes his head no. David too.

                    ASST. COACH WEATHERS
          We're gonna need a whole lot of Icy
          Hot patches tonight.

Shasta's offense takes the field. They break huddle, line up.

The Shasta center snaps the ball. Their QB palms the pigskin, looks downfield. He finds his target, throws a tight spiral and completes the pass to a wide open receiver.

ANNOUNCER (V.O.)
                  Touchdown Shasta!

Coach Burns fumes. He throws his hat on the ground. Shasta
takes the lead: 7-0. Just one minute into the game.

Now, it's Eric and the Threshers' turn on offense. The Kekoa
Brothers line up at scrimmage. They glare at a very nervous
Crunk, just before he hikes the ball to Eric.

The big duo steam roll over Crunk. He lays flat on the field,
watches the brothers sack Eric for a big loss.

The Thresher fans wince. Paul shakes his head no. The teams
huddle, then line up for the next play.

Eric grabs the snap. He looks downfield. Max is trapped in
double coverage. No one's open. Eric takes another sack.

Jenna tries to rally the cheerleaders. She waves her POM-POMS
in their faces. They just stare at her. Jenna sighs.

LATER

The scoreboard reads: *Miners 35. Threshers 3.*

                    ANNOUNCER (V.O.)
                  Thirty seconds left in the first
                  half, and the Miners have dominated
                  every aspect of the game tonight.
                  They have a five possession lead
                  over the battered Threshers.

The bruised and bloody Thresher players hobble towards the
sideline. Max helps Crunk off the field.

David sprints onto the divot-filled turf. He supports Crunk's
other shoulder. The big kid's really hurting.

Corporal Lane enjoys the slaughter. Hailey not so much.

Paul can't stand watching anymore. He rises up from his seat,
walks down the aisle towards the field.

Coach Burns kicks the sideline turf. His boys can't catch a
break tonight. Paul surprises him...

                          PAUL
                  You're getting crushed out there,
                  Coach. Time to make a change.

                       COACH BURNS
                  What're you talking about?

David watches Paul and Coach Burns talk.

                PAUL
Let David start the second half.

             COACH BURNS
This is no time for a publicity stunt, Paul. If David got hurt, the press would crucify me.

                PAUL
Stop treating David like he's special! My Son's just like any other kid that loves football. Trust me Coach, I know David can turn this game around.

             COACH BURNS
Get off my field! David! Escort your father back to his seat!

               DAVID
Yes, Coach.

                PAUL
Listen to m--

               DAVID
Dad please, let's go. Please?

Paul sighs, then nods yes. He obeys his son, heads back to the grandstand. David sprints down to the field. Paul takes his seat, looks at the empty aisle seat next to him.

He stands up, turns around. Facing the fans, Paul starts to chant. Louder and louder...

                PAUL
Twelve. Twelve. Twelve.

Paul stamps his feet on the floorboards in time. More and more fans start chanting. They stamp their feet in unison...

             THREHSER FANS
Twelve. Twelve. Twelve.

INT. THRESHER LOCKER ROOM - NIGHT

Coach Weathers and David assist injured players. Coach Burns looks over his team. Defeat in their weary eyes.

                    COACH BURNS
          Boys, I ain't gonna lie. We just
          played the most embarrassing thirty
          minutes of my entire coaching
          career. We have got-- What in the
          wide world of hell is that noise?!?

EXT. THRESHER FOOTBALL FIELD - NIGHT

Paul faces the stomping throng. He screams the number that he and David have worn with pride...

                    PAUL
          Twelve! Twelve! Twelve!

In the Miners grandstand, Hailey chants for David. A silent Corporal Lane sits next to her. She pokes her brother, lays her puppy eyes on him. Corporal Lane sighs, stamps his feet.

                    CORPORAL LANE
          Twelve. Twelve. Twelve.

INT. THRESHER LOCKER ROOM - NIGHT

The muted chant fills the room. The coaches look at each other. Burns shakes his head no at Weathers.

The players look to each other. Many rally around Eric. Some talk in whispers, then look at David.

                    ANNOUNCER (V.O.)
                (muted by distance)
          This crowd is crazy for their
          former all-star to return! But can
          he do it with just one arm?

Max and Crunk start to chant and clap...

                    MAX AND CRUNK
          Twelve. Twelve. Twel--

                    COACH BURNS
          You two, shut up! DelSanto! Did you
          put your father up to this?

                    DAVID
          No way, Coach. I'm sorry. I'll go
          put a stop to this right now.

                    ERIC
          Wait. Coach, I think David should
          start in the second half.

COACH BURNS
Are you out of your mind? You're
the one that got us here.

ERIC
We wouldn't be here, if David
hadn't shown me what kind of
dedication and sacrifice it takes
to be on this team.

DAVID
But this is your team, Eric.

ERIC
And this is your last game. Look,
I'll be back next year, so will our
back-up. But you, this is it. This
is your time.

David ponders the impossible comeback.

The fans chanting grows louder and louder. David listens to his number again and again. He nods yes. The team cheers.

COACH BURNS
DelSanto!

Everyone falls silent. All eyes on their head coach.

COACH BURNS
Get your gear on. You're starting
the second half.

The team rallies around their returning quarterback. David's all smiles...

Until he realizes something TERRIBLE. The team quiets down.

MAX
What's wrong?

DAVID
I can't play without a jersey. We
don't have any spares.

INT. THRESHER HIGH SCHOOL - NIGHT

An out of breath Paul sprints down a dark corridor. As if he ran all the way here from the nearby football field.

ANNOUNCER (V.O.)
(muted by distance)
Two minutes to kick off, folks!
(MORE)

Who will be the Thresher quarterback for the second half? Stay tuned!

INT. PAUL'S OFFICE - NIGHT

The only light in the room comes from the TROPHY CASE. Inside said case: David's championship JERSEY. #12.

Paul unlocks the door, bolts into the room. He tries to open the case, but it's locked. Paul rifles through his desk, then his pockets. No luck.

>PAUL
>(to himself)
>Come on! Where is it?!?

He stops searching, elbows the case. The glass holds. Paul winds up, smashes his elbow through the glass. He tosses aside shards, extracts the jersey.

EXT. THRESHER FOOTBALL FIELD - NIGHT

In the Miners grandstand, Corporal Lane and Hailey watch the Shasta players take the field. They wave to their little brother, he waves back.

>HAILEY
>Where are the Threshers?

>CORPORAL LANE
>No. You don't think...

>HAILEY
>What?

>CORPORAL LANE
>Nah, I'm not gonna say it beca--

>ANNOUNCER (V.O.)
>David DelSanto takes the field!!!

Hailey jumps up. She whoops and cheers. Corporal Lane remains seated. He shakes his head no, then sighs.

>CORPORAL LANE
>Because then it will happen.

>HAILEY
>Go Threshers!!!

That sentiment rouses Corporal Lane out of his seat.

                    CORPORAL LANE
          Miners rule!!!

David leads the team across the turf. He raises his clenched
fist high in the air.

The Thresher fans go wild. Paul screams. He jumps up and
down, like a kid watching his very first football game.

EXT. HILLSIDE - NIGHT

The spot where Paul and David spread Connie's ashes. The
faint cheers of the Thresher fans fill the air.

The distant bright lights of the football field illuminate
the lush field of WILDFLOWERS in full bloom.

                    ANNOUNCER (V.O.)
               (muted by distance)
          After spending all season on the
          sideline, can DelSanto pull off an
          impossible comeback? I wouldn't
          miss this game for the world!!!

EXT. THRESHER FOOTBALL FIELD - NIGHT

The teams break their huddles. David walks up to the line of
scrimmage, breathes in deep the musk of the game, he's back.

                    DAVID
          Set one! Set two! Hut!

Crunk hikes the ball. David FUMBLES the hand-off. The crowd
gasps. David retreats, falls on the football.

Both Kekoa brothers charge Crunk. They break through, fall on
David and try to strip the ball. They taunt David...

                    KEKOA BROTHERS
          Welcome back, water boy. Next time,
          we'll break the other arm.

                    ANNOUNCER (V.O.)
          The Kekoa brothers almost come up
          with the fumble recovery. Before
          tragedy struck, DelSanto was a top
          candidate to be nominated for the
          U.S. Army All-American Bowl team.

Max and Crunk pull the Kekoa brothers off David. He groans on
the ground. Crunk offers him a hand. He helps David up.

CRUNK
Get your head in the game, QB!

Next play. David holds onto the hike from Crunk. He hands the ball to the Thresher Running Back. The Kekoa brothers smother the runner for a loss. Next play, same thing.

The crowd boos. Coach Weathers appeals to Coach Burns.

ASST. COACH WEATHERS
Come on, let David pass the ball.

ERIC
Coach, try my hook route play.

COACH BURNS
Alright! Make it happen. Let's go!

Next play. David drops back, ball in hand. He looks down the sideline, sees Max running. David throws a sweet spiral. Max hooks around and catches the ball! Thresher fans cheer.

ANNOUNCER (V.O.)
DelSanto finds his favorite target,
Max Robinson, for forty yards!

Next play. David stands in the Shotgun formation. Crunk hikes the ball. David grabs the snap, poised to throw. But he pulls down his arm, runs past the charging Miners for a huge gain!

ANNOUNCER (V.O.)
Play action run for twenty yards!
The Miners are going to have to
completely rethink their strategy
to contain DelSanto.

Next play. David stands in the pocket. He takes the snap from Crunk, looks for an open receiver. Max finds the seam in the Miners secondary, slants across the endzone.

David throws a laser-guided spiral where his star receiver will be in three, two--

ANNOUNCER (V.O.)
Touchdown Threshers!!!

Paul screams. Hailey cheers. Corporal Lane glares at her. The endzone scoreboard updates: *Miners 35. Threshers 10.*

LATER

The teams line up for a KICK OFF to the Miners. The endzone scoreboard displays: *Miners 35. Threshers 24.*

THE COMEBACK | 419

ANNOUNCER (V.O.)
With two minutes left, the
Threshers have turned a blowout
into a two possession game.

The Threshers kick off. Crunk thunders downfield. The Miners receiver FUMBLES the ball! The receiver reaches down for it.

Crunk scoops up the ball! He huffs and puffs his way into the endzone. Crunk flexes his fat frame, spikes the football! The team rallies around him.

CRUNK
I am Crunk!

THRESHER FANS
Cruuuuuuuuuuunnnk!!!

ANNOUNCER (V.O.)
Touchdown! Crunk Miller! This is
anyone's game with forty seconds
left to play!

The Threshers special teams line up, but this time, they're going for an ONSIDE KICK. Max stands tall, eyes the kicker.

ANNOUNCER
Max Robinson's ready for the onside
kick. The Threshers have no time
outs left. If they don't recover
the ball, their season's over.

The fans fall silent. The players line up. The kicker strikes the top of the ball. The pigskin RICOCHETS high off the turf.

All the players charge the descending football. Max jumps higher than he ever has in his life, corrals the football!

ANNOUNCER (V.O.)
Threshers' ball!!!

Crunk hikes the ball. David looks downfield. Max struggles in double coverage. The Kekoa brothers charge David. He pivots.

ANNOUNCER (V.O.)
Busted play. DelSanto sprints down
the Miners sideline!

A Miner defender grabs David. He tucks the football under his stump. David STIFF-ARMS the defender with his left! He gains big yardage until he's violently shoved out of bounds.

The endzone GAME CLOCK stops at: *0:13*. The REFEREE blows the whistle. He throws a YELLOW FLAG, then keys his remote mic...

> REFEREE (V.O.)
> (through loudspeakers)
> Unsportsmanlike conduct. Number sixty-one, defense. Fifteen yard penalty, first down Threshers.

> ANNOUNCER (V.O.)
> The Threshers are thirty yards away from making history!

David falls near the Miners bench. His opponents surround him, glares on their faces. Until the Kekoa brothers make a hole. Respect in their eyes, they offer David a hand.

The Kekoa brothers set David on his feet. The trio of players return the field. All fans applaud the good sportsmanship.

The Threshers line up. David takes the snap, hands the ball to the Running Back. The runner trots a few steps, turns and tosses the ball back to David.

> ANNOUNCER (V.O.)
> It's a Flea Flicker!

The Kekoa brothers flatten the Running Back. David throws a high tight spiral. Max streaks down the sideline. He looks up, sees the football descend. Max makes the catch!

Hailey, Paul and all the Thresher fans ROAR!

Just before a Miners defender BULL-DOZES Max in the kidneys, drives him out of bounds at the ONE YARD LINE. Max writhes in pain on the ground. David and Crunk rush to his aid.

0:02 left on the clock. The Kekoa brothers look exhausted.

> ANNOUNCER (V.O.)
> The Miners punish Robinson for making that spectacular catch! There's time for one more play!

David and Crunk help Max to his feet. They support him all the way to the bench. The Coaches assist Max. David starts back towards the field. Coach Burns stops him...

> COACH BURNS
> Run it down their throats, David.

David nods, then leads his team to the line. Crunk hikes the ball, charges into the defenders. David lines up behind him.

> ANNOUNCER (V.O.)
> It's a quarterback sneak!

Crunk blasts through the Kekoa brothers. They collapse at his feet, drag him down with them. David leaps over the mass of bodies! GOAL LINE in sight, he stretches his hand.

Just as a Kekoa brother grabs David's feet and hauls him down to the turf. The ball lands INCHES SHORT from victory.

The REFEREE blows the whistle.

>   ANNOUNCER (V.O.)
>   Miners win!!! What a finish!

Paul, Hailey and all the Threhser fans fall silent. The opposing grandstand erupts with cheers and applause. Paul runs down the aisle. His departure reveals something...

There's a GOLD PLAQUE on the aisle seat: *In Memory of Connie DelSanto. Dedicated Mother. Life-long booster.*

Both teams meet at midfield, shake hands. Paul joins them, by his son's side. The MINERS COACH shakes David's hand...

>   MINERS COACH
>   I wish I had ten of you on my team.

>   PAUL
>   I'm so proud of you, Son.

David and Paul hug. Both grandstands chant...

>   ALL FANS
>   Twelve. Twelve. Twelve.

Hailey watches the embrace, looks at Corporal Lane. He sighs.

>   CORPORAL LANE
>   Go on. But if he breaks your heart--

She kisses him on the cheek, runs down the aisle. Hailey navigates through the departing crowd. She looks for David.

Paul talks with the coaches. David starts to leave. Hailey intercepts him, then lays a sweet kiss on his surprised lips.

>   DAVID
>   What's that for? I didn't win.

Hailey looks David in the eye with all the certainty a girl in love can summon...

>   HAILEY
>   Yes, you did.

They kiss each other. Their lips mingle for a while.

Someone stands by the edge of the grandstand. It's Joe! He smiles at the couple, steps back into the shadows.

The fan's cheers give way to an even LOUDER CROWD...

EXT. ALL-AMERICAN BOWL - DAY

The massive ARENA'S big enough to host an NFL game. The fans cheer for all the all-star players on the sideline.

> BOWL ANNOUNCER (V.O.)
> Welcome to the U.S. Army All-American Bowl, where the nation's elite high school players clash!

At the mouth of an ACCESS TUNNEL, Corporal Lane wears military dress uniform. He helps David with his suit and tie, fixes the collar. Corporal Lane glares at David.

> CORPORAL LANE
> Don't embarrass me in front of my superior officers, Thresher.

> DAVID
> Yes sir. Who're they clapping for?

> CORPORAL LANE
> You, dummy.

> DAVID
> Why me?

> CORPORAL LANE
> Because you're tossing the coin.

> DAVID
> Coin toss? Oh, hell no. Why didn't you tell me sooner?

> CORPORAL LANE
> Where's the fun in that?

Corporal Lane pushes David out onto the football field.

> BOWL ANNOUNCER (V.O.)
> Let's give a warm welcome to our honorary All-American high school quarterback: David DelSanto!

The crowd applauds. On the sideline: Paul, Hailey, Max and Crunk clap. Not too far from them: It's Joe and Doctor Vang!

They're chaperoning kids with PROSTHETIC LIMBS and LEGS. All of the younger kids wearing their team uniforms...

A boy with a prosthetic arm wears a basketball jersey. A girl with a prosthetic leg wears a baseball uniform. A boy in a football jersey stands on two prosthetic legs.

The young physically challenged athletes cheer. David waves to the kids, then raises his fist high, towards Heaven.

The crowd goes wild.

David gestures to his father. Paul joins his son. He sets the coin on David's thumb...

                    PAUL
     Flip it real high, Son, so your mom
     can see it.

David tosses the mint GOLD COIN high into the clear blue sky, reflecting sunlight with each flip until we...

                                            FADE TO BLACK.

ABOUT THE AUTHOR

Ron Iannone has degrees from St. Bonaventure University and University of Rochester as well as having attained his doctorate from Syracuse University, with post-graduate work at Harvard. He has written a number of books, articles, plays, and screenplays, with a particular focus on education. His books are known nationally, especially *School Ain't No Way: Appalachian Consciousness*, which has been re-issued. His other recent publications include *Consequences: Short Stories, Poems, Commentaries*; an updated edition of *An Ethnic Connection and Goals Beyond: Reflections of an Italian American Poet*; and the novels *A Boston Homecoming* and *A Not So Normal Family*. He is also the founder of West Virginia Public Theatre.

He has received two lifetime achievement awards for his contributions as a writer, educator, poet, and artist, and as an outstanding Italian American in West Virginia. In 2015, he received West Virginia University's College of Human Services Hall of Fame award.

www.ingramcontent.com/pod-product-compliance
Lightning Source LLC
Chambersburg PA
CBHW022056090426
42743CB00008B/627